CW01019971

Nietzsche's Conscience

ALSO BY AARON RIDLEY

Music, Value and the Passions

Beginning Bioethics

R. G. Collingwood: A Philosophy of Art

NIETZSCHE'S CONSCIENCE

Six Character Studies from the *Genealogy*

AARON RIDLEY

CORNELL UNIVERSITY PRESS

ITHACA AND LONDON

Copyright © 1998 by Cornell University

All rights reserved. Except for brief quotations in a review, this book, or parts
thereof, must not be reproduced in any form without permission in writing from
the publisher. For information, address Cornell University Press, Sage House,
512 East State Street, Ithaca, New York 14850.

First published 1998 by Cornell University Press

First printing, Cornell Paperbacks, 1998

Printed in the United States of America

LIBRARY OF CONGRESS CATALOGING-IN-PUBLICATION DATA

Ridley, Aaron.
    Nietzsche's conscience : six character studies from the Genealogy
/ Aaron Ridley.
        p.   cm.
    Includes bibliographical references and index.
    ISBN 0-8014-3557-9 (cloth : alk. paper)
    ISBN 0-8014-8553-3 (pbk.)
    1. Nietzsche, Friedrich Wilhelm, 1844–1900.   Zur Genealogie der
Moral.   2. Ethics.   I. Title.
    B3313.Z73R53   1998
    170—dc21   98-29695

Cornell University Press strives to use environmentally responsible suppliers
and materials to the fullest extent possible in the publishing of its books. Such
materials include vegetable-based, low-VOC inks and acid-free papers that are
recycled, totally chlorine-free, or partly composed of nonwood fibers.

Cloth printing   10   9   8   7   6   5   4   3   2   1

Paperback printing   10   9   8   7   6   5   4   3   2   1

To Ann

Contents

PREFACE

I had been fascinated by Nietzsche for a long time before daring to write about him. But when I arrived in Southampton in 1994 and found myself at last able to offer a course on him, my inhibitions began to falter—even if the course was given in the event with more trepidation than competence. And then the politics department hired David Owen, whose book *Nietzsche, Politics and Modernity* I read with a dawning sense of how a decent course on Nietzsche might actually have been put together. We started to talk, and it was David's encouragement that finally got me to put pen to paper. Since then we have thrashed through every word I've written on Nietzsche, many of those words being themselves the products of earlier thrashings through. I haven't made any attempt in what follows to flag the things I owe to him; to have done so, apart from being tedious and embarrassing, would also have been impossible. There is an art of virtual coauthorship, and David mastered it here. I must also thank the proprietors and staff of the Avenue Bar, Padwell Road, for providing the environment in which almost all of our discussions took place, as well as the vast majority of the actual writing, editing, and revising.

But then I've been fortunate across the board. The editors of the *Journal of Nietzsche Studies* and of *Nietzsche, Philosophy and the Arts* (Cambridge University Press, 1998) have kindly allowed me to reuse parts of two previously published essays in Chapters 1 and 4. My father, Brian Ridley, read an early version of the complete manuscript and persuaded me to take out some awful bits and to clarify some others. Henry Staten, who read the book for Cornell at the behest of the excellent Roger Haydon, understood what I was up to so much better than I did that his comments struck often with the force of revelation. To the extent that I have managed to incorporate or act upon his suggestions, the book is a great deal more convincing now than it was.

The book is also better, finally, if existence is a perfection, for the forbearance of my wife, Ann, who shared me patiently with Nietzsche, David, and the Avenue Bar throughout. But since she is also cover artist and dedicatee, I won't go on.

AARON RIDLEY

Southampton, England

NOTE ON SOURCES

All references in the text are to sections, not pages. So, for instance, "GM II.14" refers to section 14 of the second essay of the *Genealogy*; "D P5" refers to section 5 of the preface to *Daybreak*; "TI, Expeditions 11" refers to section 11 of the part of *Twilight of the Idols* called "Expeditions of an Untimely Man"; etc. The following abbreviations and editions have been used:

AC   *The Anti-Christ*: from *Twilight of the Idols* and *The Anti-Christ*, trans. R. J. Hollingdale (London: Penguin Books, 1968).

BGE   *Beyond Good and Evil*: trans. Walter Kaufmann (New York: Vintage Books, 1966).

BT   *The Birth of Tragedy*: from *The Birth of Tragedy* and *The Case of Wagner*, trans. Walter Kaufmann (New York: Vintage Books, 1967).

D   *Daybreak*: trans. R. J. Hollingdale (Cambridge: Cambridge University Press, 1982).

EH   *Ecce Homo*: from *On the Genealogy of Morals* and *Ecce Homo*, trans. Walter Kaufmann (New York: Vintage Books, 1967).

GM   *On the Genealogy of Morals*: from *On the Genealogy of Morals* and *Ecce Homo*, trans. Walter Kaufmann and R. J. Hollingdale (New York: Vintage Books, 1967).

GS   *The Gay Science*: trans. Walter Kaufmann (New York: Vintage Books, 1974).

HH   *Human, All Too Human*: trans. R. J. Hollingdale (Cambridge: Cambridge University Press, 1986).

TI   *Twilight of the Idols*: from *Twilight of the Idols* and *The Anti-Christ*, trans. R. J. Hollingdale (London: Penguin Books, 1968).

Z   *Thus Spoke Zarathustra*: trans. R. J. Hollingdale (London: Penguin Books, 1969).

INTRODUCTION

> May I be forgiven the discovery that all moral philosophy so far has been bor-
> ing. . . . "[V]irtue" has been impaired for me more by the *boringness* of its ad-
> vocates than by anything else.
>
> —*Beyond Good and Evil*, sec. 228

On the Genealogy of Morals is the most important piece of moral philosophy
since Kant. It has been influential, too, and much discussed, but not always
well understood. Today, of course, we have entered the realm of readings of
readings of Nietzsche, of tertiary and even quaternary material; but the effect of this is largely to make conspicuous just how little truly secondary
material there is—material that seeks to elucidate Nietzsche's ideas and arguments rather than merely to make off with them (one of the finest commentaries on *Zarathustra*, for instance, remains Delius's *A Mass of Life*). I
don't deny that the use a philosopher can be put to is often as interesting
as, sometimes more interesting than, the philosopher himself. But when a
philosopher *is* worth making use of, as so many have thought Nietzsche to
be, he must also be worth getting right. This book is intended as a contri-
bution to that strictly secondary task.

I

It may seem odd to have invoked Kant so early. Described as a "catastrophic
spider" (AC 11), as the "most deformed conceptual cripple there has ever
been" (TI, What the Germans Lack 7) and, together with Leibniz, as one of
the "two greatest brake shoes of intellectual integrity in Europe" (EH, The
Case of Wagner 2), Kant is the beneficiary of some of Nietzsche's most lav-

ish abuse: the categorical imperative, the thing-in-itself, pure reason—the whole Kantian apparatus is the object of relentless hostility.[1] But there are strong affinities between them for all that. The following, from Kant's remarkable essay "An Answer to the Question: 'What is Enlightenment?'", could almost have been written by Nietzsche:

> Laziness and cowardice are the reasons why such a large proportion of men, even when nature has long emancipated them from alien guidance, nevertheless gladly remain immature for life. . . . It is so convenient to be immature! If I have a book to have my understanding in place of me, a spiritual adviser to have a conscience for me, a doctor to judge my diet for me, and so on, I need not make any efforts at all. I need not think, so long as I can pay; others will soon enough take the tiresome job over for me. The guardians who have kindly taken upon themselves the work of supervision will soon see to it that by far the largest part of mankind (including the entire fair sex) should consider the step forward to maturity not only as difficult but also as highly dangerous. . . . Having first infatuated their domestic animals, and carefully prevented the docile creatures from daring to take a step without the leading strings to which they are tied, they next show them the danger which threatens them if they try to walk unaided. . . . Thus only a few, by cultivating their own minds, have succeeded in freeing themselves from immaturity and in continuing boldly on their way.[2]

Nor is the Nietzsche-like quality of this passage limited to its tone or rhetoric. Kant is engaged in the diagnosis of a cultural crisis: his contemporaries refuse, through laziness, cowardice, fear, and inadequate exercise of the understanding, to take the opportunities presented to them—opportunities presented by a decline in the authority of certain "alien" (i.e., irrational) claims on their allegiance, including religious claims. His contemporaries refuse to take the step to maturity and enlightenment—or, as he puts it elsewhere, to "autonomy"—because they refuse to make the effort to cultivate their own minds: and, in doing so, they sell themselves short as human beings. Kant, then, has an ideal of human life, a vision of what it would be to be fully self-governing, fully self-legislating; and this ideal will be realized once people can be brought to understand that true freedom—true freedom from "alien guidance"—lies in their discovery of themselves as *essentially* rational beings. This discovery will arm them against superstition and quackery of every kind; and it will allow them to go "boldly on their way" because

---

1. Nor should anyone who enjoys this sort of thing miss TI, Expeditions 29.

2. Immanuel Kant, *Political Writings* (Cambridge: Cambridge University Press, 1991), p. 54. The relevance of this aspect of Kant's thought to an understanding of Nietzsche was made plain to me by David Owen—see his *Maturity and Modernity* (London: Routledge, 1994).

to make that discovery is to submit oneself to the authority of reason alone, a submission which is, insofar as one is oneself rational, a submission to no one and to nothing but oneself. Thus they are to become self-legislating, autonomous, free, mature, achieved human beings, practitioners of the Moral Law (of which, being rational, they are authors, subjects, and limits), and conscious of themselves as *valuable* precisely in virtue of their discovery in themselves of that highest, indeed transcendental, faculty, the faculty of pure reason.

Kant, then, identifies an acute spiritual malaise (immaturity), suggests its causes (laziness, poor understanding, etc.) and prescribes a cure (pure reason)—a cure, moreover, to which he suspects that contemporary conditions are comparatively amenable. So if his diagnosis is unforgiving, his prognosis is optimistic: enlightenment is possible.

II

Nietzsche's project is structurally identical. He too identifies an ill, suggests its origins, and tries to prescribe a cure; he too, in his better moods at least, thinks that enlightenment is possible. But the malaise in his view is altogether deeper and more systematic than Kant had thought, its consequences more radical, and—hence—its amelioration far harder. Kant singles out pure reason as the solution. But, for Nietzsche, the Kantian understanding of reason is itself symptomatic of that profounder problem which Kant leaves untouched. In his prescriptions for "maturity," Kant accords an absolute, a priori value to the life of reason. But it can only have this value if the authority of reason is itself beyond question (i.e., if it is "pure," if it is immune to contamination from merely contingent or temporal influence). Hence he grants to reason a transcendental status: indeed he construes it as the one incursion into our contingent, temporal world (the world of appearances, of *phenomena*) by the *noumena*—by the "real" world of things as they are in themselves, as they are independently of any of their phenomenal manifestations. Thus, in man, the faculty of reason marks a unique breach in an otherwise impermeable metaphysical barrier. Man stands with one foot in each world. But since the noumenal world is the "real" world, the world in which things have their essences, and since the essence of man, on Kant's view, is his reason, it follows that man, in his innermost being, is *of* that world. Whatever does not pertain to the life of reason is therefore "alien"; which is to say, whatever pertains to temporality, to contingency, to the world of phenomena, is "alien." Man is, in effect, an exile in the world of appearances, and his best life is led in consciousness of this fact. In practicing the Moral Law, he grasps imperatives which reason itself holds to be categorical (unconditional); in submitting to them, he acknowledges their transcendental authority; in acknowledging their authority he reaffirms his own value as a being whose true home is, in the end, elsewhere.

So Kant regards the declining authority of "alien guidance"—that is, of religious and other limitations on the freedom of thought—as an opportunity (in most cases missed) for man to embrace himself as a sublimely rational agent, as a legislator to and for himself of eternal moral truths. In effect, then, Kant sees the decline of one sort of transcendental authority (e.g., the religious) as an excuse for the replacement of it by another (i.e., the rational). And it is in precisely this that Nietzsche's quarrel with him lies. If Nietzsche had flirted with various bits and pieces of Kantian metaphysics throughout the 1870s and early 1880s, chiefly as a result of his early infatuation with Schopenhauer's pessimistic, Platonizing version of them, then by 1886/7 (when *Beyond Good and Evil*, the *Genealogy*, and book 5 of *The Gay Science* were published) he had decisively rejected, not merely the bits and pieces, but the whole Kantian world-picture. He had always been much more than somewhat suspicious of the categorical imperative and its appurtenances; but now, toward the end of his effective life, he is convinced that Kant's solution to the problem of "immaturity" is itself a symptom—a distinctively late symptom—of the very same problem. Kant is a close cousin of the "scientist" discussed in the third essay of the *Genealogy*: he kicks over the traces of religion—he forbids himself the lie involved in that particular piece of transcendentalism. But he instates another piece of transcendentalism in its place, and so ensures that "transcendentalists of every kind have once more won the day—they have been emancipated from the theologians: what joy!— [But] Kant showed them a secret path by which they may, on their own initiative and with all scientific respectability, from now on follow their 'heart's desire'" (GM III.25)—their "heart's desire" being the desire to invest at least something with transcendental authority. Kant had granted that authority to reason; the Kantian "scientist" accords it to truth. God is dethroned—but is also replaced.

Nietzsche regards this outcome as the sign of a still undercultivated, still unenlightened understanding. The rejection of God as a transcendental authority is a step in the right direction. But part of what makes belief in God increasingly difficult or impossible is the thought that anything whatever might have transcendental authority: indeed, according to Nietzsche, the very idea is incoherent. God isn't merely hard to imagine or troublesomely inaccessible. He is, considered as a source of authority, self-contradictory—a condition which he shares with his Kantian successor. Nietzsche's reasons for claiming this are as follows. Absolute, transcendental authority can be claimed only from a standpoint that is logically indefeasible, that is, universally valid; a standpoint can only be universally valid if it is independent of all particulars (e.g., the vagaries of time and place); no standpoint can possibly be independent of every particular (a view is always a view from somewhere); therefore there is no standpoint from which absolute, transcendental authority can be claimed (GM III.12). There isn't, in other words, and never has been and couldn't be, a view from nowhere—whether that view is supposed to be enjoyed by God, by the sublimely rational agent of Kantian metaphysics, or by the scientist who claims at last to have arrived at the Grand Unified Theory of Everything. Nor, consequently, have there ever been those things that the view from nowhere is supposed to be a view *of*: those things-as-they-are-in-themselves, those essences which are logically distinct from any of their possible appearances, those noumenal truths that are, quite literally, beyond reason. Insofar as Western metaphysics since Plato has been committed to such things, Western metaphysics, according to Nietzsche, has been a mistake.

In his view, then, Kant's project of enlightenment constitutes one relatively short step within a much larger movement—a movement away from transcendentalism of all kinds, as the unintelligibility of the metaphysics of transcendence becomes increasingly apparent. From this perspective, the opportunities presented by the decline of religious authority are altogether further reaching than Kant suspected: not only might man be emancipated from the "alien guidance" of priests (not to mention the assorted experts that people seem all too ready to subject themselves to instead)—he might be emancipated from the very conditions that make claims to such transcendentalizing authority possible, including the claims of "pure" Kantian reason. Thus Nietzsche's critique of Kant is a rational critique of the pretensions of Kantian reason, not a critique of reason itself (a project about which Nietzsche is scathing: see, e.g., D 3 or BGE 210). And his prescription for the modern malaise is *more* reason, not less.

If Kant wanted man to learn to stand on his own two feet, then so too does Nietzsche: but Nietzsche wants to see both of those feet planted firmly in *this* world. If the "immature" man of Kant's account won't do without the (essentially unnecessary) "leading strings" of the guardians' authority, then it seems that the "enlightened" man who is to take his place won't do without the (essentially incoherent) leading strings of transcendental authority. So when Nietzsche and Kant look around, dismayed, at their respective contemporaries, Nietzsche's dismay is the deeper: for when he looks around at his, he finds that the best of them are too much like the best of Kant's—which is to say too much like Kant. Kant, for Nietzsche, is part of the problem. Enlightenment lies on the far side of him.[3]

3. If anything is meant by calling Nietzsche a post-enlightenment philosopher, it is this. (Commentators are not always so careful: he is often, absurdly, called *anti*-enlightenment.) For a clear expression of Nietzsche's commitment to enlightenment, see D 197.

III

On the Kantian scheme of things, man, defined by his faculty of reason, is a peculiar hybrid. His defining feature is noumenal; everything else—his feelings, desires, interests, inclinations, propensities, ambitions, fears, proclivities, sufferings, whatever—is phenomenal. To himself the "immature" man seems shot to the core with temporality, contingency, embodiment, and accident; to Kant he appears lazy. Indeed the very term "alien" is employed by Kant precisely so as to label those "heteronomous" features of being human that the normal, "unenlightened" person regards as most distinctively his own. Thus Kant systematically alienates man from his most natural self (just as the Christian, with his insistence on the immortal, supernatural character of the soul, is dedicated to doing); and he bases his estimate of the *value* of life on that separation. Addressing Schopenhauer's version of Kant, Nietzsche claims that at stake is "the *value* of morality— . . . the value of [the instincts] which Schopenhauer had gilded, deified, and projected into a beyond for so long that at last they became for him 'value-in-itself,' on the basis of which he said *No* to life and to himself. . . . It was precisely here that I saw the *great* danger to mankind, its sublimest enticement and seduction—but to what? to nothingness?—it was precisely here that I saw the beginning of the end" (GM P5).

The crisis that Nietzsche claims to have seen lies in the compulsion to expel value from the world we actually inhabit into some unintelligible "beyond"—into a never-never land of metaphysical things-in-themselves. Schopenhauer exhibits this compulsion when he transcendentalizes morality. And Kant does the same: by alienating man from himself, he locates his *real* value, his value as author, subject, and limit of the Moral Law, in the world of the noumena. Both, in Nietzsche's terms, say *No* to this life and to this world in favor of a (nonexistent) other. And this shocks him: for if both reject religion's claim to transcendental authority as unintelligible, they ought surely to refrain from granting it to something else instead. They should *see* that this "beyond"—this otherworldly home of value, whether Christian, Kantian, or whatever—just doesn't add up. Yet they continue to denude the world in its favor anyway.

Nietzsche's name for this compulsion is the "ascetic ideal." First Plato, then Christ (more strictly, St. Paul) and now Kant and Schopenhauer have propounded it. But why? Why would embodied, contingent, temporal souls insist on the worthlessness of their own embodiment, contingency, and temporality? Nietzsche's short answer is "sickness; self-hatred." But that is a deep cause. More accessible is the reason why particular transcendental devaluations of man's real—that is, nontranscendental—nature have been found so captivating: and that, according to Nietzsche, is the want of a sufficiently, or remotely, historical perspective. We have values foisted upon us from birth. Kantian Man treats them as given. Nietzschean Man wonders where they came from. Kantian Man decides that most of them constitute the unwitting deliverances (by the unenlightened understanding) of what the enlightened understanding would have come up with anyway. Nietzschean Man reflects on the need for a "*typology* of morals":

> Just because our moral philosophers knew the facts of morality only very approximately in arbitrary extracts or in accidental epitomes—for example, as the morality of their environment, their class, their church, the spirit of their time, their climate and part of the world— . . . they never laid eyes on the real problems of morality; for these emerge only when we compare *many* moralities. In all "science of morals" so far one thing was *lacking*, strange as it may sound: the problem of morality itself; what was lacking was any suspicion that there was something problematic here. What the philosophers called "a rational foundation for morality" and tried to supply was, seen in the right light, merely a scholarly variation of the common *faith* in the prevalent morality; a new means of *expression* for this faith; . . . indeed, in the last analysis a kind of denial that this morality might ever be considered problematic. (BGE 186)

Thus the moral philosophers have simply *assumed* that the values they are used to are absolutely authoritative, and have then sought to explain that absolute authority by grounding it in a realm of eternal truth (the style of explanation that Kant calls "transcendental deduction"). So—paradoxically—it is the very parochialism of their outlook that leads them to propose extravagant, otherworldly considerations in its favor. Nietzsche calls this the "typical" prejudice of all metaphysicians: the conviction that "the things of the highest [or at least of unquestioned] value must have another *peculiar* origin—they cannot be derived from this transitory, seductive, deceptive, paltry world. . . . Rather from the lap of Being, the intransitory, the hidden god, the 'thing-in-itself'—there must be their basis, and nowhere else" (BGE 2).

But this prejudice begins to look absurd (as well as self-contradictory) as soon as it is appreciated how local and contingent the values attributed to the "lap of Being" really are. In *Beyond Good and Evil* the method for exposing this contingency is described as "typology." But in Nietzsche's next book—said on its title page to be "A Sequel to My Last Book . . . , Which It Is Meant to Supplement and Clarify"—the "typology of morals" has become "the *genealogy* of morals."

In relation to Kant, then, Nietzsche's project is fourfold: to expose (as irrational) the granting of transcendental authority to anything whatever; to show how contingencies can lead to the elevation of local truths into (alleged) eternal verities; to show how the compulsion to alienate man from himself, and hence to alienate value from the world, is itself the product of contingency; and to suggest what possibilities for maturity and enlightenment await us if we can free ourselves of that compulsion. The *Genealogy* represents Nietzsche's most sustained effort to do all of these things.

IV

Genealogy—most succinctly—is the attempt to show us how we have become what we are, so that we may see what we might yet become; and Nietzsche begins his at the beginning.

Man, originally, is little more than an animal—instinctive, cruel, and stupid. And so he would have stayed were it not for the fact that some men are stronger than others. These stronger men—the "nobles"—enslave the weaker men and force them to do their bidding. To the nobles this seems entirely proper and natural: their whole scheme of values is based on their affirmation of themselves *as* strong, *as* powerful, *as* dominant. They unreflectingly think of themselves as "good" and of whatever is least like them as "bad." To the weaker men, on the other hand, enslavement is traumatic. Their instincts are denied natural outlet, their natural physicality denied expression. They become repressed; they turn in on themselves and develop an inner life, a soul, on which they can vent all the aggression and cruelty that their position at the bottom of the pile prevents them from venting on anyone else. This new interiority is thus a locus of great and seemingly unassuageable suffering. But it is also a locus of increasing ingenuity. So the slave develops in two ways that the noble does not: he suffers more, and thus resents the conditions of his existence and feels rancor against those who have thrust them upon him; and yet, because he is forced to invent and cultivate inner resources for coping with existence, he also becomes more cunning than his oppressors. These twin developments come together and culminate in the "slave revolt in morals"—an inversion of the values of the nobles. The slave confers the label "evil" on the noble, his oppressor, and grants himself the contrasting label "good." Thus in opposition to the primitively self-affirming good/bad distinction of noble morality appears the rancor-inspired good/evil distinction of slave morality. And according to Nietzsche, it is this latter variety—its virtues mimicking the qualities of the weak (humility etc.), its vices mimicking the qualities of the strong (pride etc.)—that has won out. Indeed it has won out so convincingly that moral philosophers like Kant have taken it as given, natural, as beyond question.

But there is more to come. Slave morality allows its proponents to take verbal revenge against the powerful. But this doesn't yet resolve the underlying problem—the problem of the slaves' suffering, the suffering that makes them rancorous in the first place. So a further step is taken, now under the aegis of a more sophisticated kind of noble (the priest) who sees in the slaves a great opportunity for power. The priest exploits the unresolved resentment of the down-trodden in two complementary ways: he persuades them that their suffering is in fact their own fault (guilt, sin), thus driving their suffering to new heights; but at the same time he persuades them that there is a god who will forgive the humble and punish the proud, so promising eventual recompense (revenge) for the suffering that makes the slaves' existence intolerable. In effect, then, he persuades them to make their rancor against life and the world absolute—to apply the "evil" side of their new distinction to *everything* temporal, immanent, this-worldly, and the "good" side of it to whatever lacks these qualities—to the "beyond," to God, to heaven. Thus the priest teaches the ascetic ideal: he makes existence bearable by demonizing it, by portraying it as a mistake or as a kind of exile from the "true" home of everything good. He evacuates all value from *this* world and transcendentalizes it (appointing himself its spokesperson at the same time). And again this move has been found so captivating that every metaphysician (e.g., Kant) still insists on assigning the origin of whatever he thinks most valuable (e.g., reason, the Moral Law) to some otherworldly, transcendental realm. Transcendentalism is the product, then, not of pure reason or divine revelation, but of rancor against life.

The ascetic ideal, however, fosters other capacities than self- and world-hatred. It also, for instance, fosters increased repression, increased ingenuity and—thanks to the exigencies of having to find oneself guilty for everything—increased powers of self-scrutiny, of *truthfulness* with and about oneself. And this latter capacity, according to Nietzsche, sets up a kind of countercurrent within asceticism's own precincts. For as one becomes harsher with oneself, and increasingly steels one's heart against one's own most comforting fantasies, one eventually realizes that the priest's stories (about God, heaven, and the rest) are just that—comforting fantasies; one is forced to admit that God is a fiction, a fiction one ought truthfully to do without. And so it is that Western culture becomes more secular. But it doesn't thereby become less transcendentalized: for God is simultaneously abolished and replaced—by reason (for its own sake), by truth (for its own sake). *These* values are now accorded absolute authority. But the countercurrent can't stop there. The ascetic ideal must eventually end by eating itself away from the inside, as people become ever more truthful with themselves and realize at last that transcendental values of *every* kind are a comforting fantasy, a fiction, a sublimated compensation for the horrors of existence. This, in Nietzsche's view, is the point to which we have now come (or ought to have). Here, too, is the great crisis that Kant missed: the ascetic ideal—which has succeeded for two thousand and more years in making existence and suffering bearable (by making them, at bottom, illusions)—is coming to an end. So what—if anything—is to take its place? Where do we go from here?

V

Kant's crisis, in effect, is that we are not truthful enough—that we won't face up to our transcendental responsibilities as rational beings. Nietzsche's crisis is that we are now more truthful than Kant. Our commitment to the ascetic ideal (for instance, to Kantianism) allowed us to cope with existence at the price of a certain amount of self-deception. But we can no longer (or should no longer) permit ourselves to pay that price. So we have left ourselves in the lurch: now even more richly endowed with the capacity for suffering, owing to the increased internalization engendered by asceticism, we suddenly find ourselves without those resources which, hitherto, we had used to deal with it. We find ourselves faced with an entirely detranscendentalized existence—with the problem of living, and of living with suffering, immanently. The nearest thing we possess to a virtue—our "extravagant honesty" (BGE 230)—obliges us to construct value, if we are to construct it anywhere, here. It is in this sense that morality has become a problem: once one recognizes, first, that *no* value has transcendental authority and, second, that traditional—that is, slave—morality is founded on a hatred of life, one is left to wonder *which* values might serve us best.

Nietzsche can see us adopting any of three measures in response to this crisis. The least attractive to most of us, although not very obviously to Nietzsche, is nihilism. We might simply throw up our hands in horror: existence is full of suffering; we are quite incapable now of making transcendental sense of that suffering; therefore life, existence, the world—everything—is intolerable. Sooner destruction than existence on these terms. Less apocalyptic—although not necessarily, in Nietzsche's view, more desirable—is to do what in fact we have done: to try to abolish suffering (BGE 225). We can attempt to mobilize our institutions, our technology, our science in an all-out war against pain and discomfort (and thus, in Kantian terms, embrace the "leading strings" of our guardian-experts). But this recourse, according to Nietzsche, is undesirable for at least two reasons. First, it is insufficiently truthful: suffering cannot be abolished, and the pretense that it can be is a comforting fantasy that we should be honest enough to do without. Second, it threatens to instate certain values—comfort, security, longevity—as un-

questionably authoritative: that is, it threatens, in effect, to transcendentalize the contingent benefits brought by an efficient dislike of pain, or, to put
it another way, it threatens to transcendentalize complacency. (If Nietzsche
had had *us* for contemporaries, his dismay upon looking around would surely
have been still greater.) Or finally—and this is Nietzsche's prescription—
we can truthfully face up to a life of immanence (suffering and all) and attempt to affirm it for what it is. We can try, in other words, to turn suffering somehow to account, so that life becomes valuable to us not in spite of
the suffering it inevitably contains, but at least partly in virtue of it. We can
try—somehow—to harness our pain so that it turns us toward life and the
world rather than away from it. The original nobles affirmed themselves and
their lives more or less instinctively: the world and existence were "good"
simply for having them in it. Nietzsche's hope—his ideal for human living—
is that we should succeed in discovering a new nobility, a way of living that
recaptures the original nobles' sense of themselves as immanently valuable,
but which constructs that sense out of the capacities (internalization, truthfulness, etc.) that two millennia of asceticism have bequeathed to us. The ascetic adventure sustained us, indeed it turned man into *"an interesting animal"* (GM I.7); but what we have to do now is to find a way of accepting
ourselves as the interesting animals we have become.

This is the challenge that Nietzsche interprets the modern condition as
posing. It is, in effect, Kant's challenge (think for yourselves; submit yourselves to that highest part of yourselves—to reason) squared. Whereas maturity, for Kant, is both to be achieved by, and transcendentally underwritten by, the use of reason, maturity for Nietzsche rests with us alone (as, inter
alia, rational beings); and it is to be underwritten, if at all, only by the joy
we can take in being (immanently) ourselves. And just as the challenge that
Nietzsche identifies is that much more challenging than Kant's, so the temptation to shirk it—whether through laziness or cowardice—is that much
greater too. Indeed, Nietzsche's own deepest challenge is to try to persuade
us that the arduous, pain-embracing prescription he favors is really better for
us than the alternative that we have, on the whole, chosen. We are bound to
ask him: if dreaming of the abolition of suffering involves giving up on our
one remaining virtue—our "extravagant honesty"—well . . . so what? Are
we any *worse off* for that? Why be enlightened?

It is at this point that Nietzsche begins to look more fondly upon nihilism.

VI

Kant was able to think of himself as someone who had taken the final step
to maturity, as one of those who continue "boldly on their way." Not so

Nietzsche. He is painfully aware that he is a creature of the crisis rather than its resolution: no one knows yet exactly *how* a new nobility is to be achieved, or whether it can be. And this fact, and his awareness of it, lends a strained and sometimes fractured quality to his argument.[4] The difficulty is in some ways particularly acute in the *Genealogy*, where the complexities arising from Nietzsche's implication in his own problem are all too easy to under-estimate—especially when he appears to be offering a ready-made naviga-tion kit in the shape of a fairly simple set of dichotomies and oppositions. Good/bad, noble/slave, strong/weak, natural/unnatural—one reads these, and one assumes that by holding firm to them one will emerge from the far side of the *Genealogy* in full possession of Nietzsche's meaning. Thus one can find oneself, again all too easily, concluding that Nietzsche regards us as hav-ing once been good, noble, strong, and natural; as having become bad, slav-ish, weak, and unnatural; and as looking forward to our becoming good, noble, strong, and natural again. But this, while not utterly unconnected to it, is at best a caricature of Nietzsche's position. And what prompts the cari-cature is precisely the too-easy identification of those friendly-looking pairs of opposites as navigational aids. In truth, they are what need to be navi-gated. At one point Nietzsche describes mankind as being in "unstable equi-librium between 'animal and angel'" (GM III.2); elsewhere he speaks of man as *"pregnant with a future,"* as "an episode, a bridge, a great promise" (GM II.16) whose "future digs like a spur into the flesh of every present" (GM III.13). In *Beyond Good and Evil* this condition features as a "mag-nificent tension of the spirit the like of which had never yet existed on earth: with so tense a bow we can now shoot for the most distant goals" (BGE, Preface); and reflection on this condition, in the *Genealogy*, "gives rise to an interest, a tension, a hope, almost a certainty" (GM II.16). The provisional, *un*certain quality of what is given rise to exactly matches the uncertainty of what gives rise to it: and in both cases the watchword is *tension*, for Nietzsche's conception of his problem (man) is precisely, because reflexively, bound up in the same unstable equilibrium that allows man to figure as "an episode, a bridge" and as a tightly drawn bow. To expect, in light of this, that Nietzsche's dichotomous pairs should function as solid path markers is to ex-pect quite the wrong sort of thing. Instead, one should expect that good/ bad, slave/noble, and so on would mark out fields of tension—treacherous zones within which man has his natural/unnatural habitat, and from within which Nietzsche attempts to imagine what man's great pregnancy might

---

4. The stress fractures and faults in Nietzsche's hugely ambivalent relationship to his own proj-ect are traced brilliantly by Henry Staten in his *Nietzsche's Voice* (Ithaca: Cornell University Press, 1990).

promise. Certainly that is what one finds. If one wants to get anywhere with the *Genealogy*, then, one must tread carefully, especially in the vicinity of Nietzsche's more solid-looking pieces of apparatus, which are often the least reliable of the lot. According to one commentator, indeed, the *Genealogy* performs "dialectical reversals" about these terms "at a rate that only just prevents the virtuosic from sliding into the chaotic" until it eventually reaches "a point of subtlety, often disguised by the crude vigour of its expression, which admits that the phenomena are no longer susceptible of intelligible ordering."[5]

The purpose of the present book is not to refute that conclusion but to defer it for as long as possible—for as long as sense allows. It is true that the *Genealogy* courts and sometimes succumbs to confusion and contradiction. But it spends a lot of its time not doing that, and precisely where those points of impossible subtlety are reached is a question deserving circumspection. Nietzsche is infuriatingly unbothered about the elements of philosophical etiquette—things like consistency of terminology, clear labeling of problems and conclusions, identification of opponents, and indication of where, at any given point, he is coming from. And this disregard can prompt his readers either to let themselves be swept along on a wave of what feels like thought or else to despair too quickly of ever making proper sense of any of it. But the *Genealogy* is, I think, a good deal more coherent than it sometimes seems. The strictly ancillary task (attempted here) of filling in the gaps can clarify a reasonable amount; and it can, at times, transform a near-unintelligible morass of invective and indirection into something quite closely resembling argument. Under the "*essence* of interpreting," Nietzsche lists "forcing, adjusting, abbreviating, omitting, padding, inventing" and "falsifying" (GM III.24). I haven't knowingly refrained from any of these—but I have always attempted to deploy them to the end of producing a maximally consistent and plausible reconstruction of Nietzsche's position. Nietzsche himself calls for an "art of exegesis" and alleges himself to "have offered in the third essay [of the *Genealogy*] an example" of what he means: "an aphorism is prefixed to this essay, the essay itself is a commentary on it" (GM P8). But when one turns to the relevant page, one discovers a prefixed quote from *Zarathustra* of which, with the best will in the world, the subsequent essay cannot be construed as an elucidation, a commentary, or anything else. Nor does one's grip on Nietzsche's art of exegesis improve when one recalls that "whoever writes in blood and aphorisms does not want to be read but to be learned by heart" (Z, Of Reading and Writing). In short, I am sure that what I have attempted here is not only *not* an example of the "art

5. Michael Tanner, *Nietzsche* (Oxford: Oxford University Press, 1995), p. 70.

of exegesis," or learning by heart, but is in fact something which, in its wholly ancillary ambitions, would have earned Nietzsche's undying contempt. But I hope it will be found useful even so.

There is a further problem in making sense of the *Genealogy*. This is that Nietzsche is an intensely *personal* thinker—not just in the sense that his thought is an unusually direct expression of the sort of person he was, nor merely in the sense that, reading him, one gets the feeling of being personally buttonholed, but in the sense that he thinks through particular types of person, that he uses these personalities as arguments. For him, these types function as magnets for issues or for aspects of issues which are then pursued, psychobiographically, through a disquisition on the personality types that exemplify them. It is in an attempt both to capture and to clarify this aspect of Nietzsche's thought that I have arranged his themes here under character headings. Just as the slave, for instance, acts as a focal point for the investigation of *ressentiment*, bad conscience, and self-aggrandizement, so the priest serves to focus issues about asceticism, transcendentalism, and power. The point of the distinction between ideals and procedures, and of the subtly different kinds of self-relation which seemingly identical procedures can signify, emerges through discussion of the philosopher; beauty, style, and the aesthetic dimension of interpretation emerge through the artist; the scientist attracts questions about truth, intellectual integrity, and the self-overcoming of the ascetic ideal; while the noble vivifies the problems of nihilism, immanent living, and the Last Man. If, as Nietzsche famously remarks, "every great philosophy so far has been . . . the personal confession of its author and a kind of involuntary and unconscious memoir" (BGE 6), then the *Genealogy* is no exception—except perhaps in this, that it reads more like a civil war between various factions within Nietzsche's personality than like a confession or a memoir *of* it. Nietzsche shows every sign of knowing each of the six characters discussed here at first hand. And to this extent, at least, the present book is as much about him, or about refereeing between the various factions he comprises, as it is about the *Genealogy*.

A word in conclusion about sources. I have predictably taken my lead and the vast majority of my cues from the *Genealogy*. But I have not hesitated to range further afield wherever that has seemed helpful or expedient (most often, perhaps, to *The Gay Science* and *Beyond Good and Evil*). What I have not done, however, is to avail myself anywhere of the material that Nietzsche left unpublished—even when he makes remarks there that one wishes he had made in print. Unpublished notes may be evidence of many things, but they are not evidence of what a thinker finally thought. So I judge Nietzsche on what he judged to be worth reading (or learning by heart, or whatever). The published sources will have to speak for themselves.

THE SLAVE

The long and serious study of the average man . . . —this constitutes a necessary part of the life-history of every philosopher, perhaps the most disagreeable, odious, and disappointing part.

—Beyond Good and Evil, sec. 26

The "slave revolt in morality" is probably the single most important event in Nietzsche's reconstruction of our moral past. It is therefore—given the nature of Nietzsche's project—a crucial element in his attempt to imagine our moral future. If one gets the slave revolt wrong, the chances are that not much else will work out either. The revolt comes in two stages—an immanent phase (the subject of the present chapter) and a transcendental phase (the subject of the next)—and it matters that the two are distinct. But it matters even more that the slave revolt, although described as a revolt in morality, should be seen as marking, above all, a revolt in human self-understanding. It is this that makes Nietzsche's account of it a part of his positive project rather than just a (questionable) piece of history. For what Nietzsche is reconstructing, and is attempting to provoke a successor to, is a revolution of *conscience*. Conscience, in ordinary speech, is a mode of self-relation: one reflects upon oneself (have I done well? badly?) with a view, potentially, to acting on oneself (for reinforcement or reform). To have a conscience, then, good or bad, is to be not merely conscious but self-conscious: it is to have the capacity to make oneself the object of one's own consciousness and a corresponding potential to make oneself the object of one's own will. To focus on conscience, then, is to focus on a crucial site of contact between a distinctive human capacity (reflexive consciousness) and a distinctive human possibility (self-transformation): conscience is therefore, and in the same ordinary sense, the site on which human values are forged and tested. Genealogy, I said in the Introduction, seeks to ask: where might we go next, given where we are and how we've come to be here? And in the context of conscience that question becomes: what future ways of relating to ourselves are possible, what ways of forging and testing values are possible, given our current self-relations and how we have come to stand in them? The slave revolt in morality—*that* drama of conscience—tells the background story. But its final significance, if Nietzsche is right, must lie in the future— in acts as yet unwritten.

I

The slave revolt overturns the noble mode of valuation. It forges its own values—"good" and "evil"—and substitutes them for the noble values "good" and "bad." Noble values spring from self-affirmation: "the 'good' themselves, that is to say, the noble, powerful, high-stationed and high-minded . . . felt and established themselves and their actions as good, that is, of the first rank, in contradistinction to all the low, low-minded, common and plebeian. It was out of this *pathos of distance* that they first seized the right to create values and to coin names for values" (GM I.2).

Thus the noble concept "good" precedes the concept "bad," which is merely a negation, a lack: the noble man "conceives the basic concept 'good' in advance and spontaneously out of himself and only then creates for himself an idea of 'bad' . . . an after-production, a side issue, a contrasting shade" (GM I.11). The noble's positive valuation of himself and of all that characterizes him is an affirmation of his own feeling of power, of his sense of himself as dominant in his relation to others. It is a rule, Nietzsche says, "that a concept denoting political superiority always resolves itself into a concept denoting superiority of soul" (GM I.6); and so the noble's power over others is interpreted by him as virtue, as a signification of his own goodness. According to this scheme of things, the politically inferior—the weak and impotent—are marked simply by their lack of those qualities that the noble affirms in himself, and so are characterized (by negation) as "low," "common," and "*bad*." The slave revolt, then, is the revolt of the "bad" against the "good"—or, perhaps better, of the oppressed against the style of valuation that labels the oppressor "good." And it begins when "*ressentiment* itself becomes creative and gives birth to values: the *ressentiment* of natures that are denied the true reaction, that of deeds, and compensate themselves with an imaginary revenge. While every noble morality develops from a triumphant affirmation of itself, slave morality from the outset says No to what is 'outside,' what is 'different,' what is 'not itself'; and *this* No is its creative deed" (GM I.10). Slave morality, then, begins with a creative negation— it labels the "good" of noble morality "evil," the "good one" of noble valuation the "evil one." And this latter is the slave's "basic concept, from which he then evolves, as an afterthought and pendant, a 'good one'—himself!" (GM I.10).

This reversal of noble morality is the eventual expression of the slave's own painful relation to himself. Triumphant self-affirmation isn't possible for him: he is too weak and powerless. But he longs for it nonetheless, and his unassuaged desire serves only to make his situation more painful. His experience of himself, his understanding of himself, in the terms set by noble values—as "low, low-minded," "*bad*"—fills him with rancorous self-loathing (*ressentiment*); and it is only when his *ressentiment* turns "creative" that he is able to counterfeit a form of self-affirmation (I am "good") by the expedient of first labeling all genuine self-affirmers "evil." Thus the slave's morality is the "imaginary revenge" through which he seeks compensation for the hell and misery of being himself. This complex set of moves, through which the slave comes, in effect, to understand himself as "good" *because* he loathes himself, exemplifies precisely that interplay between reflexive consciousness and value which I have referred to under the heading "conscience." And it as "conscience," too, one of the commonest words in his vocabulary, that Nietzsche seeks to understand its dynamic—although what he comes up with is so convoluted that one might almost despair of making sense of it. The problem lies partly in his cavalier attitude to terminology, partly in his determination to be consistently nice about the nobles and nasty about the slaves, and partly, too, in the sheer amount he tries to do at once. But the resultant tangle of argument is absolutely essential to his project. What he does, at bottom, is to offer more or less simultaneous explanations of how conscience is possible at all, of why it takes various forms, such as good and bad, and of what follows from its taking them. That Henry Staten, author of probably the best book ever written on Nietzsche, finds himself talking about a "*good* 'bad conscience'" and a "bad, passive form of bad conscience" should indicate something of the difficulty of the *Genealogy* at this point.[1]

I follow Staten's lead, however. What one discovers, once one picks the tangle apart,[2] is a sense of "conscience," confusingly described by Nietzsche as "bad," which is neutral and ubiquitous (i.e., the common quality of noble and slave); a bad version of this "bad" conscience which is distinctively

1. Henry Staten, *Nietzsche's Voice* (Ithaca: Cornell University Press, 1990), pp. 20, 54.
2. I have tried to pick the tangle apart in a more laborious and only doubtfully clearer way in "Nietzsche's Conscience," *Journal of Nietzsche Studies* 11 (1996), 1–12.

slavish; and a good version of it—a noble version—which Nietzsche never directly attributes to the nobles at all, presumably because he'd then have to admit, at apparent odds with his pro-noble sentiments, that they too are characterized by the neutral kind of conscience which Nietzsche, confusingly, calls "bad." But it might be best to begin with something else that Nietzsche does, and does first: he gives a sort of foretaste of the (enlightened) conscience of the future (a taste, however, whose forward-looking qualities will have to wait until Chapter 6). The suggestive passage is this:

> The ripest fruit is the *sovereign individual*, . . . the man who has his own independent, protracted will and the *power to make promises*. . . . The proud awareness of the extraordinary privilege of *responsibility*, the consciousness of this rare freedom, this power over oneself and over fate, has in his case penetrated to the profoundest depths and become instinct, the dominating instinct. What will he call this dominating instinct, supposing he feels the need to give it a name? The answer is beyond doubt: this sovereign man calls it his *conscience*. (GM II.2)

Conscience, then, is related to the capacity to make promises; and that capacity, Nietzsche tells us, requires "a real *memory of the will*"—it requires that man should "have become *calculable, regular, necessary*, even in his own image of himself, if he is to be able to stand security for *his own future*, which is what one who promises does!" (GM II.1). A "real *memory of the will*," however, is not come by painlessly. It is developed by living in the "social straitjacket" (GM II.2), under customs backed up by the "mnemotechnics" of punishment. Through punishment one learns to abide by the customs that make one calculable, "one finally remembers five or six 'I will not's,' in regard to which one had given one's *promise* so as to participate in the advantages of society" (GM II.3). Subjection to custom and punishment, then, are necessary for acquiring the capacity to make promises, for acquiring a conscience. But customs and punishments don't just appear out of nothing. They need to be imposed by someone—by someone, moreover, who himself has the capacity to make promises: the basic form of custom imposition, after all, is "Do this, or else . . . " (a threat, a promise). And this means that the imposer of customs must himself have a memory of the will and have become calculable, which means in turn that he must have been subjected to custom and punishment. The point here is not that Nietzsche's account is circular: any account of the origins of a social institution is bound to be reflexive. Rather, the point is that both the subject *and* the originator of a given custom must have had the experience of living under customs—as Nietzsche signals when he speaks of the nobles (the powerful, the imposers) as "men who are held so sternly in check *inter pares* by custom, respect, usage" (GM I.11). In this much, the nobles and the slaves are in the same boat.

What Nietzsche is sketching out here is the neutral, ubiquitous form of conscience I mentioned a moment ago. Man requires certain qualities—calculability, regularity—if he is to live as a social animal; and these qualities are fostered by the repression of his natural impulses (by punishment, by holding him "so sternly in check"). These qualities, moreover, are sophisticated and self-reflective—man must be made calculable and regular "even in his own image of himself." They are, in other words, qualities not merely of consciousness but of self-consciousness. Nietzsche is quite explicit about the role of repression in this development: "All instincts that do not discharge themselves outwardly *turn inward*—this is what I call the *internalization* of man: thus it was that man first developed what was later called his 'soul.' The entire inner world, originally as thin as if it were stretched between two membranes, expanded and extended itself, acquired depth, breadth, and height, in the same measure as outward discharge was *inhibited*" (GM II.16). The "depth, breadth, and height" which the inner world acquires—these "distances within the soul itself" (BGE 257)—are the spaces across which man is now able to reflect upon himself, to have an "image of himself." Nor does the internalization of man merely engender self-reflection. It creates the possibility of self-directed action too, of the revision of one's image of oneself: for when "the instinct for freedom" is "pushed back and repressed," it is "finally able to discharge and vent itself only on itself" (GM II.17)—"the material" it vents itself on, and upon which it is now capable of "imposing form," being "man himself, his whole ancient animal self" (GM II.18). To have the power to make promises, then, the power which the "sovereign man" calls his "*conscience*," is to have developed, through repression, the capacity for self-reflection and the potential for self-transformation.

This, in outline, is Nietzsche's account. But the way he actually advances it is confusing in the extreme. Internalization, he says, the repression of instinct, "that, and that alone, is what *bad conscience* is in its beginnings" (GM II.17)—which has the effect of disguising the neutrality of what he has in fact described. He does attempt here and there to redress the balance: he refers to the bad conscience as "an illness"—"but as pregnancy is an illness" (GM II.19), that is, as something that could go either way, good *or* bad. And elsewhere—having asked how "that other 'somber thing,' the consciousness of guilt, the 'bad conscience,'" came "into the world" (GM II.4)—he answers, "as a piece of animal psychology, no more": repression is "the sense of guilt [the 'bad conscience'] in its raw state" (GM III.20). But "bad" conscience in its "raw state"—the "pregnancy" that is only potentially bad—is efficiently hidden from view during most of what Nietzsche says, to the detriment not only of the reader's understanding of Nietzsche but also of Nietzsche's understanding of Nietzsche. Specifically, his failure to bear in mind the neutrality of "bad" conscience leads him, at times, to think that he must protect the nobles from its taint at any cost. When they impose customs on a "formless and nomad" populace, for instance, they become a "pack of blond beasts of prey": "Their work is an instinctive creation and imposition of forms; they are the most involuntary, unconscious artists there are" (GM II.17).

The point of this, no doubt, is to distinguish the nobles from the "populace"—from the slaves—as sharply as possible; and since the populace is about to have its instincts repressed (which is what "*bad conscience* is in its beginnings") Nietzsche decides to make his nobles as unrepressed (as un-"bad") as he can: he turns them into beasts. But the problem, of course, is that only the custom-governed—that is, the repressed—can become custom imposers, and that makes it very hard to portray the nobles in the way that Nietzsche wants. He tries to wriggle out of this difficulty in the very passage where he acknowledges that the nobles are, indeed, custom-governed: "these 'good men,' . . . the same men who are held so sternly in check *inter pares* by custom, respect, usage . . . once they go outside are not much better than uncaged beasts of prey. There they savor a freedom from all social constraints, they compensate themselves in the wilderness for the tension engendered by protracted confinement and enclosure within the peace of society, they go *back* to the innocent conscience of the beast of prey" (GM I.11). But this is incoherent. *Back* to the innocent conscience of the beast of prey? "To breed an animal *with the power to make promises*," Nietzsche asks, "is not this the paradoxical task that nature has set itself in the case of man?" (GM II.1). The power to make promises is exactly what distinguishes man from the beasts; and insofar as the power to make promises is a power engendered by living under customs—by internalization, by the development of conscience in its "raw state"—a conscience, innocent or otherwise, is just what a beast cannot have, however much of an "artist" he is said to be. So there is nothing there for the nobles to go "back" to.

What Nietzsche is evading in all this, of course, is the recognition that the nobles need a "bad" conscience themselves even before they can create the conditions required to produce it in others. When Nietzsche says, "It is not in *them* that the 'bad conscience' developed—but it would not have developed *without* them" (GM II.17), his claim is—from the point of view of the present act of oppression—literally true. One doesn't get a bad conscience from oppressing someone. But one does get one from being repressed; and it is only by being first repressed that one has the wherewithal—the memory—to oppress somebody else. That Nietzsche does at some level recognize this is plain from his description of the nobles "once they go outside": "they savor a freedom from all social constraints, they compensate themselves in the wilderness for the tension [i.e., the repression] engendered by protracted confinement and enclosure within the peace of society." But the fact that they are able to "compensate" themselves for their "tension" doesn't really help. For to experience that tension at all is sufficient for "*bad conscience* in its beginnings," even if its further developments are somehow forestalled by going "outside." The portrayal of the nobles as beasts of prey, then, with their illicitly "innocent" consciences, is a nonstarter. The nobles need a "bad" conscience to do what they do.

One must conclude, then, that man, insofar as he is at all social, is necessarily the possessor of a "bad" conscience.[3] But because what Nietzsche calls "bad" here is really neutral, it doesn't follow—as Nietzsche, when he loses track of his terminology, appears to think it does—that this "bad" conscience is actually "bad" in the noble sense, that is, bad in the way that the "low, low-minded, common and plebeian" are "bad." It doesn't follow, in other words, that the "bad" conscience in its "raw state" is a *slavish* conscience—the kind of conscience that eventually reverses the noble scheme of values. Nietzsche knows this, too—as he makes clear in a remarkable passage:

> One should guard against thinking lightly of this phenomenon [bad conscience] merely on account of its initial painfulness and ugliness. . . . This secret self-ravishment, this artists' cruelty, this delight in imposing form upon oneself as a hard, recalcitrant, suffering material and in burning a will, a critique, a contradiction, a contempt, a No into it, this uncanny, dreadfully joyous labor of a soul voluntarily at odds with itself that makes itself suffer out of joy in making suffer—eventually this entire *active* "bad conscience"—you will have guessed it—as the womb of all ideal and imaginative phenomena, also brought to light an abundance of strange new beauty and affirmation, and perhaps beauty itself. (GM II.18)

Here the "pregnancy" of "bad" conscience has become a "womb"; but its progeny is the very opposite of slavish *ressentiment* (a condition, Nietzsche tells us, whose "action" is always "fundamentally reaction" [GM I.10]). This "active" bad conscience enjoys the blessing of some of Nietzsche's most laudatory words and phrases: "delight in imposing form," "joyous labor," "affirmation"—"activity" itself. (Nor is it an accident, surely, that this reference to the "artists' cruelty" of the bad conscience appears immediately after the nobles, in their guise as beasts of prey, have been described as "the most involuntary, unconscious artists there are," and their work as "the instinctive

---

3. Thus Dan Conway has called the bad conscience the "opportunity cost" of living within the walls of society and peace: "Nietzsche, Heidegger, and the Origins of Nihilism," *Journal of Nietzsche Studies* 3 (1992), 28.

creation and imposition of forms." The strain of trying to keep the nobles and the bad conscience apart proves too much here, for all Nietzsche's insistence on instinct and the like.) In short, "bad" conscience—the inevitable possession of man insofar as he is even minimally socialized—is, in itself, neither good nor bad. The pregnancy, the repression, which the "bad" conscience is in its beginnings, can go either way: it can become the *bad* bad conscience of slavish *ressentiment*; or it can become the *good* bad conscience of that affirmative, joyous, form-giving activity which Nietzsche, when he's straight with himself, calls nobility and mastery.

II

Bad conscience in its "raw state," then, characterizes nobles and slaves alike. Both are repressed to some degree, both are internalized to some degree. But despite its essential neutrality—its potential to issue in good *or* bad—the bad conscience does nevertheless pose a problem: it may be like a "pregnancy," but it is still an "illness." Indeed man, because of it, is "*the* sick animal" (GM III.13). The reason for this is that an instinct repressed is not thereby deprived of its force—only of its natural outlet. And so, as Nietzsche says, it turns "*inward*," it carves out the inner spaces of consciousness and creates surprising new capacities there, but—like the pressure in a steam engine—must always be channeled, harnessed to something, discharged, if it is not to become "the most dangerous of all explosives" (GM III.15).

The inability to harness or discharge repressed instinct leads to frustration and rancor—to the state that Nietzsche calls *ressentiment*. And it is *ressentiment* that eventually gives birth to slave morality, to the values of the *bad* bad conscience. The nobles too, of course, are prone to *ressentiment*, since they too have a "raw" bad conscience; but "*Ressentiment* . . . , if it should appear in the noble man, consummates and exhausts itself in an immediate reaction, and therefore does not *poison*: on the other hand, it fails to appear at all on countless occasions on which it inevitably appears in the weak and impotent" (GM I.10). The noble's knack for dealing with *ressentiment* is impressive, no doubt, but then it ought to be. He, after all, is no slave. He is able to "go outside" and work off his frustrations there; and even without going "outside" he can take it out on those beneath him. In short, although repressed and "held so sternly in check *inter pares* by custom, respect, usage," he is not nearly as repressed as those at the bottom of the pile.[4] *Ressentiment* is a relatively minor problem for him—and hence relatively unlikely to issue in a *bad* bad conscience.

4. For discussion of the relative degrees of repression at issue here, and of their consequences, see David Owen, "Nietzsche, Enlightenment and the Problem of Noble Ethics," in John Lippett, ed., *Nietzsche's Futures* (London: Macmillan, forthcoming).

Not so the slave. One can see, says Nietzsche, in an unhelpfully condensed formula, "who has the invention of 'bad conscience' on his conscience— the man of *ressentiment!*" (GM II.11). The slave, denied release from the tensions of his "raw" bad conscience—"denied the true reaction . . . of deeds"— becomes resentful; and when his *ressentiment* turns creative he takes his "imaginary revenge" by inventing the values of the *bad* bad conscience: "This inversion of the value-positing eye—this *need* to direct one's view outward instead of back to oneself—is of the essence of *ressentiment*: in order to exist, slave morality always needs first a hostile external world— . . . its action is fundamentally reaction" (GM I.10).

There is, on the face of it, a problem with the mechanics here. We are told initially that the slave revolt begins when "*ressentiment* itself becomes creative and gives birth to values," from which it is plain that there is a noncreative form of *ressentiment* which precedes, and is a condition of, the creative form of *ressentiment*—which precedes, that is, the creation of values. But almost immediately afterward Nietzsche announces that "of the essence of *ressentiment*" is "This inversion of the value-positing eye" where, on any reading, such inversion just *is* the slave revolt in morality. So it looks as if *ressentiment* is somehow a precondition of its own essence.

The natural way out of this is to construe the second claim as referring exclusively to *ressentiment* in its creative form (so that the essence of creative *ressentiment* is the inversion of the value-positing eye), of which noncreative *ressentiment* can then intelligibly be held to be a precondition. And this, I suggest, is the way to take it. Indeed one can go further. For in the same passage Nietzsche seems to veer between the creative and the noncreative versions of *ressentiment* in almost every sentence, a movement that can be traced quite easily if the creative version of *ressentiment* is understood as a solution to the predicament signaled by the noncreative version. Predicament: being "denied the true reaction, that of deeds." Solution: compensation by means of "an imaginary revenge." Predicament: the "*need* to direct one's view outward instead of back to oneself." Solution: the "inversion of the value-positing eye." Predicament: "a hostile external world." Solution: "slave morality."

It is impossible to say whether Nietzsche consciously intended *ressentiment* to bear this double meaning—but if he didn't, he should have.[5] For one thing, the passage is self-contradictory if construed otherwise. And for another, it helps to make sense of the noble's occasional and quickly discharged experience of *ressentiment*. If the inversion of the value-positing eye

5. I think the point has escaped his readers. Walter Kaufmann, for instance, says that "the *Genealogy* contains several examples of misleading slogans, but *ressentiment* is actually not one of them. That term is univocal." *On the Genealogy of Morals*, trans. Walter Kaufmann and R. J. Hollingdale (New York: Vintage, 1967), p. 7.

really were the essence of *ressentiment* in all its forms, the noble would be profoundly—however briefly—implicated in the slave revolt in morality, and it is impossible to believe that Nietzsche intended that. What marks the noble, after all, is precisely that he does *not* go in for such inversions. It seems altogether more plausible to suppose instead that the noble experiences *ressentiment*, when he does, in its pre-creative form, and that he discharges it before it has a chance to "give birth to values"—values which would be the exact opposite of his own. The present reading gives the noble that room for maneuver: his conscience renders *ressentiment* a possibility; but his *ressentiment*, being of a protean, noncreative kind, does not eventuate in the slavish evaluations of a *bad* bad conscience.

I propose, then, to hang on to Nietzsche's implicit distinction between noncreative and creative *ressentiment*, and to take the former as a condition of the latter—that is, as a condition of the slave revolt in morality. Noncreative *ressentiment* signals the predicament of being "denied the true reaction, that of deeds," of having the "*need* to direct one's view outward instead of back to oneself" and of feeling oneself to inhabit "a hostile external world." The noble, one may suppose, although briefly stymied, pulls himself together and engages either in the "true reaction" that he momentarily fancied denied to him or else in some other compensatory measure, such as going "outside." The slave, on the other hand, has no such alternative. For him, the bottling up of his instincts is something he can do nothing about, except fume inwardly. His eventual inversion of the noble's values, Nietzsche says, "listened to calmly and without previous bias, really amounts to no more than: 'we weak ones are, after all, weak; it would be good if we did nothing *for which we are not strong enough*'; but this dry matter of fact, this prudence of the lowest order which even insects possess . . . , has, thanks to the counterfeit and self-deception of impotence, clad itself in the ostentatious garb of . . . virtue" (GM I.13). This "prudence"—this acknowledgment of powerlessness—is the slave's only recourse before the revolt. "We are not strong enough," better not to do "too much": in a "hostile external world," incomparably more powerful than one is oneself, one feels the "*need* to direct one's view outward instead of back to oneself"; which is to say, one feels driven to regard the outside world as the source and the shaper of one's destiny, as the actor in the drama of which one's own life is merely the residue. Unlike the noble, who feels and affirms his own efficacy, the slave's experience of agency is minimal and derivative, a mere reflection of his own impotence in the face of those larger forces by which he is surrounded and repressed. In such a position, "the true reaction, that of deeds," is simply unavailable. In a nutshell, then, noncreative *ressentiment* is the rancorous, impotent sense that one is on the receiving end of life, that one is a *reactor*, not an actor, an undergoer, not an undergone. That this is nonetheless the condition in which *ressentiment* can become creative and give birth to values is made plain in one of Nietzsche's less attractive passages:

> There is a soft, wary, malignant muttering and whispering coming from all the corners and nooks. . . . Weakness is being lied into something *meritorious*, no doubt of it. . . . The inoffensiveness of the weak man, even the cowardice of which he has so much, his lingering at the door, his being ineluctably compelled to wait, here acquire flattering names, such as "patience," and are even called virtue itself; his inability for revenge is called unwillingness to revenge, perhaps even forgiveness. . . . They also speak of "loving one's enemies"—and sweat as they do so. (GM I.14)[6]

Here, in the furtive, prudential world of noncreative *ressentiment*, we are shown the slave revolt in morality at its inception, the value-positing eye at the moment of its inversion.

III

Let's pause here for a second. The distinctions I have been trying to tease out—particularly those between the "raw," *good* bad, and *bad* bad consciences—are, I think, fundamental to Nietzsche's project, and they are certainly fundamental to my reading of him. So it would be as well to make sure that I have drawn them as clearly, now, as I possibly can, or as the text allows.

"Bad conscience," I have suggested, means three quite distinct things in the *Genealogy*. In its most basic and universal sense it means the "raw" bad conscience—the bare capacity for self-reflection made available by "internalization." This is the common possession of man insofar as he is socialized at all. The experience of "raw" bad conscience is inherently uncomfortable, disconcerting. "The situation that faced sea animals when they were compelled to become land animals or perish," Nietzsche suggests, "was the same as that which faced these semi-animals" when "they were reduced to their 'consciousness,' their weakest and most fallible organ! I believe there has never been such a feeling of misery on earth" (GM II.16). But the "raw" bad conscience is a site of potential as well as of discomfort. In its discomforting aspect it may elicit (noncreative) *ressentiment*—a condition of rancorous frustration directed inwardly at oneself for being as one now is and outwardly at the causes of one's being so. If this frustration is allowed no outlet, it mounts, and in mounting it further increases the dimensions and the dis-

6. Although I am using Kaufmann's translation, I follow Nietzsche's paragraphing.

comforts of the inner world which elicited it in the first place. Eventually, Nietzsche claims, the greater interiority of the most repressed makes possible a set of conceptual innovations (detailed in the following two sections) that allow *ressentiment* to turn "creative," to give birth to values—and it is these values which are definitive of the *bad* bad conscience. The slave revolt in morality takes place, then, when the inwardly and outwardly directed rancor of those least able to discharge it finally brings about a transformation in the slaves' understanding, first outwardly, of the strong ones who oppress them (as "evil"), and then inwardly—"as an afterthought and pendant"— of themselves (as "good"). But the "pregnancy" of the "raw" bad conscience need not turn out this way. It can instead, Nietzsche suggests, issue in the kind of "active" self-relation that I have called the *good* bad conscience— a self-relation in which an "artist's cruelty," a "delight in imposing form upon oneself," brings "to light an abundance of strange new beauty and affirmation, and perhaps beauty itself." And this, given the ubiquity of bad conscience in its "raw" state, must be the best that we or Nietzsche can hope for—a mode of conscience which does not derive from the creativity of *ressentiment*, but rather, one supposes, from its overcoming. The later chapters of this book attempt to discover what Nietzsche may have meant by that. But for the moment it is enough if the fundamental mechanics of Nietzsche's way with conscience (raw, good, and bad) are in place. The genealogical drama is driven by them.

IV

But what actually prompts the slave revolt? What catalyst permits an impotent state such as noncreative *ressentiment* suddenly to give birth to values? How does the slave's wretched relation to himself give him the resources for invention?

The short answer is "cleverness." His position at the bottom of the pile— as the most repressed, the most internalized, the most tormented—means that his "inner world" acquires a great deal of "depth, breadth, and height": "he understands how to keep silent, how not to forget, how to wait, how to be provisionally self-deprecating and humble. A race of such men of *ressentiment* is bound to become eventually *cleverer* than any noble race; it will also honor cleverness to a far greater degree: namely, as a condition of existence of the first importance" (GM I.10). This cleverness, born of enforced prudence, is the ace up the slave's sleeve. It is his intellectual superiority, his greater inwardness, that allows him to invent his new morality, to have "the invention of 'bad conscience' on his conscience." And this invention consists of three elements: a distinction between doers and deeds, the idea of free will, and a moralized conception of guilt. When all three of these elements have been invented, the slave revolt in morality is a fait accompli. The remainder of the present section is devoted to the first two.

The slave's high degree of internalization leads him to develop a contrast between "inner" and "outer." The "inner"—the theater of his own private torment—is himself; the "outer" is that hostile external world which has made him as he is. And this contrast, as Nietzsche argues in a famous and brilliant passage, allows the slave to commit some fruitful "errors":

> To demand of strength that it should *not* express itself as strength . . . is just as absurd as to demand of weakness that it should express itself as strength. . . . and only owing to the seduction of language (and of the fundamental errors of reason petrified in it) which conceives and misconceives all effects as conditioned by something that causes effects, by a "subject," can it appear otherwise. For just as the popular mind separates the lightning from its flash and takes the latter for an *action*, for the operation of a subject called lightning, so popular morality also separates strength from expressions of strength, as if there were a neutral substratum behind the strong man, which was *free* to express strength or not to do so. But there is no such substratum; there is no "being" behind doing, effecting, becoming; "the doer" is merely a fiction added to the deed—the deed is everything. (GM I.13)

There are actually two errors diagnosed here—the one made by the "popular mind" and the one made by "popular morality," and it is helpful to keep these a good deal more distinct than Nietzsche does. The error of the popular mind is to conceive of "all effects as conditioned by something that causes effects"; in the context of human deeds, this error comes to the belief that there is "a neutral substratum behind the strong man," that "there is a 'being' behind doing." This error (if it is one) is not the error of popular morality. That error is made only when the "neutral substratum" of the popular mind is held to be "*free* to express strength or not to do so," when the fictional "doer" is held to have chosen "the deed." That these are distinct issues becomes clear when one recalls that determinism, a doctrine that explicitly construes every event as the effect of some antecedent cause, has not always been thought an obvious counterpart of the doctrine of free will; or when one notes that the (real) temptation to think of a lightning flash as the "operation of a subject called lightning"—as the flash *of* the lightning—need not result in the thought that the lightning is somehow free to flash or not to flash. In other words, one might in principle separate the doer from the deed without going on to think of the doer as being free to do otherwise. It is in virtue of this that what Nietzsche goes on to say next makes sense: "our entire science still lies under the misleading influence of language and has not disposed of that little changeling, the 'subject' ...; no wonder if the sub-merged, darkly glowering emotions of vengefulness and hatred exploit this belief for their own ends and in fact maintain no belief more ardently than the belief that *the strong man is free* to be weak and the bird of prey to be a lamb—for thus they gain the right to make the bird of prey *accountable* for being a bird of prey" (GM I.13). If the belief in the subject and the belief that the strong man is free to be weak were not different beliefs, the former would not need to be "exploited" to yield the latter—a point underlined when Nietzsche suggests that the neutral independent subject "(or, to use a more popular expression, the *soul*) has perhaps been believed in hitherto more firmly than anything else on earth because it makes possible to the majority of mortals, the weak and oppressed of every kind, the sublime self-deception that interprets weakness as freedom, and their being thus-and-thus as a *merit*" (GM I.13). The belief in the subject, note, "makes possible" the self-deception of the weak: it is not itself that deception. Thus the slave revolt in morality exploits the doer/deed distinction in such a way that "the weakness of the weak—that is to say, their *essence*, their effects, their sole ineluctable, irremovable reality" is interpreted as "a voluntary achievement, willed, cho-sen, a *deed*, a *meritorious* act" (GM I.13). Or, to put the matter another way, the slave revolt involves the supplementation of the fictitious doer/deed dis-tinction by the fiction of freedom of the will.

If my reading of this is right, it is possible to divide the events recounted into three stages. First, there is the error of "the popular mind"—the gen-eral misconception of "effects as conditioned by something that causes effects." Second, there is the specific application of this misconception to people, so that a distinction is introduced between doer and deed. And third, there is the invention of free will, which permits the doer to be held *ac-countable* for his deeds. The transition from the first stage to the second is required by minimal standards of consistency, while the transition from the second to the third requires a radical imaginative leap.

This way of taking Nietzsche's argument has consequences that may seem surprising. For instance, it follows from what I have said that there is noth-ing to prevent the noble going through all three of the stages just mentioned, yet without inverting his value-positing eye. How? Well, although the first two stages do represent a mistake and its application, they represent a mis-take and an application that are pretty easy to make, particularly if Nietzsche is right in saying that they owe their appeal to "the seduction of language." One needn't be a slave or impotent to be misled into thinking that deeds re-quire doers. Nor, in principle, need one be either of those things in order to make the imaginative leap that construes doers as the *choosers* of deeds. That leap is implicated in the inversion of noble values only when made from the standpoint of impotence—from the "instinct" of the *weak* "for self-preservation and self-affirmation" (GM I.13). There could, in other words, be a style of noble morality that, like slave morality, utilized and exploited the fiction of the free subject—a mode of valuation that (mis)construed the nobles' "*essence*, their effects, their sole ineluctable, irremovable reality" as "a voluntary achievement, willed, chosen, a *deed*, a *meritorious* act." Made from the standpoint of strength—from the "instinct" of the *strong* "for self-preservation and self-affirmation"—such valuations would remain wholly uninverted.

It is not hard to see why Nietzsche doesn't canvass this possibility in his discussions of the slave revolt. For one thing, it would have muddied the waters. For another, it would have been superfluous. The nobles don't need the sophisticated fiction of a free will in order to affirm and to preserve themselves. Their "*essence*, their effects, their sole ineluctable, irremovable reality," the fact that they are and feel themselves to be powerful in any case, renders that extra imaginative leap unnecessary. Not being denied the "true reaction, that of deeds," the nobles require no "imaginary revenge": they're already on top and they needn't ice the cake. But none of this affects the point that such a style of valuation is, in principle, available to them—as Nietzsche, at one point, seems to recognize:

> The moral philosophers of Greece later imagined the eyes of God looking down upon the moral struggle, upon the heroism and self-torture of the virtuous: . . . virtue without a witness was unthinkable for this nation of actors. Surely, that philosopher's invention, so bold and so fateful, which was then first devised for Europe, the invention of "free will," of the absolute spontaneity of man in good and in evil, was devised above all to furnish a right to the idea that the interest of the gods, in man, in human virtue, *could never be exhausted*. (GM II.7)

The opposition "in good and in evil" may suggest that the slave revolt in morality has already happened. But when one recalls that "these Greeks used their gods precisely so as to ward off 'bad conscience,' so as to be able to rejoice in their freedom of soul," it seems improbable that Nietzsche meant his "Greeks" to be taken for slaves (GM II.23). More likely is that Nietzsche's evaluative terminology has been briefly thrown out of kilter by his own abrupt connection of the Greeks ("those noble and autocratic men") with the concept of free will. Under the circumstances this would be understandable, even if, on the present reading, it might also have been unnecessary. The significant point, though, is that a mode of noble valuation which can, if needs be, make use of the idea of free will is not ruled out even by

Nietzsche (however queasy the thought may make him). The slave revolt is, as a matter of fact, launched from the standpoint of impotence; but this does not, by itself, preclude the use of its conceptual machinery by the strong—a fact whose long-term consequences are significant (see Chapter 6).

V

The argument of the previous section indicates that the doer/deed distinction and the fiction of the freely choosing subject are necessary conditions of the slave revolt. But they are not sufficient. What's missing, if the nobles are to be held *accountable* for being noble, is the concept of guilt.[7]

It is important to understand the slave's strategy at this point. If he can hold the nobles accountable—can find them guilty—for being as they are, he has what he needs if he is to label them "evil"; and if he can label them "evil" he can then label himself, by contrast, "good"—which is what he's after. To realize this end, however, he may have to make sacrifices. Specifically, he may find that in order to deprive the nobles of their (as yet) unchallenged right to be called "good," he has first to take upon *himself* the mantle of "guilt," only afterward extending its use to cover the nobles. Certainly some such sacrifice appears to be involved in Nietzsche's reconstruction—which is why the concept of guilt emerges first in the context of the slave's relation to himself. Guilt, Nietzsche suggests, has a long prehistory which ends, momentously, in its being "moralized," although it isn't ideally clear what Nietzsche understands by that term. I have argued that the bad conscience in its "raw state" can develop either into a *good* bad conscience or into a *bad* bad conscience, which is the conscience of *ressentiment* turned creative: and it is of this latter that Nietzsche asks: "But how did that other 'somber thing,' the consciousness of guilt, the 'bad conscience,' come into the world?" (GM II.4); to which the answer when it finally arrives is: through the "moralization" of the concept of debt, through its being "pushed back into the *bad* conscience" (GM II.21). Squaring these remarks with one another isn't a problem if the "*bad* conscience" into which the concept of debt is "pushed back" is construed as bad conscience in its "raw state." But how does the moral concept "guilt" emerge from the nonmoral concept "debt"? The answer, Nietzsche suggests, lies in the prehistory of punishment:

> Throughout the greater part of human history punishment was *not* imposed *because* one held the wrong-doer responsible for his deed, thus *not* on the pre-

7. I am assuming here that free will *is* necessary for accountability—that is, I'm assuming that the religious doctrine of predestination is incoherent as well as repulsive.

supposition that only the guilty one should be punished: rather, as parents still punish their children, from anger at some harm or injury, vented on the one who caused it—but this anger is held in check and modified by the idea that every injury has its *equivalent* and can actually be paid back, even if only through the pain of the culprit. And whence did this primeval, deeply rooted, perhaps by now ineradicable idea draw its power—this idea of an equivalence between injury and pain? . . . [I]n the contractual relationship between *creditor* and *debtor*. (GM II.4)

In injuring someone the culprit becomes a debtor—one who owes recompense to his creditor; and the injured party, in the role of creditor, exacts payment from the debtor in the form of pain, or rather in the form of pleasure derived from either causing or witnessing the debtor's pain. This sense of "punishment, as requital, evolved quite independently of any presupposition concerning freedom or non-freedom of the will"; indeed, the thought that the criminal should be punished because he could have acted otherwise is "an extremely late and subtle form of human judgment and inference" (GM II.4). At this stage, then, the idea of debt is operating in a nonmoral sense and has not yet undergone the transformation that turns it into the concept of guilt—a transformation which, not unexpectedly, involves the notion of free will.

In the pre-moral phase, the culprit suffers "no 'inward pain' other than that induced by the sudden appearance of something unforeseen" (GM II.14); he thinks "'here something has unexpectedly gone wrong,' *not*: 'I ought not to have done that'" (GM II.15). The experience of "inward pain" and the thought "I ought not to have done that," therefore, are characteristic of guilt proper. Fairly evidently, then, the moralization of debt into guilt involves the augmentation of an outwardly caused pain (that of punishment, repayment) by an inwardly caused one (guilt),[8] by a sense that one is somehow a worse person for doing what one did. And certainly this captures something of what Nietzsche means by the moralization of guilt.

But a crucial factor is missing. As it stands, the sketch just offered implies a strong commitment to the essential unity of inner and outer. The guilty person regards an externally instigated misfortune (that of being obliged to make amends) not merely as a regrettable fact but as a regrettable fact about himself. As a doer he embraces his deed. "I ought not to have done that," he says, "but I did. *Therefore* I am contemptible." Yet "guilt" is supposed to be conditional on the radical separation of doers and deeds—as (resentfully)

8. What Arthur Danto calls the addition of "intensional" to "extensional" suffering: "Some Remarks on *The Genealogy of Morals*," in Robert Solomon and Kathleen Higgins, eds., *Reading Nietzsche* (Oxford: Oxford University Press, 1988), p. 21.

interpreted in the light of presuppositions "concerning freedom . . . of the will." The missing factor can be glimpsed in the following passage:

> It was precisely through punishment that the development of the feeling of guilt was most powerfully *hindered*. . . . For we must not underrate the extent to which the sight of the judicial and executive procedures prevents the criminal from considering his deed, the type of his action *as such*, reprehensible: for he sees exactly the same kind of actions practiced in the service of justice and approved of and practiced with a good conscience: spying, deception, bribery, setting traps, . . . violence, defamation, imprisonment, torture, murder . . . —all of them therefore actions which his judges in no way condemn and repudiate *as such*, but only when they are applied and directed to certain particular ends. (GM II.14)

So guilt involves not merely "inward pain" and the thought "I ought not to have done that," but also the thought that one's deed, the type of one's action *as such*, is reprehensible. The introduction of an emphasis on types of action as such serves to reanimate the distinction between doer and deed, which seemed a moment ago almost to have dropped out. To condemn and repudiate an action purely on the grounds that it is an action of a certain *kind* is to condemn it no matter whose action it is, and is thus to evaluate the deed in isolation from the doer. This emphasis helps to explain what Nietzsche means elsewhere when he speaks of the "morbid softening and moralization through which the animal 'man' finally learns to be ashamed of all his instincts" (GM II.7): again, it is a type of action *as such*—this time instinctive action—that attracts the condemnation of the moralized conscience.

In the beginning, then, "debt" signifies merely a kind of fact—a fact which, in the context of contractual relationships, might be expected to have certain consequences (for instance, attempts at recovery on the part of the creditor). The debtor's attitude toward the fact is primarily prudential; he may regard it as inconvenient, but doesn't regard himself as a worse person for his indebtedness. Then, as a concomitant of the distinction between doer and deed, debt-incurring actions come to be repudiated *as such*: one comes to think "I ought not to have done that; I ought to have done otherwise"— one interprets one's indebtedness as freely chosen, as a crime. This now hurts, now constitutes the "inward pain" of "guilt," for one is turning the fact of one's indebtedness back against oneself, as something with which to torment oneself. Why? Because the instinct for cruelty is repressed and turned inward by living under customs. In the absence of any other outlet, one makes oneself suffer "out of joy in making suffer" (GM II.18); and holding oneself accountable for one's own actions is a particularly efficient way of doing this. Guilt, then, as one of the many products, or potential products, of

the internalization of man, is most likely to be invented by the most internalized, the most repressed—by the slave. The slave's place at the bottom of
the pile permits him very few opportunities for the outward venting of his
instinct for cruelty, and so he turns it back on himself. So once again the
slave's oppressed circumstances serve as a condition of his own peculiar
brand of creativity, the creativity of *ressentiment*.

At this point the slave may appear merely to have discovered a new way of
lowering his sense of his own worth. But he has actually achieved rather
more than this. Specifically, because he has discovered how to hold himself
accountable for his own actions—how to construe himself as guilty for his
own deeds—he now has the conceptual wherewithal to construe others as
guilty for theirs, to condemn and to repudiate the nobles, for instance, for
their oppressive actions *as such*. At the price, then, of some real extra discomfort, the slave has got the nobles where he wants them. He has the doer/
deed distinction; he has the idea of free will; and now, with his new moralized conception of guilt, he has the last piece of the jigsaw. The nobles, construed as guilty of freely chosen acts of oppression, have become "evil." The
slave has become "good"—a "goodness" perhaps amplified by the fact that
he, unlike the noble, is ready to acknowledge his own "guilt." His sacrifice,
from this point of view, has been well worth making: some extra torment in
exchange for (at least a kind of) self-affirmation.

VI

I suggested at the beginning of this chapter that the slave revolt in morality
came in two distinct phases—an immanent and a transcendental. I have now
sketched out what I take to be the first of these. But it cannot be denied that
there is a strong temptation to read the *Genealogy* as if the slave revolt were
an all or nothing affair, as if the overturning of noble values were inseparable
from the invention of a transcendental realm, of God, of Christianity—as
if the inversion of the value-positing eye were itself a denial of this-worldly
in favor of otherworldly values. And there seems to be no question that
Nietzsche himself often thought of the revolt in this light: in the section of
Ecce Homo devoted to the *Genealogy*, for instance, he says that "the truth of
the *first* enquiry is the birth of Christianity: the birth of Christianity out
of the spirit of *ressentiment* . . . —a countermovement by its very nature,
the great rebellion against the dominion of *noble* values" (EH, Genealogy of
Morals). And a little later, we hear that

> Whoever uncovers morality also uncovers the disvalue of all values that are
> and have been believed; he no longer sees anything venerable in the most ven-

erated types of man, even in those pronounced holy. . . . The concept of "God" invented as a counterconcept of life—everything harmful, poisonous, slanderous, the whole hostility unto death against life synthesized in this concept in a gruesome unity! The concept of the "beyond," the "true world" invented in order to devaluate the only world there is—in order to retain no goal, no reason, no task for our earthly reality! The concept of the "soul," the "spirit," finally even "*immortal* soul," invented in order to despise the body, to make it sick, "holy." (EH, Why I am a Destiny 8)

If the slave revolt *is* all or nothing then the slave has already, on the account given so far, gained the promise of eternal bliss, as spiced up by the promise of watching the nobles suffer in hell—gloatingly reported by Nietzsche through the gloating testimony of Tertullian (GM I.15). But even in the longer of the passages just quoted there is a movement from earlier to later ("the 'soul,' the 'spirit,' finally even '*immortal* soul'"); and this prompts the suspicion that the slave revolt is less a sudden coup d'état than a gradual progression toward that "gruesome unity," God. The question then is whether the invention of the freely choosing subject and the moralized concept of guilt require transcendental moves to be made. If not, then the slave revolt indeed comes in two phases—an immanent phase supplemented by a transcendental one.

So: is the inversion of the value-positing eye *already* a transcendentalizing event? When man was internalized he "first developed what was later called his 'soul'" (GM II.16)—but how much later? Nietzsche is slippery on this. Sometimes he uses the term "soul" in contexts where it is clear that nothing transcendental is going on, as when he speaks of the "rule that a concept denoting political superiority always resolves itself into a concept denoting superiority of soul" (GM I.6) or speaks of the Greeks and "their freedom of soul" (GM II.23). At other times he appears to treat the invention of the freely choosing subject as already tantamount to the invention of the soul, as when he says that "the subject (or, to use a more popular expression, the *soul*) has perhaps been believed in hitherto more firmly than anything else on earth" (GM I.13). But is there anything in the development traced so far that actually *requires* the freely choosing subject to be a transcendental soul (an "*immortal* soul")? I think not.[9] I have already argued that Nietzsche oughtn't to think so: his occasional, and in my view warranted, readiness to countenance the idea of nobility and freedom going together scarcely suggests an indissoluble link between freedom, as such, and transcendence. But

9. In *Beyond Good and Evil* Nietzsche is emphatic: the immortal soul should be "expelled from science!" But this doesn't mean that it is "at all necessary to get rid of 'the soul' at the same time, and thus . . . renounce one of the most ancient and venerable hypotheses" (BGE 12).

even if Nietzsche does consider that link indissoluble, establishing that it is so would require an argument not given in the *Genealogy*. The concept of free will is, to put it no higher, a notoriously difficult one. There is no philosophical consensus over its status; nor is there, so far as I am aware, the least reason to think that it proves any more tractable when predicated of a transcendental subject than of a material one. In short, if "could have done otherwise" equals "free," then there is no presumption that the question "*what* could have done otherwise?" must receive an otherworldly answer. And this is so whether the words "free will" denote something real or something fictional. I suggest, then, that the freely choosing subject need not be thought of as a "soul" in any religious or transcendental sense. Nothing in this, though, rules out a move *from* the freely choosing subject to the soul, or *from* the slave revolt to the kingdom of heaven. It may well be that the overturning of noble values does lead to the invention of a transcendental realm, or that the inversion of the value-positing eye does lead to the banishment of value from "the only world there is"; and it may well be that these leadings are in some way (psychologically rather than logically) ineluctable.[10] All I am suggesting is that it doesn't follow from the existence of these tendencies that the creativity of *ressentiment*—the conjuring up of a weakness that chooses to be weak—is always and already transcendentalizing.

Nor is this conclusion much undermined when one turns to consider guilt, even if the evidence is rather mixed and Nietzsche's use of the concept infuriatingly changeable. Sometimes he uses it as a synonym for the bad conscience—which settles nothing (e.g., in GM II.4). Sometimes he ties it explicitly to religion, as when he glosses the moralization of guilt as "the involvement of the *bad* conscience with the concept of god" (GM II.21)—which appears to make guilt dependent on prior transcendental moves. Sometimes he suggests that religious concepts, such as sin, arise through "the exploitation of the *sense of guilt*" by "the priest, that artist in guilt feelings" (GM III.20)—which implies that guilt feelings are already there to be exploited. And sometimes he speaks of the moralization of guilt as a process that culminates in religious notions: guilt is turned back

> against the "debtor" first of all, in whom from now on the bad conscience is firmly rooted, eating into him and spreading within him like a polyp, until at last the irredeemable debt gives rise to the conception of irredeemable penance, the idea that it cannot be discharged ("*eternal* punishment"). . . . that will to self-tormenting, that repressed cruelty of the animal-man made inward and scared back into himself . . . —this man of the bad conscience has seized upon the presupposition of religion so as to drive his self-torture to its

10. The psychological ineluctability of this development is discussed in Chapter 2.

most gruesome pitch of severity and rigor. Guilt before *God*: this thought becomes an instrument of torture to him. . . . In this psychical cruelty there resides a madness of will which is absolutely unexampled: the *will* of man to
find himself guilty and reprehensible to a degree that can never be atoned for;
his *will* to think himself punished without any possibility of the punishment
becoming equal to the guilt. . . . This should dispose once and for all of the
question of how the "holy God" originated. (GM II.21–23)

These remarks suggest that man arrives at a moralized conception of guilt
first, and only then turns it to religious or transcendental account; and this,
as far as I can make out, does seem to be the main thrust of the later sections
of the second essay of the *Genealogy*, however much it may also be true that
Nietzsche sometimes says the opposite.

We have three options here. First, we can decide that the narratives of the
first and second essays can be reconciled by construing the moralization of
guilt in the manner just suggested, as a precondition of transcendental ideas.
On this reading, the moralization of guilt is—together with the ideas of the
subject and free will—one of the factors that makes the slave revolt in
morality possible. The main drawback with this interpretation is Nietzsche's
intermittent tendency to portray moralization as always and already transcendentalizing. Second, we can decide that the narratives of the first and
second essays can be reconciled by construing the moralization of guilt as essentially tied up with transcendental moves. On this reading, if the moralization of guilt is a precondition of the slave revolt, the slave revolt is always
and already transcendentalizing. One chief difficulty with this way of taking
Nietzsche is that his critique of transcendentalism often appears to suppose
that the concept of guilt is available *before* transcendental ideas; another difficulty is that there seems to be no good reason for thinking that the moralization of concepts must involve transcendental moves. Third, we can decide
that the narratives of the two essays need not be reconciled. On this construction, Nietzsche's account of the slave revolt is complete as it stands (the
first essay), and a fully moralized conception of guilt is not a necessary condition of the slave's holding the nobles accountable for being as they are and
doing as they do. The first essay describes how the inversion of the value-
positing eye leads in the end to transcendental ideas, while the second essay
recounts how the same ideas are separately encouraged by the transformation
of the concept of debt into the concept of guilt. The most unsatisfactory
thing about this third reading is that, in giving up on the attempt to fit the
evolution of "guilt" somewhere into the inversion of noble values, it presents
a weaker and more fragmentary version of Nietzsche's case than the apparent parallels between essays 1 and 2 would lead one to expect or to hope.

Of these options, I am least inclined to favor the second. It seems to me that just too much of the textual evidence points the other way, and that Nietzsche nowhere provides the arguments that would be needed to establish that "guilt" is necessarily a transcendental concept. But if the price for construing the slave revolt as always and already transcendentalizing looks too high to me, it must nonetheless be admitted that neither of the other options comes free. The third is perhaps the cheapest in terms of interpretative violence: to relax the demand that essays 1 and 2 should somehow fit closely together is to allow more latitude to the arguments apparently advanced in each. On this reading, one could have a nontranscendentalizing slave revolt whether or not the moralization of guilt depended on the "involvement of the *bad* conscience with the concept of god" (GM II.21). But this should be a last resort. For if we can—at the price of ignoring only a little of what Nietzsche says—come up with an account that makes tolerable sense not only of both essays individually but of the fit between them, and that does so in a fairly commonsensical way, it seems to me that we should prefer it. So I prefer the first option—the one that construes the moralization of guilt as one of the conditions of the slave revolt, and that construes the slave revolt as not necessarily involving anything transcendental. This reading shares with the second option the drawback of clashing with at least some of what Nietzsche says, but not with as much of it; and it shares with the third option the advantage of following the text fairly closely, but without rendering the relation between essays 1 and 2 completely opaque. I conclude, then, that the slave revolt does have an initial, immanent, this-worldly phase—a phase made possible by the invention of the freely choosing subject and the moral concept "guilt."

VII

This conclusion gains force when one considers what the slave has gained by his revolt (assuming that eternal bliss is still around the corner). The most striking thing he has gained is a share in the noble right to "create values and to coin names for values." Indeed, "the lordly right of giving names extends so far that one should allow oneself to conceive the origin of language itself as an expression of power on the part of the rulers: they say 'this *is* this and this,' they seal every thing and event with a sound and, as it were, take possession of it" (GM I.3). Through the inversion of the value-positing eye, the slave too begins to "seal" things and to take possession of them, he too begins to express his power.

Before, the slave's own status and worth could only be construed through the value-positing eye of the noble. The slave regarded himself from the nobles' points of view as "low, low-minded, common and plebeian," as exemplifying the lack of every quality that the nobles affirm in themselves. Before the revolt, the slave was, for himself, literally worthless, "bad," without value, a creature whose only recourse was to prudence, caution, and impotent *ressentiment*. But with the creative leap to the concept of "evil" this changes. The slave now has a value with which to oppose the "good" of the nobles: in labeling the nobles, their characteristics and deeds "evil," the slave has for the first time opened up a space in which it is possible for him to affirm *himself*. Admittedly the affirmation made available is of a pale and derivative sort: "*the Evil One* . . . is his basic concept, from which he then evolves, as an afterthought and pendant, a 'good one'—himself!" (GM I.10); or, in more pastoral vein, "these birds of prey are evil; and whoever is least like a bird of prey, but rather its opposite, a lamb—would he not be good?" (GM I.13). Yet for all its negative, reflected quality, by its very existence this mode of affirmation changes the evaluative landscape decisively. Not only are there now two competing pairs of evaluative oppositions, good/bad and good/evil, but—and for the first time—there are two competing groups, each determined to affirm its own way of being as uniquely valuable.

But even so, what *real* good does the slave's self-affirmation do him? (He's still the oppressed one, after all, and the nobles are still on top.) This is rather like asking what real good being happy does someone, and it invites only the same kind of hand-waving in response. To experience oneself as utterly worthless and low, prompted to live by nothing more than an uneradicated instinct for survival and a fear of death, is to experience the worst, and it is not only a trendy style of chat-show therapy that would urge the absolute value of self-esteem in the face of it. Any kind of self-affirmation, however pale and reflected, is more livable than none; and when the self-affirmation concerned is capable not merely of according one some minimal worth but, as the slave's is, of portraying one to oneself as *better* than those who regard one as worthless, it is more livable still. That one lacks the material wherewithal to impress one's superiority on those who thoughtlessly insist on oppressing one is, from this perspective, secondary. It is enough that one no longer regards oneself through their eyes as a mere lack, a null, a perfectly natural and inevitable object of violation.

The inversion of the values of the powerful is, then, in the end, a response to the problem of suffering—an acute problem for the slave, since he does more of it than anybody else. The slave's experience of oppression, powerlessness, and *ressentiment* ensures that suffering is the basic condition of his existence. And before the revolt, his suffering, being after all *his*, is worthless from his own point of view. He doesn't yet have a way of affirming himself *through* it. From the point of view of the nobles, on the other hand, the slave's suffering may be eminently worthwhile. Nietzsche is unflinching in his insistence on the basic human appetite for the suffering of others:

> To see others suffer does one good, to make others suffer [does] even more: this is a hard saying but an ancient, mighty, human, all-too-human principle to which even the apes might subscribe; for it has been said that in devising bizarre cruelties they anticipate man and are, as it were, his "prelude." Without cruelty there is no festival: thus the longest and most ancient part of human history teaches—and in punishment there is so much that is *festive!*— . . .
>
> Today, when suffering is always brought forward as the principal argument *against* existence . . . one does well to recall the ages in which the opposite opinion prevailed because men were unwilling to refrain from *making* suffer and saw in it an enchantment of the first order, a genuine seduction *to* life. (GM II.6, 7) [11]

"What really arouses indignation against suffering," Nietzsche says, "is not suffering as such but the senselessness of suffering" (GM II.7); "every sufferer instinctively seeks a cause for his suffering" (GM III.15) and thirsts "for reasons—reasons relieve" (GM III.20). The slave's suffering, from the nobles' point of view, certainly isn't senseless: it does them good, it enhances their feeling of power. But from his own point of view, the best that the slave can do is to see his own suffering through their eyes, as being good for *them* (i.e., at least as good for something, as having a reason). And this, of course, is exactly the tactic that Nietzsche imputes to the nobles in their efforts to make sense of their own suffering: they "understood all suffering in relation to the spectator or the causer of it" and "knew of no tastier spice to offer their gods to season their happiness than the pleasures of cruelty" (GM II.7).

The seeking of reasons or causes is essential here. The need to construe one's experience as meaningful is a corollary of becoming a self-conscious animal, of being internalized by living under customs. We have already seen that "the lordly right of giving names" is "an expression of power on the part of the rulers: . . . they seal every thing and event with a sound and, as it were, take possession of it." And this is part of a process. As David Owen puts it, "insofar as one develops consciousness at the expense of instinct, so the feeling of power is increasingly mediated through meaning" until "the instinct for [power] turned fully back on itself becomes the conscious desire for the feeling of [power], where this is entirely mediated through meaning." [12] The attempt to render one's suffering intelligible, then, is the attempt to feel

---

11. The slave may occasionally experience pleasures of this kind—although Nietzsche is vague on the point. See GM II.5.

12. David Owen, *Nietzsche, Politics and Modernity* (London: Sage, 1995), p. 65.

powerful with respect to it, to take possession of it: "whatever exists . . . is again and again reinterpreted to new ends, taken over, transformed, and redirected by some power superior to it; all events in the organic world are a subduing, a *becoming master*, and all subduing and all becoming master involves a fresh interpretation, an adaptation through which any previous 'meaning' and 'purpose' are necessarily obscured or even obliterated" (GM II.12). Nietzsche's specific subject here is punishment, but the point is a general one: in attempting to take possession of one's suffering, to subdue it, one imposes an interpretation on it, one gives it a reason, so that interpretation becomes the *means* of exercising one's power.

Before the revolt, the slave's interpretative resources are thin and unsatisfactory. To construe one's suffering as being for the benefit of the causers of it is better than nothing, no doubt. Yet it scarcely constitutes a decisive subduing and becoming master. To be a spectator sport may perhaps be enough for the nobles, since they have less systematic suffering to make sense of, and are anyway usually on the delivering end; but for the slave something more is required. And this is what the immanent phase of his revolt gives him— for by turning the noble interpretation of things upside down, he does indeed now begin to master and subdue his suffering. No longer content with construing it from the point of view of those who cause it, the slave at last has his own reasons for suffering, and with them the means to affirm himself precisely *as* a sufferer. By holding his oppressor accountable for oppressing him, by labeling the cause of his suffering "evil," the slave imposes a meaning on that suffering, which not only redeems it from senselessness but also establishes the slave himself as a better, more valuable man than the man who makes him suffer. Through this ingenious reinterpretation, the slave turns his suffering to account and now understands his pain as valuable— as his most powerful and self-affirming defense against a "hostile external world."

This really *is* a revolution in conscience. From the least promising of starting conditions the slave has discovered a way of turning his problem into its own (partial) solution. Burdened with the torments of repressed instinct, unable to discharge it in the natural way, he exploits the internalized resources that his condition has thrust upon him in order to effect a transformation in "his own image of himself." He no longer understands himself as a worthless site of suffering: he understands himself instead as "good" *because* he suffers. He has forged the values he needs—the *bad* bad conscience he needs—if his existence is to be even minimally tolerable to him. His revolt has begun to pay. But its dividends haven't yet reached their heights— and they won't until, thanks to the priest, the slave's relation to himself takes its decisive transcendentalizing step. That is the subject of the next chapter.

CHAPTER TWO

THE PRIEST

The sight of the saint awakened a suspicion in them: such an enormity of denial, of anti-nature will not have been desired for nothing, they said to and asked themselves. There may be a reason for it, some very great danger about which the ascetic . . . might have inside information.

—*Beyond Good and Evil*, sec. 51

In the preceding chapter I set out what I take to be the opening phase of the slave revolt in morality—an essentially immanent phase, during which the slave reaps the first fruits of his inversion of the value-positing eye. In this chapter I turn to the second, transcendentalizing phase of the revolt, the momentous brainchild of the "ascetic priest." This phase is again complex, and Nietzsche's attitude to it, if anything, still more so. His ambivalence is rooted in his high regard for what the priest has achieved: the priest completes the revolution in conscience which the first phase of the revolt initiates—with the most drastic consequences for the self-understanding of its participants. After the priest, the slave understands himself not as a suffering, this-worldly animal who must shift for himself as best he can, but as an otherworldly "soul" temporarily exiled into a realm of embodiment, contingency, and pain. The forging and testing of values takes the form, from this standpoint, of denigrating the immanent in favor of the transcendental—of evacuating value from this world into another. The priest's masterstroke consists in exploiting, to these ends, the momentum of the process that has made the slave as he already is. The slave's instincts have all been turned inward, repressed; he lacerates himself and feels *ressentiment* toward the external conditions that have (so painfully) internalized him. So the priest simply completes the circle: he encourages the repression and the internalization of the slave's one remaining impulse—his *ressentiment*—and so drives him to such a pitch of self-hatred that nothing of a this-worldly character—that is, nothing pertaining to contingency and embodiment—can possibly seem "good" to him. Transcendental consolation is now an essential requirement; and the priest—through his invention of that "gruesome unity," God—is able to promise it. The audacity of this move takes Nietzsche's breath away. Partly he is shocked and horrified: so successful has the priest been that he half-suspects that man has been ruined by him, and ruined for ever. But partly he is encouraged: if a revolution in conscience on this scale has proved possible once, why not again—only this time in the opposite direction?

I

The immanent phase of the revolt has brought the slave some benefits. From the inner resources generated by his position as the most repressed, he has created the wherewithal to think of the nobles as "evil" for oppressing him, and at the same time he has opened a space within which he can affirm himself precisely *as* a sufferer. He has, as it were, laid hold of his own suffering and reinterpreted it to his own greater glory—and so is incomparably better off than he was when he could only see his suffering from the nobles' point of view, as essentially good for *them*. Yet the benefits he has gained are still not all he might hope for. "What really arouses indignation against suffering," says Nietzsche, "is not suffering as such but the senselessness of suffering" (GM II.7). The slave has brought a certain kind and amount of suffering under a self-empowering interpretation. Most notably, because he now has the conceptual machinery required to hold the nobles accountable for oppressing him, he has brought the suffering caused by the nobles under a self-empowering interpretation. But this leaves an awful lot still to be accounted for.

The "inversion of the value-positing eye" is described by Nietzsche as an "imaginary revenge"—and one can see why. It does have some real effects: for instance, it permits the slave a minimal degree of self-affirmation. But it does nothing at all to rectify the circumstances that made revenge desirable in the first place. The "evil" nobles still oppress the "good" slaves, the "good" slaves still find their instincts remorselessly turned inward; they still lacerate themselves under the conditions that originally filled them with *ressentiment* and then turned their *ressentiment* "creative." Moreover, because they now regard the nobles as guilty for what they do, yet lack the power to make the nobles either acknowledge or pay for their guilt, the impotence of their situation, always galling, must now strike them as grotesque. The "good" man, the "better" man, seems destined to live under the yoke of the "evil" man forever—destined to live and to die oppressed. And death itself is a horizon for the clever man, a finality for him as it is not for the noble. The noble can *act*: he has the capacity to impose himself on the world, to leave a trace of himself, of his having existed, inscribed into it: he emerges from his depredations "convinced" that he has "provided the poets with a lot more material for song and praise" (GM I.11). In this way, the (not too clever) noble achieves a tolerable accommodation with the prospect of his own death. Not so the slave: no one will sing of him—true deeds are denied him. When he dies, his death will be the end of him, as if he had never lived. How senseless! Suffering, says Nietzsche, is often "brought forward as the chief argument *against* existence" (GM II.7); and to the slave—a self-conscious sufferer, whose sole means of self-affirmation consists in affirming himself *through* his suffering—that argument is apt to look particularly strong. Uninterpreted suffering is fatal to him, a standing reproach not just to the manner of his existence but to the fact of it: his problem, as a self-conscious, mortal sufferer, destined for permanent repression, becomes: Why exist at all?

The problem here, in effect, is that creative *ressentiment* is still *ressentiment*. The slave still suffers from his inability to discharge his instincts, from the weakness that restricts his vengeance to the imaginary. He still suffers from the "dreadful heaviness" of "consciousness": "I believe there has never been such a feeling of misery on earth, such a leaden discomfort—and at the same time the old instincts had not suddenly ceased to make their usual demands! Only it was hardly or rarely possible to humor them" (GM II.16)—and in the slave's case not possible at all. This condition is, of course, the bad conscience in its "raw" state, a condition whose discomforts the slave is unable to discharge or to turn (entirely) to his own advantage. His impotence in the face of them poisons him, makes him malignant—he longs for revenge against the forces that make his impotence possible. But even his best, most creative form of revenge is only imaginary. Real redress—that is, the elimination or resolution of repression—is altogether beyond him. And so he is still consumed with *ressentiment* against the conditions that have made him what he is—and what, once internalized, he is destined to remain. For the slave, then, for "the man of *ressentiment*," the problem is not so much individual bits and pieces of suffering (for which imaginary compensations are available) as the whole business of being alive, of existence on the terms that lead him to suffer from being himself in the first place. He is soured against himself and against the world by the sheer burden of his own inexpressible rancor.

The slave's existence, in the first phase of his revolt, is only partly justified: the question Why live? remains unresolved. Nor, as yet, do the resources that he has marshaled furnish him with any obvious next step, however strong

his craving. The next step, the step from immanence to transcendence, requires not merely a further inference but—as with the earlier move from the
doer/deed distinction to the idea of the freely choosing subject—a radical imaginative leap. It is this further leap that constitutes stage two of the
revolt.

II

Here is where the priest comes in. Or, to put it more accurately, here is where
the priest becomes essential. In construing the immanent phase of the slave
revolt in morality as entirely the slave's own work I have, more or less deliberately, excluded the priest from the account. But I don't insist on his exclu-
sion. It is possible that the priest should be credited with inspiring the first
phase of the revolt too—with the initial twist that allows *ressentiment* to become creative. Perhaps he is the only one ingenious enough to make these
opening immanent moves. But there is no real reason why one would have
to be a priest in order to make them, and until now I've left him out so as to
avoid the distraction of introducing an implicitly transcendentalizing figure
(the priest) to account for a series of essentially nontranscendental inventions. At bottom, though, not much hangs on the question: Who was clever
enough? The answer is simply: someone very internalized, very repressed.
And that someone could, on the face of it, have been either slave or priest.

But if the priest *is* involved in stage one of the revolt, it is important to
recognize—as Nietzsche sometimes does not—that he must be involved as
orchestrator rather than participant. This possibility is expressed very clearly
in *The Gay Science* (on the assumption that the priest can be seen as the
founder of a religion); the priest's distinctive achievement is

> first: to posit a particular kind of life and everyday customs that have the ef-
> fect of a *disciplina voluntatis* and at the same time abolish boredom—and
> then: to bestow on this life style an *interpretation* that makes it appear to be
> illuminated by the highest value. . . . [T]he way of life . . . was usually there
> before, but alongside other ways of life and without any sense of its special
> value. The significance and originality of the founder of a religion usually
> consists of his *seeing* it, *selecting* it, and *guessing* for the first time to what use
> it can be put, how it can be interpreted. (GS 353)

That the priest ought not to be seen as a participant in the first stage of the
revolt becomes clear when one notes that "the priestly mode of valuation"
branches "off from the knightly-aristocratic" mode of valuation, and that
"the priestly caste and the warrior caste" are identified as two distinct kinds

of noble (GM I.7). As a noble, the priest already affirms himself for what he is, and so has no immediate personal interest in overturning the noble scheme of values. So if he does orchestrate the first stage of the revolt, he does so for rather remoter reasons than those of its participants.

But with Nietzsche things are never so simple. Section 7 of the first essay, from which a chief warrant for regarding the priest as a variety of noble derives, is peculiarly difficult to make sense of. "One will have divined already," Nietzsche says, "how easily the priestly mode of valuation can branch off from the knightly-aristocratic and then develop into its opposite" (GM I.7). But despite his blithe assurance, it is well worth asking how. How is one meant to have divined this? And this question, which is a question about what kind of noble the priest is supposed to be, becomes the more pressing when one notes how contradictory Nietzsche's claims about the priest sometimes are. In GM I.7, where Nietzsche seems most concerned to mark the contrast between the priestly and the warrior castes as vividly as possible, the priest is portrayed as one of the "truly great haters in world history"—hatred being the reactive, vengeful response of the impotent. But in the third essay, where Nietzsche is more concerned to emphasize the sheer ingenuity of the priest's inventions, and seems himself to be half seduced, the priest has become an "animal that despises more readily than it hates" (GM III.15)—the capacity to despise having earlier been marked out as characteristic of the (nonpriestly) noble (GM I.10). If the priest really is a noble of some kind, we should presumably take his propensity to despise more seriously than his propensity to hate. But then, immediately afterward, the priest appears to be transformed into a slave:

> All that has been done on earth against "the noble," "the powerful," "the masters," "the rulers," fades into nothing compared with what the *Jews* have done against them; the Jews, that priestly people, who in opposing their enemies and conquerors were ultimately satisfied with nothing less than a radical revaluation of their enemies' values, that is to say, an act of the *most spiritual revenge*. For this alone was appropriate to a priestly people, the people embodying the mostly deeply repressed priestly vengefulness. It was the Jews who, with awe-inspiring consistency, dared to invert the aristocratic value equation . . . , saying "the wretched alone are the good; the poor impotent, lowly alone are good . . . , alone are blessed by God, blessedness is for them alone— and you, the powerful and noble, are on the contrary the evil . . . ; and you shall be in all eternity the unblessed, accursed, and damned!" (GM I.7)

The revaluation of values here is clearly the slave revolt in morality; and the priests appear to be taking part in it, to be participants. Doubtless this accords reasonably well with the claim that the priestly mode of valuation develops into the opposite of the knightly-aristocratic. But it accords very ill with the claim that the priestly mode of valuation "can *branch off*" from the knightly-aristocratic, or with the portrayal of the priestly mode of valuation as the "priestly-*noble* mode of valuation." What are we to make of this?

One move would be to lean quite heavily on the distinction between being a priest and being priestly. On this reading, "the Jews, that priestly people" need not themselves be priests; rather, they might merely be a people peculiarly under the sway of priests, so that their revolt is conducted under the auspices of priests but not with their participation. This way of taking the passage certainly has the advantage of restoring the priest to an orchestrating role, and so of preserving his status as a variety of noble. But it isn't very persuasive even so. For to take the priest/priestly distinction this seriously is at once to credit Nietzsche with a concern for the minutiae of terminological exactitude that nothing else in the *Genealogy* encourages, and at the same time to limit the scope of that exactitude quite drastically (and arbitrarily): surrounding passages abound with "priestly" references that are obviously references to priests. Instead, I think, we should take GM I.7 to mark a moment at which Nietzsche is simply trying to do too much at once. The whole of the slave revolt (both phases) is presented here in the most compressed form, and if distinctions are elided and valuations conflated as a result, one ought not perhaps be too surprised (or too keen to extract from the passage any perfectly consistent meaning).[1] That the priest is involved in *some* way in the slave revolt in morality is hardly unexpected. But I suspect that if we wish to learn exactly how, we will do better to seek the bulk of our evidence elsewhere.

The first step is to try to make sense of the claim that the priest is a kind of noble. To be a noble, in the first essay, is to regard oneself as the source and exemplar of value, to conceive "the basic concept 'good' in advance and spontaneously out of" oneself before going on to create "an idea of 'bad'!" (GM I.11). In "the majority of cases," the nobles "designate themselves simply by their superiority in power (as 'the powerful,' 'the masters,' 'the commanders'). . . . But they also do it by a *typical character trait*: and this is the case that concerns us here. They call themselves, for instance, 'the truthful'" (GM I.5). And "to this rule that a concept denoting political superiority always resolves itself into a concept denoting superiority of soul it is not necessarily an exception . . . when the highest caste is at the same time the *priestly* caste and therefore emphasizes in its total description of itself a predicate that calls to mind its priestly function. It is then, for example, that

---

1. Nietzsche is more expansive elsewhere. But the account I am about to unpack from the *Genealogy* is consistent with Nietzsche's lengthier discussions: see, e.g., AC 25 and surrounding passages.

'pure' and 'impure' confront one another for the first time as designations of station" (GM I.6).

Thus the priestly mode of valuation is, to begin with at least, in perfect conformity with the *style* of valuation one would expect from a variety of noble, even if the content of it diverges from that of the more knightly styles of valuation. It is this, presumably, that leads Nietzsche to assume that one should "have divined already how easily the priestly mode of valuation can branch off from the knightly-aristocratic"—although since the priestly mode, just like the knightly-aristocratic mode, is a central instance of noble valuation, it seems a bit partial to describe the former as "branching off" from the latter.

As to the priestly mode developing into the opposite of the knightly-aristocratic, or at any rate into something less healthy than the knightly-aristocratic, Nietzsche has this to say: "it is clear from the whole nature of an essentially priestly aristocracy why antithetical valuations [i.e., 'pure' and 'impure'] could in precisely this instance soon become dangerously deepened, sharpened, and internalized" (GM I.6)—a claim that deserves some attention, especially since Nietzsche is about to attribute to "the priestly form" of human existence the fact that "man first became *an interesting animal*" (GM I.6). Why is it said to be "clear from the whole nature of an essentially priestly aristocracy" that their antithetical valuations would "soon become dangerously deepened, sharpened, and internalized," when the same dangers are obviously supposed not to arise from the "whole nature" of an essentially knightly aristocracy? The answer to this lies in the "typical character traits" through which each aristocracy affirms itself. While the value judgments of the knight presuppose "a powerful physicality, a flourishing, abundant, even overflowing health" (GM I.7), those of the priest presuppose circumspection, thoughtfulness, inwardness. Their contrasting responses to the internalization engendered by living under customs underlines this difference. The knights release their "tension" by "going outside" and engaging in "a disgusting procession of murder, arson, rape, and torture, exhilarated and undisturbed of soul" (GM I.11), while the priests, whose "habits . . . turn them away from action," are ungenerously said to "alternate between brooding and emotional explosions" instead (GM I.6). Are the priests, then, denied the true reaction, that of deeds? Is their greater repression forced upon them by someone more powerful? The answer must be no. In the first place, if their "whole nature" were the product of externally imposed oppression, they would be indistinguishable from the slaves, which is clearly not Nietzsche's understanding; and in the second place, it would be unintelligible that the "priestly caste" should ever be also the "highest caste," as Nietzsche indicates may happen. Rather, it seems that the priest has to be seen as *foregoing* the more exuberant reaction of the knight (his "habits" turn him away from action). That he is none the less aggressive for his forbearance, however, nor any less bent on his own brand of domination, is amply witnessed by that two-thousand-year reign of his of which the *Genealogy* is both a diagnosis and a critique.

One could wish, though, that Nietzsche had troubled to explain how the priest came by his "habits," or why he chooses to forego "the true reaction." But Nietzsche didn't, so one can only speculate. Partly, one supposes, the answer must have to do with a simple difference in natural endowment: perhaps the nobles who became priestly nobles were just less physically robust or more shortsighted than their knightly peers, and so correspondingly less suited to action. In this much, the priests might well be expected to develop some rather unknightly "habits," including the habit of refraining from deeds. But then the question arises: how is a deedless noble a noble? How does the priest enter into the economy of noble living as a participant rather than a mere spectator? The answer, I suspect, lies in the noble capacity to deal with the thought of death — for this presupposes a division of labor: the knightly noble, having gone "outside," is "convinced" that he has "provided the poets with a lot more material for song and praise." So the noble economy needs poets. And it needs mythologizers too. The first two essays emphasize just how resourceful the nobles were in devising gods and stories through which to affirm themselves — and someone (someone noble) must have had the ingenuity to do the devising. So it is tempting to construe the priests as the ingenious ones — as a caste of poets and mythologizers, perhaps marked out for the part by a comparative lack of "powerful physicality," whose inventions and interpretations permitted the noble class as a whole to go about its business "undisturbed of soul" (GM I.11). If so, one can perhaps begin to glimpse in the priest's position the seeds of a problem: though a noble, a natural self-affirmer, he nonetheless performs an ancillary function (however essential). He finds himself on the service side of the noble division of labor. And it isn't hard to imagine that this might rankle. It isn't hard to imagine, in other words, that the priest might be on the lookout for some rather more directly self-affirming end to which his powers of invention might be turned. And perhaps that is why he is alert in the first place to the opportunities that the slavish way of life offers: one doesn't "select" something, after all, if one isn't looking for something.

This all seems plausible to me, even if it must be conceded that Nietzsche nowhere actually indicates that the priest might have functioned as a kind of poet. But whether it is plausible or not, one can at least be reasonably confident of the following: the priest is a self-affirming noble who spontaneously conceives a nonmartial concept of "good" out of himself; he foregoes the macho reaction to repression favored by his knightly peers; he nurtures the internal resources (the bad conscience) so engendered; and he finds himself, in consequence, far better placed to detect and exploit the opportunities for dominion over those whose own will to power has, as a result of oppression, become mediated entirely through consciousness, through meaning, than a mere knight ever could be. The knights are liable to misunderstand the slave: when their "mode of valuation blunders and sins against reality, it does so with respect to the sphere with which it is *not* sufficiently familiar, against a real knowledge of which it has inflexibly guarded itself: . . . that of the common man, of the lower orders" (GM I.10). The priest, by contrast, comprehends the slave very well, through having nurtured in himself the very conditions which the slave finds thrust upon him. The slave represents the priest's natural constituency, then; and the priest's originality—when confronted with the slavish way of life—"consists of his *seeing* it, *selecting* it, and *guessing* for the first time to what use it can be put, how it can be interpreted." And it is in this role—the role of master interpreters—that priests make "the *most evil enemies*" (GM I.7). We can now see that, contra Nietzsche, the priestly mode of valuation doesn't strictly *develop* into the opposite of the knightly-aristocratic, as he says. Rather, insofar as the knightly-aristocratic is characterized by its ("inflexibly guarded") resistance to the mediation of power through meaning, the priestly mode is opposed to it essentially, and is opposed to it from the beginning.

Nietzsche unquestionably finds it difficult to keep the priest in his place— as a noble whose mode of valuation is the "opposite" of the knights' and who is yet no slave. And when he does slip up, it is, as we have seen, almost invariably in the slavish direction. Nietzsche claims, for instance, that the life of the priest is ruled by "a *ressentiment* without equal" (GM III.11), which invites one to think of the priest as being, like the slave, at the bottom of the pile, as having his situation thrust upon him. But the priest (the priestly *noble*) is a primal self-affirmer; so his relation to *ressentiment* must be different from the slave's. Specifically, the priest embraces the conditions of slavish *ressentiment* willingly, out of a recognition of its possible value (to him) as a route to power. This difference—which Nietzsche is always tempted to blur—does sometimes find its way onto the page: "If one has grasped in all its profundity . . . how it cannot be the task of the healthy to nurse the sick and to make them well, then one has grasped one further necessity—the necessity of doctors and nurses *who are themselves sick*; and now we understand the meaning of the ascetic priest and grasp it with both hands. . . . He must be sick himself, he must be profoundly related to the sick—how else would they understand each other?" (GM III.15). At first it seems that the priest is tarred with exactly the same brush as the slave: "He must be sick himself."

But then Nietzsche retracts: "he must be profoundly related to the sick"—and in this retraction the difference that makes all the difference is acknowledged, however grudgingly. The priest's relation to the "sick," albeit intimate, profound, and necessary, is not one of identity. It is rooted instead in imagination, in imaginative identification.

I have spoken of the priest as "orchestrating" the slave revolt in morality. But perhaps a more fruitful analogy is to be found in the idea of a conductor. To the question, Is the conductor himself a member of the orchestra? a range of answers can be given, a range that shadows the options on offer in the present context. Yes, the conductor *is* a member of the orchestra in the sense that he too is a musician, and in the sense that he too is indispensable to the music that the orchestra makes. But no, he isn't a member of it in the sense that, say, the second oboist is, nor is he—unlike the oboist—constrained by any other musician, except in the sense that the musicians constituting the orchestra may be more or less suited to the use for which he has, as it were, selected them. The conductor must himself be a musician, must be profoundly related to the musicians constituting the orchestra; but the relation between the two is complex, a matter of imaginative identification rather than simple identity. Nietzsche's inclination to conflate the repression (bad conscience, sickness) of the priest with that of the slave precisely mirrors the temptation to conflate the sense in which the conductor is a member of the orchestra with the sense in which its instrumentalists are.

The analogy gains force when Nietzsche goes on. As well as being profoundly related to the sick, the priest "must also be strong, master of himself even more than of others, with his will to power intact, so as to be both trusted and feared by the sick, so as to be their support, resistance, prop, compulsion, taskmaster, tyrant, and god." It is in this conductorly (and unmistakably noble) role that the priest fulfills his "tremendous historical mission. *Dominion over the suffering* is his kingdom, that is where his instinct directs him, here he possesses his distinctive art, his mastery, his kind of happiness." (GM III.15).

III

If the priest detects remarkable possibilities for himself in the slavish way of life, and even collaborates with the slave through his cultivation of inwardness, then he is nonetheless also a natural ruler. Like the knightly noble, he regards the "lower orders" as the proper objects of oppression and so as providing proper occasions for self-affirmation. So, like the knight, the priest has an interest in keeping the slave in his place and in perpetuating the arrangements whereby the slave is kept there: to save "the herd and herdsman is his essential art, as it is his supreme utility" (GM III.15). This means that the priest's relation to *ressentiment* is more complex than I have suggested so far. For *ressentiment* provides the priest not only with an opportunity (for dominion) but also with a problem; and one way of seeing the priest's genius is to appreciate how his remedy—his solution to the problem—at the same time constitutes his realization of the opportunity with which it presents him.

The problem, to which Nietzsche repeatedly alludes, is that a populace consumed with unresolved *ressentiment* is a dangerous, unstable, unruly populace, which it is in the interests of the higher castes somehow to subdue and keep subdued. The slaves' experience of life on the receiving end ensures a pent-up vengefulness:

anarchy and ever-threatening disintegration within the herd, in which the most dangerous of all explosives, *ressentiment*, is constantly accumulating. . . . The suffering are one and all dreadfully eager and inventive in discovering occasion for painful affects; they enjoy being mistrustful and dwelling on nasty deeds and imaginary slights . . . ; they tear open their oldest wounds, they bleed from long-healed scars, they make evildoers out of their friends, wives, children, and whoever else stands closest to them. (GM III.15)

The dangerousness of slavish *ressentiment* poses an identical problem for both priest and knight. Both must discover channels into which it can be directed in some comparatively harmless way—comparatively harmless, that is, to the social hierarchy which it is in the interests of each to maintain. One measure to which Nietzsche devotes considerable space is the institution of limits to the quantity of punishment that a given offense may bring upon its perpetrator. Without such limits, "every kind of hostility may be vented upon" the criminal (GM II.9)—literally limitless revenge; but as "the community" becomes stronger, it begins to defend "the malefactor against this anger, especially that of those he has directly harmed, and takes him under its protection. A compromise with the anger of those directly harmed by the criminal; an effort to localize the affair and to prevent it from causing any further, let alone a general, disturbance; attempts to discover equivalents and to settle the whole matter" (GM II.10). Thus Nietzsche denies that the ideas of law and justice are rooted in vengefulness. Rather, the law represents

the struggle *against* the reactive feelings. . . . Wherever justice is practiced and maintained one sees a stronger power seeking a means of putting an end to the senseless raging of *ressentiment* among the weaker powers that stand under it (whether they be groups or individuals)—partly by taking the objects of *ressentiment* out of the hands of revenge, . . . partly by devising and in some cases imposing settlements, partly by elevating certain equivalents for injuries into norms to which from then on *ressentiment* is once and for all directed. (GM II.11)

The maintenance of social order, then, depends upon a tariff system—an eye for an eye, say, but no more than that—under which (potentially) limitless vengeance is ruled out.

But this legal response to mass *ressentiment* is deeply problematic. It may serve to curtail mayhem in certain cases, as intended. Yet in the long term it surely exacerbates the dangerousness of *ressentiment* rather than neutralizing it: you screw the lid down more tightly and the pressure builds up inside; you deny "the weaker powers" one outlet for *ressentiment* and you merely give them one more thing to bear a grudge against. Nietzsche remarks of the priest's solution to *ressentiment* that in stilling "the pain of the wound *he at the same time infects the wound*" (GM III.15): but precisely the same might be said of the legal solution.

Nietzsche finds himself on tricky ground when it comes to the law. He clearly admires the way in which "the supreme power" acts "against the predominance of grudges and rancor" (GM II.11)—and one would assume, fairly automatically, that he intends this action to be attributed to the (knightly) nobles. They, after all, are the only ones in a position to apply the appropriate kind and degree of coercion. Yet Nietzsche is oddly coy. In the three sections devoted to the question (GM II.9–11) the nobles are nowhere mentioned, and all we get are vague references to the "community" and the "stronger power," to the "supreme power." His bashfulness becomes intelligible, however, when one notes what the consequences are of "elevating certain equivalents for injuries into norms": there is an "increasingly definite will to treat every crime as in some sense *dischargeable*, and thus at least to a certain extent to *isolate* the criminal and his deed from one another" (GM II.10): "from now on the eye is trained on an ever more *impersonal* evaluation of the deed" (GM II.11). Nietzsche alleges that this move to the impersonal is "the exact reverse of that which is desired by all revenge that is fastened exclusively to the viewpoint of the person injured" (GM II.11)—but this is surely a piece of desperation, and false to boot. For it is perfectly clear that what is going on here is precisely that separation of doer from deed (the "error" of the popular mind) which marks a crucial moment in the first stage of the slave revolt in morality. Thus the "increasingly definite will" of the legislator to regard every crime as "*dischargeable*" turns out to be profoundly implicated not in the taming of *ressentiment*, as Nietzsche implies, but in its capacity to turn creative. No wonder he is reluctant to credit the institution of the law to the nobles.

Yet he should credit it to them even so. As I've already remarked, no one else could have instituted the law. Nor, as I argued in the previous chapter, is there anything about the doer/deed distinction—or even about the idea of free will—which renders it necessarily unavailable to someone who buys into the noble scheme of values. In other words, if the institution of the law makes the problem posed by *ressentiment* in some respects more acute, and if it even encourages and exploits a piece of conceptual machinery that is central to the slave revolt, then it is nonetheless perfectly *intelligible* to see this development as the work of the knightly noble. This highlights two things: first, that Nietzsche's real position in the *Genealogy* is once again incompatible with his desire to keep the knightly noble completely free of slavish taints. And second, that the role of the noble in imposing customs and laws on the lower orders actually tends, in the long run, to make more likely the victory of their style of valuation over his. This last is a question to which I return in Chapter 6. For the moment, though, it is sufficient to note that the legal solution to *ressentiment* is a deeply equivocal one. In providing a sharper and more limited focus for the rancor of the oppressed, the legal solution in effect sharpens up the rancor itself and turns it into a still more dangerous force against the oppressors.

It is against this background that the priestly solution to the problem needs to be seen and appreciated. For rather than seeking to provide a narrower and more finely honed target for *ressentiment*, the priest instead "*alters the direction* of *ressentiment*" (GM III.15). The legal solution leaves the basic direction of *ressentiment* unaltered—it is still aimed outward, at the hostile external world and the injurious deeds it contains. The priest, however, turns *ressentiment* back in upon the sufferer, so that the sufferer himself becomes the object of his own rancor and, as it were, consumes within himself those disruptive forces that previously threatened to be unleashed outward. But how is this possible? How could someone be persuaded to resent himself for his own suffering?

The first thing to say is that the priest requires a pretty sophisticated class of sufferer to go to work on. He needs sufferers who have already inverted the value-positing eye—that is, sufferers who are thoroughly internalized, who have labored under customs, laws, and punishments, who have distinguished doers from deeds, who have invented the idea of free will; he needs "lambs" who have gained "the right to make the bird of prey *accountable* for being a bird of prey" (GM I.13). He needs, in other words, slaves who have already completed the first stage of their revolt in morality, "lambs" who have grown up into "sheep": "'I suffer: someone must be to blame for it'— thus thinks every sickly sheep. But his shepherd, the ascetic priest, tells him: 'Quite so, my sheep! someone must be to blame for it: but you yourself are this someone, you alone are to blame for it—*you alone are to blame for your-self!*'—This is brazen and false enough: but one thing at least is achieved by it, the direction of *ressentiment* is *altered*" (GM III.15).

Only to those whose *ressentiment* has already become creative is the priest's response even intelligible. The whole moral language of blaming (of "guilt") is predicated on the reversal of the noble scheme of values, and the second phase of the revolt—inaugurated by the priest's redirection of *ressentiment*—is conceivable only on that premise. "Someone must be to blame" thinks the sheep, thus showing himself to be a sheep who has already come a long way. "Yes, you" replies the priest, seizing his opportunity—and revealing himself at last "as the predestined savior, shepherd, and advocate of the sick herd" (GM III.15).

IV

We have seen how it is possible that the slave might be persuaded to see his suffering as his own fault, at least in the sense that we have seen how it is not impossible for him to understand what is being proposed. But this certainly isn't enough to explain why he *is* persuaded. What's in it for him? Why should he turn against himself in this way? Why embark on stage two of the revolt?

The answer is simply that the question Why live? still awaits a satisfactory reply. The senselessness that characterizes the slave's existence as a whole—as an impotent, mortal sufferer—still constitutes a powerful "argument *against* existence"; and it is this argument that the priest seeks to defuse. His tactic is beautifully direct: retain the idea of blaming something for the fact that one is as one is, but get rid of the idea of blaming something external. No external object can ever be held fully and convincingly accountable for *all* of your suffering. So blame the one thing that is never absent from you, the one thing that stands in an absolutely necessary and unavoidable relation to you for as long as you live: blame yourself. If you can find a way of doing that, you'll have brought every conceivable kind of suffering that might ever befall you under an interpretation. Your life, as a sufferer, will finally make sense.

This gives us the slave's motivation. It remains only for the priest to tell the kind of story that will make it not merely logically possible and existen-tially desirable for the slave to blame all of his suffering on himself, but psy-chologically plausible as well. And this turns out to be a transcendental story: the priest interprets "a whole mysterious machinery of salvation into suf-fering" (GM II.7)—machinery that he renders persuasive, I suggest, by ex-ploiting three further aspects of the slave's experience. First, the slave already associates a certain amount of suffering with punishment, with the idea of being *guilty* of something (i.e., of breaking a custom or law). He has moralized the concept of "debt"; and this moralization is now to be generalized: *all* suffering is to be seen as punishment. Guilt is transformed into Sin: the slave, thirsting "for remedies and narcotics, at last takes counsel with one who knows hidden things, too—and behold! he receives a hint, he receives from his sorceror, the ascetic priest, the *first* hint as to the cause of his suffering: he must seek it in *himself*, in some *guilt*, in a piece of the past, he must understand his suffering as a *punishment*. . . . [T]he invalid has been transformed into 'the sinner'" (GM III.20).

Second, the priest exploits the community's attitude toward its ancestors. Nietzsche claims that in "the original tribal community"

> The conviction reigns that it is only through the sacrifices and accomplishments of the ancestors that the tribe *exists*—and that one has to *pay them back* with sacrifices and accomplishments: one thus recognizes a *debt* that constantly grows greater. . . . The *fear* of the ancestor and his power, the consciousness of indebtedness to him, increases, according to this kind of logic, in exactly the same measure as the power of the tribe itself increases, as the tribe itself grows ever more victorious, independent, honored, and feared. . . . If one imagines this rude kind of logic carried to its end, then the ancestors of the *most powerful* tribes are bound eventually to grow to monstrous dimensions through the imagination of growing fear and to recede into the darkness of the divinely uncanny and unimaginable: in the end the ancestor must necessarily be transfigured into a *god*. (GM II.19)

On the face of it, this might seem rather remote from the slave's concerns. His lot is a miserable one, after all, and it's hard to see what he might have to feel indebted for. Moreover, the god that stands at the end of the process just outlined is not the Christian, transcendental God, but a god of the nobles, "who indeed paid back their originators, their ancestors (heroes, gods) with interest all the qualities that had become palpable in themselves, the *noble* qualities . . . (which should not be confused with [the gods'] becoming 'holy')" (GM II.19). So it seems that the priest's only use for ancestor reverence would be to try to seduce the (knightly) nobles with it, since they are the ones who must find most in the founders' achievements to appreciate. And perhaps there is something in this: it might be, for instance, that it is through some such set of moves that the priestly noble first conceives the idea that his own indebtedness (toward his ancestors) might be transformed into other people's guilt (before God). But the priest can also do better than this: for despite the fact that the slave might not be among those most inclined to feel indebted to his ancestors, he is nonetheless a part of the tribe, and during his pre-revolt stage he had no option but to frame his own valuations from the nobles' point of view. In other words, the slave has *had* the experience of re-

garding the (nobles') ancestors as "divinely uncanny and unimaginable"—
and this is something that the priest can use. Furthermore, it is not as if the
slave had absolutely no stake in the tribe. Even he has some reason to feel
grateful for its power, as he is prompted to recall when he breaks its laws:
"The lawbreaker is a debtor who has not merely failed to make good the advantages and advance payments bestowed upon him but has actually at-
tacked his creditor: therefore he is not only deprived henceforth of all these
advantages and benefits, as is fair—he is also reminded *what these benefits are
really worth*" (GM II.9). The slave may be oppressed, then; but he also benefits from the fact that others are oppressed too. The law under which he is
obliged to live holds others in check as well, and even he has some reason
to appreciate the protection which that affords. This gives the priest just
enough to go to work on. Since the slave already grasps "the presupposition
of religion"—the idea of a "god" to whom one should make repayments—
he can now, by the priest, be incited "to drive his self-torture to its most gruesome pitch of severity and rigor. Guilt before *God*"—in which resides "the
will of man to find himself guilty and reprehensible to a degree that can
never be atoned for" (GM II.22).

The third feature of the slave's experience that the priest can be seen as ex-
ploiting is *repression*—and this, really, is his masterstroke. The slave is more
accustomed than anyone else to having his instincts repressed, to having them
turned back in on himself. In the first place his bad conscience expressed itself reactively, as a kind of rancorous prudence—and this, presumably, was
a perfectly natural response to having the outlets for his instincts dammed
up. Certainly Nietzsche doesn't suggest that he might have responded differently. Indeed, one might say that the instinct of an animal whose instincts
have been repressed is precisely to rub "itself raw against the bars of its cage";
and when *all* of the "old instincts upon which his strength, joy, and terrible-
ness had rested hitherto" (GM II.16) have been repressed—that is, when the
"true reaction" of deeds has become an impossibility—the *new* instinct, *ressentiment*, is the only "natural" expression of himself that the slave is left with.
In the first stage of the slave revolt, this new instinct turns creative and gives
birth to values, as the slave seeks a way of making sense of himself as a sufferer. But just as this solution turns out to be partial and hybrid, owing to
the character of the suffering he needs to account for, so the slave's very nature at this point is partial and hybrid. He has come far in his interpretation
of suffering, but not far enough. He has become adapted to living under customs, but not adapted enough. For he still has that one instinct which, despite and because of the repression of all the others, continues to threaten
disruption, continues to be directed outward. *Ressentiment*, seen under this
light, is an anomaly, an inconsistency; and the slave cannot hope to become

perfectly adjusted to his enclosure "within the walls of society and of peace" (GM II.16) until it, too, has been repressed, so that he is left with no outwardly directed impulses at all. By appealing to the slave's abundant experience of repression, then, it is possible for the priest to portray the redirection of *ressentiment* inward as the natural culmination of the slave's experience of all of his instincts. What could be more fitting than that the slave's own most sophisticated response to internalization—stage one of his revolt in morality—should itself be internalized in stage two?

Nietzsche describes this transformation as "unnatural"; and it may well be, from the perspective of unfettered instinctive behavior. But seen from "within the walls . . . of peace," it has another character. The slave acquires a second nature, and the "*bestiality of thought*" that "erupts as soon as he is prevented just a little from being a *beast in deed*" (GM II.22) represents a consistent—and in the form which the priest gives it, a psychologically plausible—response to the slave's predicament. The price, of course, and what is "bestial" about the thought, is that the slave is now committed to the "conception of irredeemable penance, the idea that it cannot be discharged ('*eternal* punishment')"; and *this* thought can only be made bearable by that "whole mysterious machinery of salvation" that the priest interprets into it: "God himself sacrifices himself for the guilt of mankind, God himself makes payment to himself, God as the only being who can redeem man from what has become unredeemable for man himself" (GM II.21). To change the direction of *ressentiment*, then, is to make transcendental stories essential; and to tell them, to offer otherworldly solutions to the problem of this-worldly suffering, is to seek, as the priest seeks, to achieve "*dominion over the suffering.*"

V

I have said nothing yet about the fact that Nietzsche calls the priest the *ascetic* priest; and this must now be addressed. It is tempting to take the following passage as definitive:

> The idea at issue here is the *valuation* the ascetic priest places on our life: he juxtaposes it (along with what pertains to it: "nature," "world," the whole sphere of becoming and transitoriness) with a quite different mode of existence which it opposes and excludes, *unless* it turn against itself, *deny itself*: in that case, the case of the ascetic life, life counts as a bridge to that other mode of existence. The ascetic treats life as a wrong road . . . , or as a mistake that is put right by deeds—that we *ought* to put right: for he *demands* that one go along with him; where he can he compels acceptance of *his* valuation of existence. (GM III.11)

This passage suggests, among much else, that to be ascetic and to accept a transcendental, otherworldly account of the value of life in this world are one and the same thing. Thus, on this construction, the slave is turned into an ascetic at the moment at which he embarks on stage two of his revolt and embraces the priest's "mysterious machinery of salvation," and is an ascetic precisely to the extent that he embarks on the one and embraces the other. Asceticism appears to be identical to the Manichean denial of the value of the real world in favor of some fictive transcendental world in which suffering is finally overcome.

But this is to run much more together than the argument of the *Genealogy* warrants. The "ascetic ideal," Nietzsche says at the beginning of the essay devoted to it, "has meant so many things to man"—for instance, "in the case of the physiologically deformed and deranged (the *majority* of mortals) an attempt to see themselves as 'too good' for this world, a saintly form of debauch, their chief weapon in the struggle against slow pain and boredom; in the case of priests the distinctive priestly faith, their best instrument of power, also the 'supreme' license for power" (GM III.1). To the "majority" of mortals—the slaves, in other words—asceticism does indeed mean an acceptance of an otherworldly devaluation of this world. But to the priests? Do *they* accept such a devaluation? The answer to this is complex. On the one hand, it seems that asceticism or the promulgation of asceticism are the priest's means to entirely nontranscendental ends. The "power" that asceticism brings him is not to be exercised in another world: it is immanent through and through (even if transcendental license is claimed for it), and it consists in "*dominion over the suffering*" here and now. To call the priest "ascetic," then, as Nietzsche almost always does, appears to be different from accusing him of *personally* believing that "this life counts as a bridge" to some other life, however much the priest may encourage such beliefs in the slaves. On the other hand, however, the priest seeks by his interpretation "to become master not over something in life but over life itself, over its most profound, powerful, and basic conditions" (GM III.11)—and this is very different. The distinction is between mastering those who suffer (i.e., the slaves, "something in life") and mastering suffering itself (i.e., life's "most profound, powerful, and basic conditions"). In his latter capacity, the priest does indeed appear committed to the denial of this world in favor of another. But there is no contradiction here (even if the priest himself is said to be a "self-contradictory type"). For it is precisely by portraying the priest's transcendentalizing devaluation of the world as, at the same time, a bid for power within it that Nietzsche is able to describe "this *life-inimical* species" as being "in the *interest of life itself*" (GM III.11). The priest affirms himself (is in the interest of life) by denying life, and it is in his capacity to do the one via the other that his fascination for Nietzsche lies.

But what, in light of this, are we to make of the "ascetic"? It may be help-ful to draw a distinction. Nietzsche says a great deal about ascetic "ideals," but he also speaks of ascetic "procedures"—as in this discussion of punishment: "In a certain sense, the whole of asceticism belongs here: a few ideas are to be rendered inextinguishable, ever-present, unforgettable, 'fixed,' with the aim of hypnotizing the entire nervous and intellectual system with these 'fixed ideas'—and ascetic procedures and modes of life are means of freeing these ideas from the competition of all other ideas, so as to make them 'unforget-table'" (GM II.3). In this case, the "ascetic procedures" of vigorous and cruel punishment serve, inter alia, to improve the memory. Elsewhere, the ascetic procedures of "poverty, humility, chastity" allow "*la bête philosophe*" to real-ize the most "favorable conditions under which it can expend all its strength and achieve its maximal feeling of power." The philosopher sees in these pro-cedures "an optimum condition for the highest and boldest spirituality and smiles—he does *not* deny 'existence,' he rather affirms *his* existence and *only* his existence" (GM III.7). In neither of these cases are ascetic procedures re-lated to a denial of this world in favor of a transcendental one, and in the second case, at least, any such relation is expressly denied. So the mere adop-tion of ascetic procedures does not by itself amount to the adoption of the ascetic ideal as that ideal is understood by the slave. An ascetic procedure, I suggest, is nothing more at bottom than a piece of self-denying behavior, adopted for some purpose, of a kind that would be impossible for an animal, say, which lacks the degree of internalization required to forbid itself things, but that is eminently possible for any creature suffering from bad conscience in its "raw" state. The capacity to forbid oneself things, then, exactly like the capacity to make promises, is a consequence of the repression engendered by living under customs.

The priest, as we have seen, foregoes the knightly nobles' response to re-pression, denies it to himself, and in doing so plainly engages in ascetic pro-cedures—referred to by Nietzsche as his "habits." Just how minimal these habits need be is something that Nietzsche is keen to emphasize: purity, the original priestly character trait, is "altogether *unsymbolical* in meaning to a degree that we can scarcely conceive. The 'pure one' is from the beginning merely a man who washes himself, who forbids himself certain foods that produce skin ailments, who does not sleep with dirty women of the lower strata, who has an aversion to blood—no more, hardly more!" (GM I.6). There is nothing in these procedures that necessitates a move to the tran-scendent. Such refrainings are simply among the options—often prudent, practical options—that the acquisition of an inner world makes available. There may, as Nietzsche says, also be a degree of pleasure attached to the ca-pacity to deny oneself: "This secret self-ravishment, this artists' cruelty, this delight in imposing a form upon oneself as a hard, recalcitrant, suffering material and in burning a will, a critique, a contradiction, a contempt, a No into it, this uncanny, dreadfully joyous labor of a soul voluntarily at odds with itself that makes itself suffer out of joy in making suffer" (GM II.18).

Internalization provides one with the opportunity to go to work on one-self—to give that style to one's character which, in *The Gay Science*, Nietz-sche declares is the one "needful" thing (GS 290)—and ascetic procedures are integral to the work done.[2] Even the procedure of blaming oneself for one's own suffering can, in some cases, have wholesome results: it can "di-rect the *ressentiment* of the less severely afflicted sternly back upon them-selves ('one thing is needful')—and in this way . . . *exploit* the bad instincts of all sufferers for the purpose of self-discipline, self-surveillance and self-overcoming" (GM III.16). It is clear from these and similar passages that as-cetic procedures—construed as self-denying practices—carry no automatic negative charge in the *Genealogy*. They needn't be associated with the evac-uation of value from this to another world.

The ascetic *ideal*, however, is another matter, at least as sold by the priest to the slave. Here the otherworldly impetus is essential, and it is unimagin-able that the slave would buy the ideal without the transcendental consola-tion it provides. But the ascetic ideal is more than a simple amalgamation or systematization of ascetic procedures. It is rather an exaggeration of and ex-trapolation from them. In order to engage in an ascetic procedure, one needs to have developed an inner world within which one can, as it were, oppose oneself: and one can do this without denying the real world: "a severe and cheerful continence with the best will . . . belongs to the most favorable con-ditions of supreme spirituality" (GM III.9). But to move from the procedure itself—which may be useful, enjoyable, *immanently* productive—to a con-tempt for and a downgrading of that which one opposes in oneself, and then to universalize that contempt, is to be in the grip of an ascetic ideal. Sexual abstinence, for instance, may be a procedure that brings immanent advan-tages to certain ways of living. But extrapolated into a loathing for everything fleshly, it constitutes a retreat from the world, from existence. And elevated into an ideal, it necessarily presupposes a set of transcendental *counter*claims if the idealist is not to destroy himself on the spot: in the ascetic ideal "suf-fering was *interpreted*; the tremendous void seemed to have been filled; the door was closed to any kind of suicidal nihilism" (GM III.28).

It is not simply ascetic procedures, then, that the priest encourages in the slave, nor even their preconditions. It is rather—and crucially—the view that existence itself is just one big procedure to be engaged in ascetically. As soon as one accepts this, the end to which the procedure is directed—which

---

2. A matter to be explored further in Chapters 4 and 6.

in the case of ordinary ascetic procedures is something immanent, something within the ascetic's own life—is inevitably deferred elsewhere, outside of life, to another realm. That the slave can be persuaded to engage in his life as if it were one great ascetic procedure is readily explained by the fact that his existence as a whole is characterized by suffering—suffering to which any merely immanent interpretation eventually proves inadequate; and that the priest understands this about the slave is a result of his own cultivation of ascetic procedures, of his own imaginative exploration of the advantages to be gained by encouraging the worst kind of bad conscience in those most consumed by *ressentiment*.

Nietzsche's ambivalence about the value of the "ascetic" precisely mirrors his ambivalence about the priest, who is denounced, rehabilitated, admired, warded off, and condemned again—alternately held up as an exemplar of everything that's worst and of everything most estimable.[3] There are many reasons why it is extremely hard for Nietzsche to maintain a stable attitude to the priest, several of which we've already considered; but one more reason may lie in what he says about the noble response to opposition: "Here alone genuine 'love of one's enemies' is possible—supposing it to be possible at all on earth. How much reverence has a noble man for his enemies!—and such reverence is a bridge to love.—For he desires his enemy for himself, as his mark of distinction; he can endure no other enemy than one in whom there is nothing to despise and *very much* to honor!" (GM I.10). Nietzsche, presumably, would like to ally himself with the nobles here: but the attitude he describes would require a quite astonishing degree of "self-surveillance and self-overcoming," if one's enemy really were a formidable person and one whom one sincerely did want to vanquish. But that Nietzsche regards the priest as his enemy seems, for the most part, beyond doubt. To the ideal that he has fostered in the very repressed, Nietzsche attributes "the most terrible sickness that has ever raged in man; and whoever can still bear to hear . . . how in this night of torment and absurdity there has resounded the cry of *love*, the cry of the most nostalgic rapture, of redemption through *love*, will turn away, seized by invincible horror.—There is so much in man that is hideous!— Too long, the earth has been a madhouse!—" (GM II.22). The priest so far has been entirely successful: he has orchestrated a "revolt which has a history of two thousand years behind it and which we no longer see because it—has been victorious" (GM I.7). The priest, for Nietzsche, represents the ultimate enemy—the enemy in whom, one might say, there is *all too much* to honor; and in desiring this "enemy for himself, as his mark of dis-

3. For a marvelously acute discussion of Nietzsche's attitude to the priest, see Henry Staten, *Nietzsche's Voice* (Ithaca: Cornell University Press, 1990), chap. 2.

tinction" Nietzsche places himself in an almost impossible position. For not only has the priest been successful, but he has been so successful that his success has become invisible; so Nietzsche needs first to expose his enemy, to get him out into the open as a powerful and dangerous adversary, before he can even begin to take him on. And the strain that this places on the noble requirement for that "reverence" which "is a bridge to love" is well-nigh intolerable.

But his problems run still deeper. For he also wants to *praise* the priest for his achievements—which he regards as calamitous, to be sure, but not as unequivocally calamitous. Indeed, it may be that the priest has even been in-dispensable. The ideal which he promulgates appears to represent "life *against* life"; and this is

> physiologically considered and not merely psychologically, a simple absurdity. It can only be *apparent*. . . . Let us replace it with a brief formulation of the facts of the matter: *the ascetic ideal springs from the protective instinct of a de-generating life* which tries by all means to sustain itself and to fight for its ex-istence; it indicates a partial physiological obstruction and exhaustion against which the deepest instincts of life, which have remained intact, continually struggle with new expedients and devices. The ascetic ideal is such an expedi-ent; the case is therefore the opposite of what those who reverence this ideal believe: life wrestles in it and through it with death and *against* death; the as-cetic ideal is an artifice for the *preservation* of life. (GM III.13)

So the priest is on the side of life, the ideal he promulgates is a preserving force. The "degeneration" of which Nietzsche speaks here is in fact that *alteration* that man undergoes when he becomes socialized, repressed, and *interesting*; and Nietzsche's attitude toward *that* veers almost immediately: man, "*the* sick animal," is "the great experimenter with himself, discon-tented and insatiable, wrestling with animals, nature, and gods for ultimate dominion—he, still unvanquished, eternally directed toward the future, whose own restless energies never leave him in peace, so that his future digs like a spur into the flesh of every present—how should such a courageous and richly endowed animal not also be the most imperiled, the most chron-ically and profoundly sick of all sick animals?" (GM III.13).

In this passage, Nietzsche is back in the mood to discern in the repression of the instincts a condition "*pregnant with a future*," giving "rise to an inter-est, a tension, a hope, almost a certainty" (GM II.16)—and it is this condi-tion which the priest has found a way of rendering tolerable, and so of pre-serving. Indeed, he has found the only way so far. The ascetic ideal has given the one comprehensive answer to the question—inevitable for a creature who suffers from the problem of his meaning—"why man at all?" "This interpretation—there is no doubt of it—brought fresh suffering with it, deeper, more inward, more poisonous. . . . But all this notwithstanding— man was *saved* thereby, he possessed a meaning . . . he could now *will* something; no matter at first to what end, why, with what he willed: *the will itself was saved*" (GM III.28). Thus the priest has served as the guarantor of any worthwhile and interesting future that man might have; and it is of course precisely this future that Nietzsche now seeks to open up for exploration and habitation. His struggle with the priest is a struggle for the right to succeed him, for the right to exploit his achievements in ways that the priest himself is unwilling or unable to do. And it is this almost Oedipal quality that renders Nietzsche's enmity toward the priest so fraught with contradiction. "Here alone," he says, "genuine 'love of one's enemies' is possible"; but at once he adds, "supposing it to be possible at all on earth." And for him one is driven to conclude that it isn't possible: for in his battle with the priest he is already far too *close* to the enemy to build bridges to him—or even, really, to desire him "as his mark of distinction." The transcendental stage of the slave revolt in morality may be something that Nietzsche deplores. But it is also something that he cannot do without. Nietzsche needs the priest.

CHAPTER THREE

THE PHILOSOPHER

A philosopher—alas, a being that often runs away from itself, often is afraid
of itself—but too inquisitive not to "come to" again—always back to himself.
                                                    —*Beyond Good and Evil*, sec. 292

The valuations of the slave revolt in morality have made us what we are. Our
relations to ourselves—our consciences—are shaped by those valuations
and we understand ourselves through them. If, as Nietzsche hopes, it is still
possible for us to relate to ourselves in other ways—in ways that are not predicated on hatred of self and world—then that transformation is going to have
to be effected through the means that we actually have to hand. Which is to
say, the required transformation will have to be launched from and founded
in precisely those slavish consciences that two millennia of priestly endeavor
have bequeathed to us. Thus Nietzsche needs to discover chinks, gaps, and
opportunities in the modern conscience. He needs his diagnosis and critique
of it to reveal not merely our corruption but also the capacities we require if
we are to change ourselves—if we are to discover newly noble ways of living, newly noble consciences. His tactic is to interrogate three character types
who appear at first sight to be neither slavish nor priestly—the philosopher,
the artist, and the scientist. How do these three relate to or exhibit the modern ascetic conscience? What, from their perspective, is the meaning of ascetic ideals? Nietzsche's hope is that by pressing these questions the chinks
and gaps that he is after—the opportunity that he is after—will somehow
emerge and open up. But the tactic is a fraught one. It's not just that Nietzsche doesn't know precisely what he's looking for. He doesn't know because
he is himself, as a modern, unavoidably ascetic. To this extent, his interro-
gations are self-interrogations; and to the extent that he interrogates himself,

we can never quite be sure that he has achieved enough distance from himself. The problem is, for obvious reasons, particularly acute in the case of the philosopher, since here a double distancing is required: from himself as a modern and from himself as a philosopher. It is tempting to conclude that the relative thinness of what comes out of these sections of the *Genealogy* is a product of that difficulty, even if the thinness shouldn't blind us to the important things that Nietzsche does, as I will try to show, let slip.

I

The first thing one notices about the pages devoted to the philosopher is their extreme restlessness. Denunciation and celebration alternate wildly as Nietzsche, without always bothering to mark the fact, flits backward and forward through time, from a murky prehistory to an apparent present which is actually, one suspects, an imagined future. "*La bête philosophe* . . . instinctively strives for an optimum of favorable conditions" under which he can attain "the highest and boldest spirituality" (GM III.7). But that this spirituality is, in the end, only a promise, an inspiration rather than a description of what philosophers have in fact attained, is signaled by Nietzsche's treatment of it—at once hyperbolic and tentative. He asserts and celebrates the possibility of such a spirituality yet gives no details; he presents it as a destination but sets up few signposts. In the last of the sections devoted to him Nietzsche offers, rather ominously, to "compress the facts" about the philosopher into "a few brief formulas":

> to begin with, the philosophic spirit always had to use as a mask and cocoon the *previously established* types of the contemplative man—priest, sorcerer, soothsayer, and in any case a religious type—in order to be able to *exist at all: the ascetic ideal* for a long time served the philosopher as a form in which to appear, as a precondition of existence. . . . To put it vividly, the *ascetic priest* provided until the most modern times the repulsive and gloomy caterpillar form in which alone the philosopher could live and creep about (GM III.10).

Until "the most modern times," he says. So presumably it is now possible for the philosopher to conduct himself differently, to leave his priestly past behind. But one must clearly do more, if one wishes to demonstrate the possibility of butterflies, than dub something a "caterpillar."

In order to try to work out what is going on here (and what more one must do) it is probably best to be schematic. The complexities of Nietzsche's discussion are, as I have noted, at least partly the product of temporal dislocation. So the first thing is to reconstruct the proper sequence of events. In the remainder of this section, then, I will set out what I take to be Nietzsche's account of the origins of the philosopher and of what, in his view, makes the "philosophic spirit" distinctive. In the next section I will turn to the history of the philosopher from his origins "until the most modern times." And in the third section I will try to explain how Nietzsche sees this (reconstructed) sequence of events extending into the future.

Philosophy arose, Nietzsche tells us, under "emergency conditions," under an "*oppression* of valuation." The earliest philosophers "found all the value judgments within them turned *against* them, they had to fight down every kind of suspicion and resistance against 'the philosopher in them.' As men of frightful ages, they did this by using frightful means: cruelty toward themselves, inventive self-castigation" (GM III.10). So the earliest philosophers adopted ascetic procedures in order to preserve "the philosopher in them"; and to the extent that they were ascetic they were also priestlike. But despite Nietzsche's claim that they had not merely "to *represent*" the ascetic ideal but had also "to *believe* in it in order to be able to represent it" (GM III.10), these philosophers cannot have been identical to priests. The "*ascetic priest*," after all, provided only a "repulsive and gloomy caterpillar form"—a "mask," a "cocoon"—for the philosopher to "live and creep about" in. I argued in Chapter 2 that one can adopt ascetic procedures without adopting the ascetic ideal, and I suggest that the difference between the philosopher and the priest lies in that distinction. In striving, through various kinds of self-denial, to attain "an optimum of favorable conditions under which it can expend all its strength and achieve its maximal feeling of power," the philosophical beast "does *not* deny 'existence'" (GM III.7)— that is, it does *not* embrace the ascetic ideal, even though it does proceed ascetically. This distinction is essential if the philosopher's kinship with the priest, although close, is not to become irretrievably close. The philosopher must be seen as having a real and ineliminable investment in priestly procedures but only a contingent, historically limited investment in the priestly ideal. If it is possible to see him in this way, then it may be possible too to hope, as Nietzsche hopes, that his procedures might one day lead him to shed his disguise and to emerge from his cocoon as a philosophical butterfly— ascetic, but not as the priest is ascetic. Procedures, then, must play some subtly different role in the self-understanding of the philosopher as compared with the priest. The priest, after all, construes and uses ascetic procedures as a model for living *tout court*—as a means not merely for mastering "something in life" but for mastering "life itself, . . . its most profound, powerful, and basic conditions" (GM III.11). Philosophers, therefore and by contrast, must restrict the scope of their procedures merely to "something in life" (even if, during their caterpillar days, they do allow themselves to be seduced by the priest's more comprehensive construal). They must, in other words, despite the risk of falling into "an ascetic self-misunderstanding" (GM III.10), discover how to proceed ascetically—but immanently. Or at least they must do this if they are ever to improve their "gloomy and repulsive" appearance.

But why was the disguise necessary in the first place? Why did "the philosopher in them" require such extravagant protection—and against what? Nietzsche says that these early philosophers "found all the value judgments within them turned *against* them." So the threat comes from within; the "emergency conditions" under which philosophy arose is an emergency in these philosophers' own souls. The "value judgments" in question—the ones that cause the problem through their fundamental opposition to "the philosopher in them"—are somehow the philosophers' own judgments, despite their contrary nature. So what would lead one to judge against oneself in this way? The answer is slave morality. The early philosopher is complicit in the inverted valuations fostered by the priest—he too finds the priest's solution to the problem of meaningless suffering persuasive; and yet he finds at the same time that these priestly valuations are at odds with his other leanings, indeed at odds precisely with the characteristic "propensities and virtues of the philosopher": "his bent to doubt, his bent to deny, his bent to suspend judgment (his 'ephectic' bent), his bent to analyze, his bent to investigate, seek, dare, his bent to compare and balance, his will to neutrality and objectivity . . . : is it not clear that for the longest time all of them contravened the basic demands of morality and conscience?" (GM III.9).

Thus the priest's ideal, the "morality and conscience" that are here "contravened," and to which the philosopher himself in part subscribes, is flatly opposed to everything that makes the philosopher a philosopher. And one can see why. The ascetic ideal demands the altogether non-"ephectic" rejection of the whole of "life as a wrong road" (GM III.11). In requiring an unconditional denigration of this world in favor of another, it owes nothing to neutrality and cannot tolerate it (or comparison, or balance): it is fundamentally opposed to "doubt." So the "emergency conditions" in the philosopher's soul are the product of a clash between his priestly propensity to judge without qualification and his philosophical propensity to suspend judgment altogether: he hears in himself the voice of an ascetic conscience raised against the philosopher in him, and he seeks to still it by adopting cruel and ascetic procedures toward himself. And he eludes detection (hides and protects the philosopher in him) by disguising himself in the "cocoon" of a "*previously established*" type—the priest.

This is dizzying. Indeed one can see how the philosopher himself might have become confused. Nietzsche speaks of the philosopher's "ascetic self-misunderstanding." But he also goes further: he suggests that the philosopher must positively have "*guarded* against 'feeling himself,' against becoming conscious of himself" (GM III.9); that is, he must have acted to preserve the philosopher in him while remaining, as far as possible, oblivious to the fact that any such philosopher was there. Thus Nietzsche's caterpillar analogy: the caterpillar has a "'maternal' instinct," a "secret love of that which is growing inside" (GM III.8), but the secret is so well kept that not even the caterpillar is fully in on it. And it is because the philosophical caterpillar is (at least partly) oblivious to himself in this way that the "emergency conditions" in his soul do not eventuate in the triumph of the slavish side of his conscience. Even to himself the philosopher presents an elusive target: his "ephectic" bent is sufficiently well concealed as to provoke from him only "suspicion and resistance," rather than the decisive frontal assault that would surely be forthcoming were it to parade itself openly.

We are now in a position to understand why Nietzsche says that the philosopher "first appeared on earth in disguise, in ambiguous form, with an evil heart and often an anxious head" (GM III.10). The "evil" in his heart was his propensity to doubt, to suspend judgment, to remain neutral where the priest's morality demanded unconditional rejection (of the whole of life as "a wrong road"). The anxiety in his head was his own priestly "suspicion and resistance" against the "evil" in his heart. And his "ambiguity" lay in this double allegiance: ascetic procedures, in his case, functioned both to emphasize his kinship to the priest and to preserve his least priestly propensities. Which made the caterpillar form provided by the priest the only possible disguise that the philosopher could have adopted (for all its attendant risks of "ascetic self-misunderstanding"). So the philosopher, in Nietzsche's sense, "first appeared on earth" when the "ephectic bent" characteristic of him came into collision with the categorical judgments and rejections characteristic of slave morality—judgments and rejections to which, as a product of priestly times, the philosopher also subscribes. His conscience is a slavish one, then—but with half-repressed propensities of another tendency entirely.[1]

II

The philosopher, insofar as he is a philosopher, is a natural doubter, analyzer, "ephectic"; and the history of philosophy, in Nietzsche's view, is the history of the evasive measures that philosophers have taken in order to avoid

---

1. These propensities, when given full rein and freed from the "demands of morality and conscience," constitute what Nietzsche calls "the intellectual conscience." See Chapter 5 for a discussion.

acknowledging the true opposition between these "propensities" of theirs and the "basic demands" of slave morality. They have managed to refrain from, have indeed "*guarded* against," recognizing the subversive character of their own "virtues." "Philosophy began," Nietzsche tells us, "as all good things begin: for a long time it lacked the courage for itself." It took refuge in the ascetic ideal: indeed, "one might assert that it was only on the leading-strings of this ideal that philosophy learned to take its first small steps on earth— alas, so clumsily, so unwillingly, so ready to fall on its face and lie on its belly, this timid little toddler and mollycoddle with shaky legs!" (GM III.9).

This is a hugely resonant passage. The philosopher's "ephectic bent," his suspicion of the unconditional, is something which "for a long time" he "lacked the courage" to exercise, to give free rein to. So he "*guarded* against" it, perhaps allowing himself only the odd, small ephectic step before submit- ting gratefully again to "the leading-strings" of the ascetic ideal. And that, in a nutshell, is Nietzsche's summary of all philosophy so far: a series of hesi- tant adventures in which philosophers have, cautiously, indulged their "bent to analyze, . . . to investigate," without quite acknowledging that the "will to neutrality and objectivity" which they thereby, if falteringly, exhibit is in- compatible with the "demands of morality and conscience." And so, not acknowledging this, they end by squaring their analyses and investigations with the ascetic ideal anyway, despite the real thrust of what they are doing. Kant exemplifies the philosopher's capitulation to "morality and conscience" perfectly, Nietzsche thinks. "Why is it," he asks in the 1886 preface to *Day- break*, "that from Plato onwards every philosophical architect in Europe has built in vain?" And his answer is that these philosophers were all "building under the seduction of morality, even Kant—that they were apparently aim- ing at certainty, at 'truth,' but in reality at '*majestic moral structures*'" (D P3). Thus, from Plato to Kant, philosophers have tried to exercise their virtues in a direction opposite to that in which they naturally tend; and it is in this sense that philosophers have masqueraded as priests to the point of falling into an "ascetic self-misunderstanding." They have philosophized at odds with the philosopher in them, and so have "built in vain."

Kant is always Nietzsche's favorite example of ascetic self-misunderstand- ing. His essay on enlightenment has already been discussed in the Introduc- tion, but I return to it here both for its Nietzschean pre-echoes and for its diagnosis of the "immaturity" of Kant's own contemporaries. Kant claims that religious or quasi-religious "guardians," having "first infatuated their do- mestic animals, and carefully prevented the docile creatures from daring to take a step without the leading strings to which they are tied, . . . next show them the danger which threatens them if they try to walk unaided. . . . Thus only a few, by cultivating their own minds, have succeeded in freeing themselves from immaturity and in continuing boldly on their way."[2] The over-lap in rhetoric is unmistakable, "leading strings" and all. But in Nietzsche's view, of course, the leading strings from which Kant's "few" bold spirits succeed in freeing themselves are, by Kant, replaced with others no less inhibiting to "maturity." The priestly interpretation of existence is analyzed and investigated, subjected to doubt—is even, to a degree, cast off. But in its place Kant erects the newly transcendentalized ideal of "pure" reason, and so turns "reason against reason": "To renounce," as Kant does, belief in one's own this-worldliness, "to deny one's own 'reality'—what a triumph!" It is a triumph that "reaches its height when the ascetic self-contempt and self-mockery of reason declares '*there is* a realm of truth and being, but reason is *excluded* from it!'" (GM III.12). As Nietzsche puts it in *Daybreak*, "to create room for *his* 'moral realm' [Kant] saw himself obliged to posit an undemonstrable world, a logical 'Beyond'—it was for precisely that that he had need of his critique of pure reason! In other words: *he would not have had need of it* if one thing had not been more vital to him than anything else: to render the 'moral realm' unassailable" (D P3). Thus, by identifying man's essence with "pure" reason, and then insisting that anything so "pure" must belong in an otherworldly realm of which "the intellect comprehends just enough . . . to know that for the intellect [it is]—*utterly incomprehensible*" (GM III.12), Kant manages to sustain the "hard-won *self-contempt* of man as his ultimate and most serious claim to self-respect":

> Is this really to *work against* the ascetic ideal? Does one still seriously believe . . . that Kant's *victory* over the dogmatic concepts of theology ("God," "soul," "freedom," "immortality") damaged that ideal?—it being no concern of ours for the present whether Kant ever had any intention of doing such a thing. What is certain is that, since Kant, transcendentalists of every kind have once more won the day—they have been emancipated from the theologians: what joy!— [But] Kant showed them a secret path by which they may . . . from now on follow their "heart's desire." (GM III.25)

—a path, that is, by which they may continue to pay homage to the ascetic ideal, to the transcendental ideal, only under another name.

What we have, then, in Kant as read by Nietzsche, is an exact case study of philosophy lacking "the courage for itself." Kant begins philosophically enough: he casts doubt on the authority of traditional (priestly) interpretations; he analyzes and investigates their claim to act as "leading strings." But then, in order to save himself from recognizing the full subversiveness of

2. Immanuel Kant, "An Answer to the Question 'What is Enlightenment?'" in *Political Writings* (Cambridge: Cambridge University Press, 1991), p. 54.

what he has done, he stumbles ("a timid little toddler and mollycoddle with shaky legs!") and discovers a "secret path" back to the very ideal he had dared to question (i.e., to the same "leading strings" under a different description). Thus he is not, in Nietzsche's view, sufficiently philosophical to break free of the "immaturity" he (partly) diagnoses, and so remains a caterpillar in the grip of an "ascetic self-misunderstanding." Another remarkable passage from *Daybreak* makes clear just how ambivalent Nietzsche's reading of Kant's relation to enlightenment is. The "Germans," he says, seeing enlightenment as a threat (presumably to the "demands of morality and conscience"), reacted against it

> and—in the words Kant employed to designate his own task—"again paved the way for faith by showing knowledge its limitations." Let us breathe freely again: the hour of this danger has passed! And strange: it is precisely the spirits the Germans so eloquently conjured up which have in the long run most thwarted the intention of their conjurers—[these spirits] one day assumed a new nature and now fly on the broadest wings above and beyond their former conjurers as new and stronger genii of *that very Enlightenment* against which they were first conjured up. This Enlightenment we must now carry further forward: let us not worry about the "great revolution" and the "great reaction" against it which have taken place—they are no more than the sporting of waves in comparison with the truly great flood which bears *us* along! (D 197)

Here, beneath the hyperbole, one sees the very same movement that Nietzsche describes, or at least longs for, in the *Genealogy*. The philosopher's characteristic "propensities and virtues"—analysis, suspension of judgment— initiate a process for which, once it is under way, he lacks the courage. He tries to arrest it and "again" pave "the way for faith." But the process, the "flood," has a momentum of its own, a momentum which—in Nietzsche's eyes—ought inevitably to culminate in fully "mature" philosophers who, having the courage for their own virtues, cast off the last of those "leading strings" which they have used as a cocoon and hiding place. They, and they alone, will "have succeeded in freeing themselves from immaturity and in continuing boldly on their way."

So the philosopher has managed to ward off self-recognition through a pure lack of nerve—while at the same time giving hesitant rein to those "propensities" of his which, because he has always played them false in the end, and reembraced the ascetic ideal, he has also managed to preserve. This is a highly equivocal and complex "secret love," to be sure—but not an empty one. Indeed it has "created in Europe a magnificent tension of the spirit the like of which had never yet existed on earth: with so tense a bow we can now shoot for the most distant goals." And it has created this tension

despite attempts "made in the grand style to unbend the bow," most recently
"by means of the democratic [i.e., Kantian] enlightenment which, with the
aid of freedom of the press and newspaper-reading,[3] might indeed bring it
about that the spirit would no longer experience itself so easily as a 'need,'"
as a tension (BGE, Preface). To shoot properly for "the most distant goals,"
then, we must go further than Kant.

III

Kant speaks of the "few" who cultivate "their own minds," and enlightenment, for him, just is that cultivation. For Nietzsche likewise. Whatever the
details of his quarrel with Kant, he too is convinced that enlightenment is
a matter of self-cultivation, of a transformation of conscience. Kant scorns
those who have "a spiritual adviser to have a conscience for" them[4]—but
then allows an otherworldly, noumenal realm to usurp the function. Nietzsche, by contrast, wants us to have our consciences for ourselves: "whoever
has at some time built a 'new heaven' has found the power to do so only in
his *own hell*," he says (GM III.10). And the new heaven that the philosopher
is to build out of his own hell is, in effect, himself.

But what would Nietzsche's version of the fully mature philosopher, the
philosophical butterfly of the future, be like? What sort of self-relation would
he have? Things now—perhaps unsurprisingly—become rather more ob-
scure. "We are unknown to ourselves, we men of knowledge," he says: "we
are necessarily strangers to ourselves, we do not comprehend ourselves, we
have to misunderstand ourselves, for us the law 'Each is furthest from himself' applies to all eternity—we are not 'men of knowledge' with respect to
ourselves" (GM P1). Assuming that we "men of knowledge" are the new
philosophers who are now, in these "most modern times," possible, why does
he say this? In part, perhaps, his comment harks back (or rather forward) to
the philosophical habit of guarding against "feeling" oneself. But there is
something else going on too. When philosophers guard against feeling themselves, after all, it is the morality-contravening character of their philosophical propensities that they suppress. But presumably the philosopher who
goes boldly on his way has come to terms with his virtues and their tendencies, and indeed welcomes them. So the self-relation hinted at, according to which "Each is furthest from himself," appears not to revolve around

3. Compare Kant's insistence on the need for "the public use of reason" and hence for free expression if "maturity" is to become widespread—"An Answer to the Question: 'What is Enlightenment?'" pp. 55–58. (Note, too, that Kant's essay itself appeared first as a newspaper article, in the
Berlinische Monatsschrift, December 1784.) *Surely* Nietzsche knew this piece.
4. Kant, "An Answer to the Question: 'What is Enlightenment?'" p. 54.

the concealment of self-knowledge, even if some sort of distance from self-knowledge does seem to be central. What Nietzsche is getting at, I think, emerges more clearly when we notice another philosophical propensity, the propensity to avoid "fame, princes, and women." The philosopher's "motto is 'he who possesses is possessed.'" The ascetic procedures of "poverty, humility, chastity" allow him to refrain from entering too much into his own present condition, from loving his caterpillar state too well. Together they express what Nietzsche calls a "will to the 'desert.'" The philosopher seeks "a voluntary obscurity perhaps; an avoidance of [him]self. . . . His 'maternal' instinct, the secret love of that which is growing in him, directs him toward situations in which he is relieved of the necessity of thinking *of himself*" (GM III.8).So the philosopher needs somehow to prise himself away from himself as he now is, if he is to flourish; and this prising away is to be accomplished ascetically (although not in the service of the ascetic ideal). It is in this sense, I think, that "we men of knowledge" are said not to be "'men of knowledge' with respect to ourselves": we refuse to subscribe to any current, settled view of ourselves, to shackle ourselves to our own self-definitions.

The philosopher's "avoidance" of himself, then, is primarily an epistemic avoidance; his instinct is to avoid "the necessity of thinking *of himself*" as a person of such-and-such a kind. His self-relation is, in short, and as we might expect, *ephectic*. He declines to hypostasize himself by making a final judgment about who he is, and so is, in that sense, a "stranger" and "unknown" to himself. Kant's mature philosopher knows himself all too well: he has made the unconditional judgment that he is, essentially, noumenal— that he is, essentially, freed from "the whole sphere of becoming and transitoriness" (GM III.11). Nietzsche's mature philosopher, by contrast, refuses to pin himself down in this way. His "ephectic bent" won't let him.

If this is correct, it allows us to mark another distinction between the philosopher and the priest. Both, as we know, exploit ascetic procedures. But, as Henry Staten remarks, Nietzsche's attitude toward such procedures in the case of the priest is "obscured by his oscillation between viewing it in terms of the priest's self-relation and in terms of the ascetic priest's relation to the masses. When he views it in terms of the former," his "admiration begins to overflow the bounds of his official attitude of condemnation." But then he can always put this right by shifting "to the latter to touch ground again with that condemnation."[5] The philosopher, then, insofar as he is distinct from the priest, is so to the extent that he occupies the first pole of Nietzsche's oscillation: his procedures are directed, however indirectly, to the end of self-cultivation. Among the masses, on the other hand, the philoso-

5. Henry Staten, *Nietzsche's Voice* (Ithaca: Cornell University Press, 1990), p. 59.

pher wishes "to go unrecognized" so that he "can talk to anyone with impunity" (GM III.8): he, unlike the priest, does *not* seek dominion over them. He, and not the priest, might exclaim with Nietzsche, "Oh how *fortunate* we are, we men of knowledge, provided only that we know how to keep silent long enough!" (GM P3). Thus the philosopher is not a leader of men. (When, in the preface to *Beyond Good and Evil*, Nietzsche describes Christianity as "Platonism for 'the people'" he is marking the same distinction: Platonism is an expression of a certain ascetic self-relation which, when sold to the people by the priest, when not kept "silent," becomes a religion— becomes an expression of the priest's relation not to himself but to the masses.)

But consider now what Staten says a little later: the difference between the philosopher and the priest, he suggests, is that the philosopher

> brings forth a work, whereas the ascetic priest works only on his own being, he does not save his energy for the production of a work but uses it to shut down the springs out of which that energy flows. . . . [So perhaps] the asceticism of the ascetic priest is the pure essence of the same will that drives the philosopher, perhaps the philosopher's will is only a slightly etiolated form of the priest's will. . . . The work that grows within is only the reflection of the philosopher's own being, not a real expenditure of his being into the outside, into the world, into time, but a way of avoiding such expenditure, of addressing a postcard to oneself.[6]

This is an acute summary of one tendency in Nietzsche's thought—the tendency to seal himself hermetically within the bounds of his own fantasy of himself. But it doesn't sort very well, I think, with the larger tendency of Nietzsche's discussion of the (mature) philosopher. It may be right to construe the priest's self-relation as one that closes the loop of his own energies so that they are discharged, ultimately, only into a fantasy called God. But I suspect that the philosopher, for whom "the law 'Each is furthest from himself' applies to all eternity," cannot be pinned down in the same way, or in any "etiolated" version of the same way. Philosophers care "from the heart," Nietzsche says, about "bringing something home": they flutter around "the beehives of knowledge . . . , being by nature winged creatures and honey-gatherers of the spirit" (GM P1). Yet their fluttering must involve the exercise of the philosophical virtues (analysis, doubt, suspension of judgment), so that what they bring "home" cannot be quite a self-addressed postcard— that is, a card whose contents are fixed and known to them in advance—

6. Ibid., pp. 63–64.

even if the card is indeed addressed to them. Staten suggests that the "work that grows within is only the reflection of the philosopher's own being." But this is to ignore the character of the philosopher's self-relation: because his ascetic procedures relieve him "of the necessity of thinking *of himself*" it is precisely not, on pain of falling into an "ascetic self-misunderstanding," some fixed picture of himself that he seeks to find reflected.[7] The philosopher, then, although painted by Nietzsche in a variety of tones, including the tone highlighted by Staten, simply isn't—at the philosopher's or at Nietzsche's best—to be seen as a mere ascetic self-regarder. Rather, his best self must be understood as that butterfly or "new heaven" which, insofar as he is true to himself, the philosopher nurtures through a certain ascetic self-*dis*regard— through the complex, almost paradoxical self-relation that Nietzsche attempts to evoke in images of caterpillars and pregnancy. Only thus, one gathers, has the philosopher a chance of "bringing something home."

If I am right in claiming that the philosopher becomes most truly himself when, and only when, his "propensities and virtues" are incorporated into and exercised upon his own relation to himself, a couple of slightly odd remarks that Nietzsche makes start to fall into place. "We philosophers," he says, "need to be spared *one* thing above all: everything to do with 'today.'" Indeed it is a mark of the philosopher that he "shuns light that is too bright: that is why he shuns his age and its 'day'" (GM III.8). On the face of it, these remarks appear to betoken nothing much more than a kind of escapism. But if one ties them to the sort of "avoidance" that goes with a philosophical suspension of judgment about oneself (to an ephectic *self*-avoidance, in other words), what emerges instead is a distinctively philosophical relation to the present. The priest, remember, is engaged in denying "the whole sphere of becoming and transitoriness." His denial is a categorical judgment against "life as a wrong road," and hence against "today" as an unqualified mistake. He hypostasizes the present, then, under a fixed description, and in doing so he closes down its futurity, its transitory character as a locus, not of (false) being, but of becoming. His commitment to the priestly ideal requires no less. And so the present, for him, is determinate precisely because he is anti-ephectic. It is in this sense—in the priestly, hypostasized sense—that Nietzsche's philosopher shuns "today."[8] Naturally ephectic, and with his ascetic self-misunderstandings behind him, he regards the present and his present self as open, as necessarily eluding the closure imposed by categori-

7. The section of *Zarathustra* called "The Honey Offering" may be to the point here. Zarathustra, on top of his mountain, having recalled his instruction to himself to "Become what you are!" rhapsodizes: "Gaze out, gaze out, my eye! Oh how many seas round me, what dawning human futures!" No fixed self-reflection here, I think.

8. This comes through clearly in, for example, GS 380.

cal judgment. His relation to the present is, in other words, the exact opposite of the priest's.

Nietzsche doesn't talk about "untimeliness" in the *Genealogy*, which is a
pity, given how often he does elsewhere. But I think that we have here a dis-
tillation of what, elsewhere, he means by it. To be "untimely" in relation to
the present is to be ephectic about it—to suspend judgment on it in the face
of its character as a locus of becoming. "Timeliness," by contrast, involves a
move to judgment: "today" is nailed down unconditionally—perhaps, as by
the priest, under the label "mistake," but at any rate under a description that
hypostasizes it. So one could posit two kinds of present: an "untimely" present of pure becoming, and a hypostasized, "timely" present of pure being. If
my suggestion here is right, the philosopher's present is an untimely one, forever prevented from coagulating into stasis by the ephectic propensity that
distinguishes him from the priest.

Nietzsche's commitment to this conception of the true philosopher is a
deep one, underwriting nearly all of his most confident and optimistic asser-
tions. Man, he insists, is *"pregnant with a future. . . .* [H]e gives rise to an interest, a tension, a hope, almost a certainty, as if with him something were
announcing and preparing itself, as if man were not a goal but only a way, a
bridge, a great promise" (GM II.16)—as if, in other words, it is in his very
untimeliness that his real and abiding value lies. So the ephectic self-relation
of the philosopher—his understanding of himself as a "bridge" rather than
as a "goal"—must, if the pages devoted to him in the *Genealogy* are anything
to go by, be somehow integral to the *good* bad conscience with which Nietzsche seeks to replace the *bad* bad conscience that has been hegemonic until
now. But for all that, and for all the encouragement which his invocation of
the philosopher undoubtedly gives him, it cannot be said that Nietzsche really succeeds in telling us very much about what such a philosopher would
actually be like, or about how such a transformed post-priestly conscience
might actually be achieved. The ratio of the vaguely if breathlessly inspi-
rational to the genuinely informative is simply too high. And he knows
it too. His last word on the philosopher, although still highly charged, aban-
dons any pretense to specificity: "Has that many-colored and dangerous
winged creature, the 'spirit' which this caterpillar concealed, really been unfettered at last and released into the light, thanks to a sunnier, brighter,
warmer world? Is there sufficient pride, daring, courage, self-confidence
available today, sufficient will of the spirit, will to responsibility, *freedom of the
will*, for 'the philosopher' to be henceforth—*possible* on earth?" (GM III.10).
Nietzsche—speaking from a present that isn't perhaps as untimely as it might
be—can only hope so. And the hyperbolic tentativeness he brings to the
hoping speaks volumes for his confidence.

I suggested at the beginning of this chapter that Nietzsche's attempt to discover promising chinks and gaps in the modern conscience was, in the case of the philosopher, beset by a double difficulty: the need to achieve enough distance from himself as a modern *and* enough distance from himself as a philosopher. And he doesn't quite bring it off. But if his discussion of the philosopher results only in a rather skeletal characterization of what Nietzsche is after (in effect, "Be reflexively ephectic!"), it nonetheless serves to rule some options out. And it serves also as a framework for the more substantial content that emerges when he turns his attention elsewhere. When he talks about the artist, for instance, we learn more of the philosopher's "new heaven" and of the kind of activity that goes into building it than was ever revealed by the philosopher himself. And in his discussion of the scientist we discover the precise sense in which the philosopher, who has "something to *do* for the truth" (GM III.8), may function not merely as a fifth columnist against the ascetic ideal, but as a successful fifth columnist against it. The philosopher himself, then, marks only the beginning of Nietzsche's efforts to imagine the enlightened conscience of the future.

THE ARTIST

The whole of morality is a long undismayed forgery which alone makes it at all possible to enjoy the sight of the soul. From this point of view much more may belong in the concept "art" than is generally believed.

—*Beyond Good and Evil*, sec. 291

The *Genealogy* is not one of Nietzsche's more art- or artist-laden books, but the role that art and artists play in it is fascinating nonetheless for that. Indeed, as I hope to demonstrate, the relatively low profile that such matters are accorded in the book is, like the dog that didn't bark, more revealing than a whole pack of references might have been. Julian Young, in his stimulating reconstruction of Nietzsche's philosophy of art, barely mentions the *Genealogy*: insofar as it figures at all, it is lumped together with *The Gay Science* and *Beyond Good and Evil* as symptomatic of the comparative lack of seriousness with which Nietzsche regarded art during the latter part of his middle period.[1] In one way that is quite right: we don't hear much from Nietzsche at this time about those redemptive and existence-justifying powers which he had attributed to art at the beginning of his career. But even if art is no longer called upon to do the rather explicit job it did before, it nonetheless—and in a manner signaled by Nietzsche's odd and somewhat cursory remarks about it in the *Genealogy*—still occupies a place at the very center of his thought. In the first section of this chapter I set out what I take to be the official aesthetic of the *Genealogy*—a rather dismissive doctrine, which appears to trivialize art and artists more or less indiscriminately and which also aligns

1. Julian Young, *Nietzsche's Philosophy of Art* (Cambridge: Cambridge University Press, 1992). I think the argument I am advancing in this chapter is broadly in line with Young's position on the *Genealogy*.

the vast majority of artists with the *bad* bad conscience. In the second and third sections I explore Nietzsche's less conspicuous unofficial aesthetic. Here one begins to glimpse something more positive—the possibility, explored further in the fourth section, that at least some artists have gone about their work with a *good* bad conscience, chiefly when their materials have been themselves. And in the fifth section I try to tease out some of the consequences of this unofficial aesthetic: specifically, I try to show that what Nietzsche needs, or believes that he needs, is a kind of counter-art of the soul with which to oppose the formidable artistry of the priest. This putative counter-art is absolutely essential to Nietzsche's attempts to imagine what the *good* bad conscience of the future might be like. Indeed, as I hope to demonstrate, Nietzsche's apparent marginalization of art in the *Genealogy* is itself, in the deepest way, an affirmation of the aesthetic and of its indispensability to his project.

I

The one remotely sustained discussion of art in the *Genealogy* comes in two brief episodes at the beginning of third essay. In the first of these Nietzsche decides that artists have little to teach us about the meaning of ascetic ideals (i.e., of ideals that deny this world in favor of some other, nonexistent "beyond"). The passage has an air of digression about it from the start, as Nietzsche, with an almost touching disingenuousness, mentions "a case I have often been asked about" to introduce what looks for all the world like an opportunistic excursus into Wagneriana (GM III.2). One thinks at once: here's something I pick away at all the time—and here I go again. And that, indeed, is how the passage mostly comes across. But let's look more closely.

"What, then, is the meaning of ascetic ideals? In the case of an artist, as we see, *nothing whatever!*... Or so many things it amounts to nothing whatever!" The reason for this is that artists "do not stand nearly independently enough in the world and *against* the world for their changing valuations to deserve attention *in themselves!* They have at all times been valets of some morality, philosophy or religion.... They always need at the very least protection, a prop, an established authority: artists never stand apart; standing alone is contrary to their deepest instincts" (GM III.5). And so, Nietzsche concludes, if one wants to learn the meaning of ascetic ideals one should bypass artists and go straight to the sources of those moralities, philosophies, and religions from which they derive their support. But why does he believe that "standing alone is contrary to" an artist's "deepest instincts"—that an artist never stands sufficiently "*against* the world" to be taken seriously? On the face of it, Nietzsche appears to arrive at this conclusion by generalizing from a single case. Wagner, he says, went over to Schopenhauer "when the latter's 'time had come,'" and so "became an oracle, a priest, indeed more than a priest, a kind of mouthpiece of the 'in itself' of things, a telephone from the beyond . . . : no wonder one day he finally uttered *ascetic ideals*" (GM III.5). Which is all very well, but it hardly, by itself, gives a reason to suppose that the same must be true of every artist.

We do better, perhaps, to turn back a page or two and look at what Nietzsche calls "the *typical velleity* of the artist." This is the wish to negate the very condition of artistry, the fact that the true artist "is to all eternity separated from the 'real,' the actual" (GM III.4). Insofar as he is genuine, an artist deifies the real world by falsifying it (GM III.25). The temptation that Nietzsche labels a *velleity* is the artist's desire to *be* "what he is able to represent, conceive and express," to become a person whose "innermost existence" is not characterized by "eternal 'unreality' and falsity": he wants "to lay hold of actuality, for once actually to *be*" (GM III.4). So the typical velleity of the artist is the fantasy of being an actor in, rather than a beautifier of, the real world.

It is important to understand the force of this claim. Nietzsche's insistence that the "innermost existence" of the true artist is unreal and false is easily misread as a criticism of it. But it isn't, for it is precisely under these conditions that the artist's "will to deception" is said to have "a good conscience" (GM III.25)—that is, to have what, in Chapter 1, I argued should be seen as the good, creative version of that "bad" conscience which is the inevitable result of repression. This indicates that the alternative attitude—the velleist's—is an expression of the bad version of the bad conscience, of a response to the exigencies of internalization that is full, not of joy and creativity, but of *ressentiment*. The typical velleity of the artist, then, is the wish to repudiate (to take revenge against) an inner existence whose nature is unbearable and from which the resources needed for self-affirmation seem lacking; and the wish "to lay hold of actuality" is the wish, characteristic of the resentful, "to direct one's view outward instead of back to oneself" (GM I.10). Even "great" artists, Nietzsche suggests in *Beyond Good and Evil*, are vulnerable—men "with souls in which they usually try to conceal some fracture; often taking revenge with their works for some inner contamination, often seeking with their high flights to escape into forgetfulness . . . —often fighting against a long nausea, with a recurring specter of unbelief that chills and forces them to languish for *gloria* and to gobble their 'belief in themselves' from the hands of intoxicated flatterers" (BGE 269). To the extent that the artist succumbs, he is a velleist. To the extent that he is a velleist, he is also slavelike; and it is in consequence of this that Nietzsche sees an intimate connection between velleity and the uttering of ascetic ideals. "Velleity," then, which is the name for *ressentiment* as it afflicts artists, constitutes the principal link between the discussion of art and the concerns of the *Genealogy* as a whole.

Since the true artist is separated from the real "to all eternity," the surrender to velleity constitutes the surrender of artistry. To resist that surrender is, as one would expect, to exhibit those exceptional qualities that the slave finds altogether beyond him. The true artist arrives at the "pinnacle" of greatness, says Nietzsche, "when he comes to see himself and his art *beneath* him—when he knows how to *laugh* at himself" (GM III.3)—when, in other words, he finds it possible to revel in the unreality and falsity of his innermost existence. This is a laugh not of self-rejection but of self-acceptance: it is the laugh of a *good* bad conscience from which the specter of *ressentiment* is, even if only for the moment, absent. But the temptation to forswear this "ultimate artist's freedom and artist's transcendence" (GM III.3) is enormous: the sheer difficulty of affirming oneself precisely *as* unreal can exhaust one, so that one becomes "weary" with the conditions of artistry "to the point of desperation" (GM III.4). Thus it is that "nothing is more easily corrupted than an artist" (GM III.25).

The effect of giving in to temptation, of being corrupted by one's own "deepest instincts"—that is, of having the goodness of one's bad conscience wrecked by *ressentiment*—is both to cease being an artist and to turn oneself into a "valet" of something other than one's art: of a morality, philosophy, or religion. Understood in this way, Nietzsche's apparent generalization from the single case of Wagner begins to look less arbitrary. If it is plausible to portray the inner life of an artist qua artist as saturated with unreality and falsity, then it is plausible too to suppose that the artist qua man might weary of this condition and wish to "lay hold of actuality" for once, to seek the "established authority" of what would nowadays probably be called "relevance." It is this wish that Nietzsche sees Wagner succumbing to when he imagines him saying to his "disciples": "it is no good! seek salvation elsewhere!" (GM III.3)—mere art is not enough; we cannot affirm ourselves *here*.

This is plausible, certainly, and psychologically acute: but it's still not the kind of thing one would want to write "Q.E.D." under. For there must be at least the possibility of resisting velleity, of being an artist whose innermost falsity is a source of joy and affirmation rather than *ressentiment*—otherwise there would be little point in talking of corruption or of the pinnacles of greatness to which artists can aspire. But Nietzsche is inclined to suppress this fact. Indeed, he goes on to speak as if velleity were not merely typical of artists—typical in the sense of being often met with, predictable—but actually essential to them. Hence his claim that "one does best to separate an artist from his work, not taking him as seriously as his work": "He is, after all, only the precondition of his work, the womb, the soil, sometimes the dung and manure on which, out of which, it grows—and therefore in most cases something one must forget if one is to enjoy the work itself" (GM III.4). This move serves to enmesh the artist still more deeply in the web of valuations that Nietzsche associates with slavishness. For now it seems that, in virtue of his (proneness to) velleity, the artist is best understood as (seeing himself as?) a doer distinct from his deeds—as, in other words, an instance of that fictitious "subject" presupposed by the morality of *ressentiment*. But of course this conclusion follows only if there are good reasons to suppose that artists must, inevitably, be velleists—and Nietzsche hasn't given us reasons to think that.

The picture we are offered, then, is this: the artist qua velleist is a distraction from what he produces qua artist, a distraction to which the velleist in the artist is himself only too prone. Thus, insofar as he is an artist he has nothing to teach us about anything, including ascetic ideals, for he is "to all eternity separated from the 'real,' the actual"—a circumstance from which Nietzsche later concludes that "art, in which precisely the *lie* is sanctified," is really "fundamentally opposed to the ascetic ideal" (GM III.25).[2] And insofar as the artist is a velleist—while he may have all sorts of things to teach us, including things about the ascetic ideal—he teaches us not as an artist but out of *ressentiment*, as, for instance, a moralist, a philosopher[3] or a priest. It is in this sense that the meaning of ascetic ideals to the artist is either "nothing whatever" (to the artist qua artist) or else "so many things it amounts to nothing whatever" (to the artist qua velleist).

There are, then, two points at issue in this discussion. One concerns an artist's relation to himself: does he have a *good* bad or a *bad* bad conscience about his own innermost falsity? The other concerns actual works of art and, as such, constitutes the only reference to them in the whole book. Here the position seems to be that works of art are either meaningless or false, and that they are best approached without reference to the people who produce them. So Nietzsche has arrived at a kind of anti-intentionalist formalism— a philosophy of art that is all Apollo and no Dionysus. It is still possible, from this point of view, to speak of the "greatness" of works of art and to go through the motions of taking them seriously. But the greatness comes to nothing more than a form of honest inconsequentiality; and to take them seriously is, at best (i.e., if the artist has a good conscience), to take seriously only the sanctification of lies. Artworks—and this appears to be the official doctrine of the *Genealogy*—are entirely trivial.

2. Precisely what sort of "lie" is at issue here is a question taken up in Chapter 5.
3. A non-ephectic philosopher, of course.

II

At the opposite pole, it seems, stands the priest, who is said to be "the actual *representative of seriousness*" (GM III.11)—a person from whom one can learn much about ascetic ideals, and whose valuations deserve and gain Nietzsche's undivided attention. Where the artist is cheerful (he looks down and laughs at the idea that his work might be redemptive, that it might offer solutions to life's suffering), the priest's "seriousness" consists in the fact that he fully intends, through *his* inventions, "to become master not over something in life" (which would be serious enough) "but over life itself, over its most profound, powerful, and basic conditions"—which is to say, over suffering *tout court* (GM III.11). If the artist (as one must suppose) falsifies or beautifies suffering, but leaves the basic senselessness of it untouched, the priest gives it a *meaning* and so makes it bearable—even desirable. "*Dominion over the suffering* is his kingdom," says Nietzsche (GM III.15).

This serves to highlight the distance apparently separating the seriousness of the priest from the triviality of the artist. But no sooner has it been established than the distance collapses: for in the kingdom to which his "instinct directs him," the priest is said to possess not only "his mastery, his kind of happiness," but also "his distinctive art" (GM III.15). There is, then, an art of seriousness—a nontrivial art that Nietzsche keeps remarkably quiet about when discussing actual artists, but to which he alludes repeatedly when Wagner and company are safely out of earshot. What is the priest's distinctive art? It is to combat "dull, paralyzing, protracted pain" by means of "an *orgy of feeling*" (GM III.19): "The chief trick the ascetic priest permitted himself for making the human soul resound with heart-rending, ecstatic music of all kinds was, as everyone knows, the exploitation of the *sense of guilt*. . . . It was only in the hands of the priest, that artist in guilt feelings, that it achieved form—oh, what a form! 'Sin'—for this is the priestly name for [it]: we possess in it the most dangerous and fateful artifice of religious interpretation" (GM III.20).

A number of things stand out about this passage, apart from its high temperature. First, the priest is allowed to be the valet of an ideal without forfeiting his claim to be an artist (if anything, the reverse is true). The second is the unmistakably Dionysian register of the writing: we haven't heard much about human souls resounding with heartrending, ecstatic music since Nietzsche's admiration for Schopenhauer was at its height in *The Birth of Tragedy*. It is hard to know exactly what to make of this. There are two other passages in the *Genealogy* in which Nietzsche invokes a Schopenhauerian conception of music, the first of which is clearly mocking, the second almost certainly so. In the first, Wagner transforms himself into a "telephone from the beyond" by accepting Schopenhauer's view that music speaks "the language of the will itself, directly out of the 'abyss' as its most authentic, elemental, non-derivative revelation" (GM III.5). The other comes later, when Nietzsche declares himself unimpressed by the pretensions of those who would see in science a vanquishing of the ascetic ideal rather than the latest expression of it: "these trumpeters of reality are bad musicians," he says: "their voices obviously do *not* come from the depths, the abyss of the scientific conscience does *not* speak through them" (GM III.23). So it is tempting to regard the present passage as a put-down too—this time of the ascetic priest. And perhaps this temptation should increase when one notes that, like the artist proper, the priest is engaged in the promulgation of a lie (although with what quality of conscience it is difficult to say—see Chapter 2): the whole telos of his heartrending music is to persuade sufferers that they themselves are responsible for their own suffering—which, as Nietzsche puts it, is "brazen and false enough" (GM III.15). So it may be that Nietzsche is either poking fun, albeit rather admiringly, at the priest for his selection of such trivial means to such undoubtedly serious ends or else is laughing along with him (on the same grounds) at the expense of those who buy the ascetic lie.

Perhaps, then, the Dionysian register of the writing *is* intended purely as satire—but one does wonder. Nietzsche's attitude toward the priest veers in the most alarming way throughout the *Genealogy*, and it is extraordinarily difficult to be sure at any point whether he is really jeering at or cheering this alter ego of his, who is also his chief opponent. The present passage—in which cheering and jeering go hand in hand—exemplifies the ambivalence. The purity of Nietzsche's mocking intentions is further called into doubt by the explicit connection of the priest's artistry to the achievement of "form" and the giving of an "interpretation"—in this case an interpretation so powerful and seemingly natural that it has become all but invisible (GM I.7).

This same connection is found in another of Nietzsche's unofficial invocations of art—and this time it is one without the faintest trace of mockery. Nietzsche is describing the process of state formation. A "pack of blond beasts of prey" fell upon a "hitherto unchecked and shapeless populace" and "went on working until this raw material of people and semi-animals was at last not only thoroughly kneaded and pliant but also *formed*." The work of these state makers "is an instinctive creation and imposition of forms; they are the most involuntary, unconscious artists there are—wherever they appear something new soon arises, a ruling structure that *lives*, in which parts and functions are delimited and coordinated, in which nothing whatever finds a place that has not first been assigned a 'meaning' in relation to the whole. . . . [T]hey exemplify that terrible artists' egoism that has the look of bronze and knows itself justified to all eternity in its 'work,' like a mother in her child. . . . [Theirs is an artist's] violence" (GM II.17). There is little enough hint in this of the "*typical velleity* of the artist"—presumably because these artists are sufficiently primitive to give the doer/deed distinction, and hence *ressentiment*, little purchase on them: their consciences are clear (GM I.11), and there is nothing to prevent them from affirming themselves directly in their real work on the real world. The reference to mothers and children underlines the point. When Nietzsche is urging the separation of an artist from his work he uses a similar image, but to different effect. Wagner, he says, could no more avoid "a kind of intellectual *perversity* . . . than can a pregnant woman be spared the repellent and bizarre aspects of pregnancy—which, as aforesaid, must be *forgotten* if one is to enjoy the child" (GM III.4). One gets no sense that Nietzsche wants to say the same about his violent mothers of the state. The fact is that we have here a version of artistry that escapes Nietzsche's censure altogether—which is, indeed, celebrated in some of the most affirmative vocabulary he can command.

The nontriviality of what the "blond beasts" achieve is emphasized immediately afterward. The natural instincts of the hitherto shapeless populace are violently repressed by enclosure within the state, with the result that, because those instincts cannot "discharge themselves outwardly," they "*turn inward*—this is what I call the *internalization* of man" (GM II.16). And here, in this new inner theater, individual men begin to go to work on themselves: "This secret self-ravishment, this artists' cruelty, this delight in imposing a form upon oneself as a hard, recalcitrant, suffering material . . . eventually . . . brought to light an abundance of strange new beauty and affirmation, and perhaps beauty itself" (GM II.18). This passage, of course, constitutes Nietzsche's description the positive, good potential of the bad conscience. Thus we have not only another of his paeans to art but also, and in the circumstances not surprisingly, a case in which the "typical velleity" of artists is ruled out in advance: for when an artist's material is himself, and his work is free of *ressentiment*, the artist/man opposition from which the velleity springs is abolished. There is no longer the space across which it would be intelligible for the artist-man to yearn "actually to *be*." This has the effect of suggesting that the problem with artists proper is really their insistence on creating works of art that are separable from themselves: had they worked instead on their own souls the problematic gap between artist and work would never have opened up. (That Nietzsche really does want to say something like this will become clearer below.) So if the priest's art appeared equivocal in certain respects—at arm's length, certainly, from the art of artists proper, but perhaps not further than that—then the work of "those artists of violence . . . who build states" (GM II.18) and the internal, affirmative work of (the best of) those whom they build them out of inhabits a different universe. The official aesthetic of the *Genealogy*—the official philosophy of *works of* art—is nowhere in sight here.

III

Art, as Nietzsche uses the term in these passages, refers to the imposition of form on raw material—whether that material be the sense of guilt, a shapeless populace, or the human soul. It also refers to the giving of meaning. The priest, in giving form to the feelings of those who suffer from guilt, gives their suffering a meaning—as punishment for "sin." The "blond beasts" impose the form of the state upon a populace and create a structure whose components are "assigned a 'meaning' in relation to the whole." Internalized man imposes form on himself and gives birth to beauty (on which more in a moment). One doesn't have to look far to find an alternative name for this kind of art. Nietzsche's name for it is "interpretation"—and the whole *Genealogy* is devoted to its history:

> whatever exists, having somehow come into being, is again and again reinterpreted to new ends, taken over, transformed, and redirected by some power superior to it; all events in the organic world are a subduing, a *becoming master*, and all subduing and becoming master involves a fresh interpretation, an adaptation through which any previous "meaning" and "purpose" are necessarily obscured or even obliterated. . . . Thus the essence of life, its *will to power*, . . . [involves] the essential priority of the spontaneous, aggressive, expansive, form-giving forces that give new interpretations and directions. (GM II.12)

One need only round out this description with references to the "egoism," "violence," and "cruelty" with which a reinterpretation is achieved to complete the picture. If Nietzsche's chief concern in the *Genealogy* is to understand how certain valuations of human existence have won out over others, his attention, necessarily, must be focused on art—or rather, on art as it is practiced by everyone except those whom we would normally call artists. And that, clearly, is why his admiration for the master-interpreters he describes, and for their master-interpretations, is couched in explicitly aesthetic terms: for we have become what we are precisely through that form-giving activity which Nietzsche (when Wagner is out of the way) calls art. This is Nietzsche's unofficial aesthetic.

IV

In the first section, I discussed one episode of Nietzsche's overt philosophy of art—where the official, trivializing doctrine is set out. But there is another episode (on the face of it also rather tangential to the main concerns of the *Genealogy*) which I think we are now in a position to make sense of. Nietz-

sche complains that philosophers of art always commit the same error—
an error exacerbated by their "lack of any refined first-hand experience" of
the beautiful: "instead of envisaging the aesthetic problem from the point of
view of the artist (the creator), [they] considered art and the beautiful purely
from that of the 'spectator,' and unconsciously introduced the 'spectator'
into the concept 'beautiful'" (GM III.6). And so it is, says Nietzsche, that we
end up with definitions of beauty like Kant's, to which even Schopenhauer
was in thrall: the beautiful calms the will; it (in Kant's words) "gives us
pleasure *without interest.*" "Without interest!" Nietzsche exclaims, and bids
us compare this spectatorial conception with that of "a genuine 'spectator'
and artist—Stendhal, who once called the beautiful *une promesse de bon-
heur* . . . ; to him the fact seems to be precisely that the beautiful *arouses the
will* ('interestedness')." It is clear enough which conception Nietzsche favors; and the point is reinforced when he concludes that Schopenhauer's insistence on disinterestedness is itself motivated by "the very strongest, most
personal interest"—that is, the wish to be free from the "torture" of sexual
desire (GM III.6).

It would perhaps be natural to focus here on the sexual aspect of Nietzsche's remarks, about which, no doubt, some interesting things might be
said. But for my present purposes it will be more convenient to forget about
sex and to focus instead on two related questions that the passage raises. Why
should aesthetic problems be envisaged from the point of view of the artist
(the "genuine" spectator) rather than the (presumably ordinary) spectator?
and What is it about Stendhal's definition of beauty that so particularly appeals to Nietzsche?

Julian Young wonders, entirely reasonably on the face of it, why one cannot have two aesthetics—an artist's and a spectator's—which complement
but do not annul one another.[4] And it is hard, indeed, to see why not: plenty
of philosophy of art *is* actually done from the artist's point of view, and it
characteristically attempts to answer different questions from the kind of investigation that privileges the spectator. If one follows this line through, I
think, one will be driven to conclude that Nietzsche's preference for the artist's perspective is nothing more than prejudice—the prejudice of someone
who, throughout his career, insisted in the teeth of abundant evidence to the
contrary that he himself was, primarily, an artist. But I think the position is
a lot less boring than that.

We need to look at the question less with reference to the philosophy of
art—that is, of *works of* art—than to what goes on elsewhere in the *Genealogy.* For if we take the *Genealogy* as our context, a precedent for Nietzsche's

4. *Nietzsche's Philosophy of Art*, p. 120.

privileging of the artist is easily found. In the first essay he takes on the "English psychologists" of value, and makes exactly the same move against them as he makes against the philosophers of art: "the source of the concept 'good' has been sought and established in the wrong place; the judgment 'good' did *not* originate with those to whom 'goodness' was shown! Rather it was 'the good' themselves, that is to say, the noble, powerful, high-stationed and high-minded, who felt and established themselves and their actions as good" (GM I.2). So again we find a value—goodness, in this case, rather than beauty—being transferred (by Nietzsche) from the jurisdiction of the passive to that of the active. In this case as much as the other, then, the "spectator" is portrayed as having been illicitly introduced into an equation which is said to be intelligible only from the vantage point of the creator. As far as the concept "good" is concerned, Nietzsche's transfer of its origin to the noble has the effect of assigning to it a meaning derived from the noble's own interpretation of himself as powerful, high-stationed, and so on, so that the term "good" now functions as a marker of his self-affirmation: indeed it "resolves itself into a concept denoting superiority of soul" (GM I.6). The alternative, "English," claim that "good" originates "with those to whom 'goodness' was shown" is not just wrong, in Nietzsche's view, but is a symptom of that wholesale inversion of values that he calls "*the slave revolt in morality*" (GM I.7)—a revolt (by those who cannot affirm themselves) precisely *against* superiority of soul. So the question, What is the meaning of "good"? becomes, almost at once, a question about what sort of soul you have.

This has implications for Nietzsche's privileging of the artist in his discussion of beauty. Indeed—if I am right that the passages on goodness and beauty run in parallel to one another—the Kantian or Schopenhauerian emphasis on the spectator's point of view can be seen as a kind of slave revolt in aesthetics. And this should come as no surprise. For what is going on here is surely a continuation of the earlier discussion of the artist's relation to himself, of his velleity, of his readiness (or otherwise) to affirm himself as one whose "innermost existence" is characterized by falsity. Does the artist have a *good* bad conscience or not? The question that Nietzsche is raising, then, is not really about the differing conceptions of beauty that the makers and consumers of works of art might favor. It is, instead, about differing qualities of soul. It is the question whether a particular person has the right to use the term "beauty" at all (a right forfeited when he succumbs to velleity). "Artists" and "spectators" are functioning here as placeholders for "superior souls" and "others."

This is the moment to raise the second of the two questions mentioned above: What is it about Stendhal's definition of beauty—as "a promise of happiness"—that so particularly appeals to Nietzsche? It can't just be that Stendhal was an artist, or that his definition was an "interested" one. Nietzsche could have found any number of definitions that would have fitted those descriptions. The answer lies in the fact that Nietzsche treats the Stendhal / Schopenhauer alternative as marking not only the artist /spectator distinction but also as marking a difference in personal qualities: Stendhal is described as a "more happily constituted person than Schopenhauer" (GM III.6). So there is something about Stendhal's conception of beauty that Nietzsche regards as importantly related to his better constitution. What might it be? The answer is surely that Stendhal, unlike Schopenhauer, goes in for that "secret self-ravishment" and "artist's cruelty" which brings "to light an abundance of strange new beauty and affirmation, and even beauty itself" (GM II.18). Stendhal, in other words, has a good conscience about himself: he is an artist of his own soul; and he gains from the experience of beauty an intimation of the form—and hence the meaning—that he might impose upon himself, that he might make out of himself. The "promise of happiness," in other words, is a foretaste of the satisfaction to be won by going to work on oneself, by interpreting oneself anew, so that one finds—in the transformation of one's own soul—that one has given birth to beauty. Read in this way, Stendhal's definition of beauty ties immediately into one of the most famous passages Nietzsche ever wrote:

> *One thing is needful.* —To "give style" to one's character—a great and rare art! It is practiced by those who survey all the strengths and weaknesses of their nature and then fit them into an artistic plan until every one of them appears as art and reason and even weaknesses delight the eye. Here a large mass of second nature has been added; there a piece of original nature has been removed—both times through long practice and daily work at it. Here the ugly that could not be removed is concealed; there it has been reinterpreted and made sublime. . . . For one thing is needful: that a human being should *attain* satisfaction with himself, whether it be by means of this or that poetry and art. . . . For the sight of what is ugly makes one bad and gloomy. (GS 290)

Beauty is a state of soul: it is the result of going to work on oneself, of interpreting oneself, of exercising upon oneself that artist's violence to which Nietzsche is so attached.[5] It is a matter of resisting the seduction to *ressentiment*, a task that requires both discipline and strength: "it is the weak characters without power over themselves that *hate* the constraint of style. They feel that if this bitter and evil constraint were imposed upon them they would be demeaned; they become slaves as soon as they serve; they hate to serve" (GS 290)—in other words, they take refuge in velleity. It is in his resistance to this temptation, surely, that Stendhal's opinion is described as an "artist's" opinion; and it is for this reason that the very idea of a "spec-

---

5. In Chapter 6 I discuss the (rather terrible) kind of beauty to be achieved by these means.

tator's" aesthetic—involving, as it would, the privileging of the *bad* bad conscience—strikes Nietzsche as a travesty. This point receives support from another passage in *The Gay Science*: "there are two kinds of sufferers: first, those who suffer from the *over-fullness of life* . . . and then those who suffer from the *impoverishment of life*. . . . Regarding all aesthetic values I now avail myself of this main distinction: I ask in every instance, 'is it hunger or superabundance that has here become creative?'" (GS 370). Stendhal, clearly, is a case of superabundance. The hungry artist, by contrast, the velleist, either destroys—"because what exists, indeed all existence, all being, outrages and provokes"—or seeks to "*immortalize*" the "real idiosyncrasy of his suffering," revenging "himself on all things by forcing his own image, the image of his torture, on them, branding them with it" (GS 370). Which comes very close to rendering analytic the suggestion, mentioned in section 2, that the real problem with artists ordinarily so-called—their typical velleity, if you like—is their tendency to produce "immortal" public objects.[6] Nietzsche really does incite one to attribute this view to him (or, certainly, the view that a work of art produced by a non-velleist is only an epiphenomenon, something strictly secondary to the genuinely beautiful business being done inside).[7]

The claim that philosophers of art have been wrong about beauty because of their "lack of any refined first-hand experience" should read rather differently now: what philosophers of art have lacked is refined firsthand experience, not of beautiful things, but of making themselves beautiful. Which shows to what extent the present episode of Nietzsche's (overt) discussion of art is intelligible only when detached from anything that would normally go under the title Philosophy of Art. The argument in GM III.6 seems really to be part of the serious, unofficial doctrine explored above in sections 2 and 3. This prompts the question: Why, when it so clearly takes second place to his concern with what a true artist of the soul can achieve, did Nietzsche bother with the official version at all?

V

Partly, no doubt, the answer has to do with Nietzsche's enduring passion for art and with his never completely resolved attitude toward Wagner. Perhaps

6. Another possible cause of Nietzsche's suspicion about public art objects is their hypostasizing character. The artist, as he says, wishes to force his own image (of himself) on things. Yet the very possession of such a self-image, if what I argued in Chapter 3 is right, betokens the absence of a sufficiently "ephectic" self-relation. In producing finished works of art, the artist exhibits a *bad* bad conscience with respect to "the whole sphere of becoming and transitoriness" (GM III.11).

7. This point receives support from the discussion in *The Gay Science* of the difference between "monological art" and "art before witnesses" (GS 367).

he would have felt moved to write about art in the *Genealogy* whether or not it had anything to do with his larger themes; and perhaps, too, he would have written about it a little less dismissively had his eye not been trained so intently on Wagner. But I am sure that that is not the whole story. For if what I have been arguing here is correct, Nietzsche had altogether deeper reasons to engage in an explicit discussion of art—and to trivialize it.

Two well-known and interestingly different claims of his are worth recalling here. In *The Birth of Tragedy* we are told that "it is only as an *aesthetic phenomenon* that existence and the world are eternally *justified*" (BT 5). By *The Gay Science* this claim has become "As an aesthetic phenomenon existence is still *bearable* for us" (GS 107). The earlier claim refers to the (Apollonian) imposition of form or meaning on a (Dionysian) reality so dreadful that, unmediated, it would destroy one. It is by transforming the true nature of the world, and so making it bearable, that the aestheticization of existence justifies (Nietzsche's version of) the ways of God to man. When he made the second claim, however, Nietzsche had abandoned the thought that there was some fundamental, metaphysical truth about the world (see Chapter 5); and so, since he no longer believed in the unspeakable Dionysian "'in itself' of things," he pulls back from any talk of existence being justified—that is, of the "real" nature of things being made acceptable by the imposition of form—for there is, in that sense, no longer a "real" nature of existence to be transformed. Rather, the *absence* of any such underlying reality is now the predicament; and it is this that is said to be made "bearable" by aestheticization. Meaninglessness, the impossibility of ultimate justification, is rendered tolerable only when life is beautified—only when one finds it possible to impose a "form upon oneself as a hard, recalcitrant, suffering material."

In this much, the remark in *The Gay Science* is entirely consonant with Nietzsche's position in the *Genealogy*. Both works present the aestheticization of existence—the transformation and reinterpretation of it—as the best that can be done in the wake of God's departure. But in another sense it would be misleading to summarize Nietzsche's position in this way. Life's being made bearable, while that may be one important motivation for its aestheticization, is, according to the unofficial aesthetic of the *Genealogy*, not ultimately more than a side effect, however desirable it might be, since *all* "events in the organic world" are said to be the product of "fresh interpretation" (GM II.12), of form giving, of aestheticization—*all* events, note, not just the ones that contribute to making life more bearable. Which means that there is a basic transformative urge (Nietzsche calls it the will to power) that is related in a necessary way to the amelioration of existence only in the trivial sense that any unsatisfied urge is unbearable. That the mere satisfaction of the urge itself is paramount—irrespective of any consequent improvement in the quality of existence—is underlined most uncompromisingly when Nietzsche insists that man would "rather will *nothingness* than *not* will" (GM III.1).

The position in the *Genealogy*, then, is not so much "As an aesthetic phenomenon existence is still *bearable*" as "As an aesthetic phenomenon is life even logically possible." The consequences of this are rather dramatic. For instance, Nietzsche's unofficial aesthetic turns out to be, in its fundamentals, nonnormative: one doesn't in the first place seek to transform the world in order to make life better (or more beautiful)—one does so merely in virtue of being alive; and if the price of transforming it is annihilation then that is, in one crucial sense, better than nothing. So the sort of thing that Nietzsche's mothers of the state get up to—which is to say, the primal imposition of form, the assignation of meaning for better or for worse, the exercise of *involuntary* artistry (GM II.17)—is basic: they satisfy their urge, they affirm themselves, as a bare condition of being. The priest and Stendhal, on the other hand, are engaged in something different and more sophisticated. They, too, are busy imposing forms. But the activity they are engaged in has acquired a normative dimension. The priest is deliberately trying to justify existence (by making it intelligible, by taking power over its most basic conditions—while, of course, concealing his artistry). Stendhal, by contrast—if it is plausible to see him as one who seeks to "give style" to his character—is deliberately trying to make life more bearable. Both, confronted with the unprecedented dilemma of internalization, want to improve the way the world is. But whereas one, the priest, invokes the otherworldly dimension that Nietzsche had rejected with his rejection of Schopenhauer (and of Dionysian metaphysics), the other, Stendhal, feeds off those rejections and strives to render *himself*, his own life, bearable—if (emphatically) not justified. So Nietzsche's unofficial aesthetic has, as it were, a purely descriptive core that functions as a condition of those normative, life-ameliorating practices at which the priest (to Nietzsche's chagrin) and Stendhal (to his delight) excel.[8]

It is this double nature of the unofficial aesthetic, I suggest, that helps to explain both the presence and the character of the trivializing doctrine that appears as the *Genealogy's* official philosophy of art. For the fact that Nietzsche is up to his elbows in the aesthetic throughout, in virtue of his emphasis on interpretation, form giving, beauty, and the like, makes it necessary for him to isolate artistry in the sense that he is concerned with from artistry as it is practiced by artists proper, like Wagner. A failure to separate the

---

8. It is unsurprising in light of this that Nietzsche nowhere gives us a genealogy of the aesthetic—for aesthetic concepts are precisely what the practice of genealogy, in his hands, presupposes.

two sufficiently would render his substantive claim—that one should be-come an artist of one's own soul and give birth to beauty *there*, specifically—strikingly undermotivated: there would be little reason to prefer (as a nor-mative expression of the basic urge to impose form) Stendhal's artistry to Wagner's, and no reason to think that the former might constitute a remotely plausible or interesting alternative to the interpretative maneuvers of the priest that would not be constituted equally well by sitting down and writ-ing an opera (or writing poetry, or designing wallpaper).

But of course Nietzsche's preference for Stendhal's way *is* motivated, in the strongest sense, for he hopes that man might somehow be cured of the damage done to his soul by thoroughgoing asceticism—that he might be re-deemed "not only from the hitherto reigning ideal but also from that which was bound to grow out of it, the great nausea, the will to nothingness, nihil-ism" (GM II.24). So Nietzsche needs a countermeasure to the priest that will meet him expressly on his own ground, a means to retrieve that "human soul," which the priest has so calamitously caused to "resound with heart-rending, ecstatic music." He needs, in other words, a counter-art of the soul, an art that will allow man to "attain satisfaction" rather than sickness with himself; and to do *that*, he needs an art with enough depth and weight to offset the "seriousness" whose "actual representative" the priest is said to be.

It might be tempting at this point to suggest that the *Genealogy* itself is somehow a performative instance or exemplar of Nietzsche's counter-art of the soul.[9] But the temptation should be resisted. That the book has some bizarre formal qualities, and some other generally estimable aesthetic ones, is not in doubt. Nor is there much question that in writing it Nietzsche in-tended to do *some* work on behalf of his longed-for counter-art. But if any-thing I've been claiming here is right, the *Genealogy* simply cannot stand for what it calls for. Works of art, for Nietzsche, are, at best, symptoms of an "overfullness of life," of a soul that has gone to work on itself, made itself beautiful, and still has energy to spare. So it is that, at best, works of art offer only a promise of happiness. The *Genealogy*, again at best, might be construed as an artful symptom of Nietzsche's own overfullness, of his own successful counter-artistry of the soul. But, if so, the *Genealogy* cannot itself be or per-form or be exemplary of that counter-art, unless at the cost of a kind of re-verse velleity—one expressly disallowed by Nietzsche when he warns that "one does best to separate an artist from his work" (GM III.4). If the typi-cal velleity of the artist is the desire to be what he represents, the typical velle-ity of the interpreter, to which Nietzsche himself was not immune, is the de-

9. Certainly people do seem to want to claim things like this: see, for instance, David Owen's *Nietzsche, Politics and Modernity* (London: Sage, 1995), pp. 126–30. In Chapter 6 I try to scotch the whole move toward exemplarity.

sire to construe the representation as a portrait of the artist rather than as a symptom of his condition. Nietzsche's own counter-artistry, if he had one, was played out in his soul, and is, at best, attested to by his books. But neither his or anyone else's soul-artistry is to be found *in* those books, or in any other kind of beautiful public object. Thus the *Genealogy* is not, and could not be, an exemplar of the counter-art it seeks to discover or to encourage.

The truth, I think, is that Nietzsche is altogether clearer about the nature and power of the priest's art than he is about his own Stendhal-inspired counter-version. He is, in other words, far more convinced of the gravity of the problem than he is of the efficacy of his solution. And it is this fact, I think, that goes a long way toward explaining the official aesthetic of the *Genealogy*. It is, among other things, a rhetorical foil against which Nietzsche's counter-art of the soul might appear, by contrast, to have something like the potency he so desperately hopes it does have. By trivializing art proper he implicitly privileges his counter-art, so that without having to say anything very particular or persuasive in its favor he can accord it a kind of negative grandeur simply in virtue of its not being the sort of thing that either priests or ordinary artists get up to. Thus it is that the artistry practiced by ordinary artists—that is, the production of beautiful public objects—is permitted to function only as a *promise* of happiness. Thus, too, his rejection of any merely spectatorial aesthetic—and, above all, his scorn for (and insistence upon) the "typical velleity" of artists. For it is this latter that allows him to drive a wedge between art proper and soul-artistry in the first place; and it is precisely this wedge that allows him to pursue the rather one-sided contrast I have just described. In the absence of his official aesthetic, then, Nietzsche's intervention against the hegemony of the ascetic ideal would have been notably more ghostly than it is, and the patina of significance accorded to it by his talk of beauty would have been rather thinner. Or so I would suggest.

One might gloss the foregoing in a series of answers to the question: What is the meaning of aesthetic ideals? From the point of view of life in general (or, for instance, of Nietzsche's artists of the state) the answer is either "everything" (because *all* meaning presupposes the purely descriptive, unofficial aesthetic) or else "nothing" (because, if all meaning presupposes that aesthetic, there is no room for talk of "ideals"). From the point of view of the priest, aesthetic ideals mean power: the priest's imposition of form on the sufferings of the internalized soul allows him to take control of the "most profound, powerful, and basic" conditions of life. From the point of view of artists proper, by contrast, the answer must be "meaninglessness, falsity"— a response made unavoidable by the "velleity" and *bad* bad conscience that Nietzsche insists or asserts is typical of them. Theirs is the least serious (if most official) expression of the unofficial aesthetic in its normative form.

And what about the artist of the soul? What will he answer? Presumably that aesthetic ideals, promising happiness as they do, provide an entirely serious alternative to ascetic ideals, a seriousness underwritten and made possible by the fact that *this* artistry is exercised upon oneself, so foreclosing that gap between artist and material which is said inevitably to result in "velleity." The artist of the soul, then, with his *good* bad conscience, is the true sanctifier of lies.

If this is right, the brief discussion of art and artists proper at the beginning of the *Genealogy*'s third essay serves to dignify Nietzsche's ideal at the expense of those with which it might (all too easily) have been confused, and the relative suppression throughout the work of aesthetics proper serves principally to highlight the depth of his commitment to that broader conception of the aesthetic which he hopes somehow to use against the priest and his nihilistic legacy. Which being so, he really did need to have an official aesthetic, and he really did need to make sure that it was a trivializing one. How peculiarly gratifying it must have been, under the circumstances, to find that both objects could be achieved by being nasty for a few pages about Wagner.

CHAPTER FIVE

THE SCIENTIST

"Knowledge for its own sake"—that is the last snare of morality: with that one becomes completely entangled in it once more.
—*Beyond Good and Evil*, sec. 64

In the preceding two chapters we have investigated the philosopher's and the artist's complex and often ambiguous relations to the ascetic ideal. These two character types furnish a minimal, preliminary sketch of the kind of anti-priestly conscience that Nietzsche is aiming at: an "ephectic," beautifying re-lation to the self. Because the philosopher and the artist succeed in offering such clues, Nietzsche considers neither figure a revealing exemplar of the ascetic ideal in its purest form. The priest, of course, is *the* agent of asceti-cism. But in the closing sections of the *Genealogy* the priest makes way for the scientist; and it is in his person that the late stages of the drama initiated by the slave revolt in morality are played out. The scientist, although in the grip of the ascetic ideal, is no mere slave—for he is also, in virtue of his ded-ication to truth, the great underminer of asceticism's most characteristic achievement: transcendental religion. The details of the scientist's role as fifth columnist are expectedly difficult to clarify: he is presented alternately as hero, parasite, and dupe, and in tones of voice that rarely occupy a settled register for long. But the key concepts are truth and truthfulness. If we can work out what is going on with those, I think, we'll be in a position to un-derstand what manner of beast the scientist is supposed to be and what his office as the harbinger of nihilism really comes to.

I

But first an outline. Nietzsche considers whether the ascetic ideal has not met its match in modern science or scholarship, "which, as a genuine philosophy of reality, clearly believes in itself alone, clearly possesses the courage for it-self and the will to itself, and has up to now survived well enough without God, the beyond, and the virtues of denial" (GM III.23). Is it not the case, he asks, that science, construed as the pursuit of truth, is capable of displac-ing that "closed system of will, goal, and interpretation" (GM III.23) which the asceticism of the priest exemplifies? Nietzsche's answer is no: the scien-tist is not an alternative to the priest.

The reason for this is teased out through a fairly foreseeable contrast be-tween two kinds of scientist—the kind with a bad conscience and the kind with a good (or at any rate a better) conscience.[1] The scientists with a bad conscience are the ones who take refuge in their work from "every kind of discontent, disbelief, gnawing worm." They "desire to keep something hid-den from" themselves, they are "*sufferers* who refuse to admit to themselves what they are, . . . heedless men who fear only one thing: *regaining conscious-ness*" (GM III.23). Nietzsche is reasonably indulgent toward these "modest and worthy laborers": "I approve of their work," he says. But their efficacy as opponents of, or as proponents of an alternative to, the ascetic ideal is nil. Devotion to truth in their case functions as a means of escape from the suf-ferings of internalization rather than as a (non-ascetic) reinterpretation of it; this kind of scientist hides from, and thus makes no attempt to master, those features of his existence most liable to produce *ressentiment*. The priest would applaud his tactics. In his "*grand struggle against the feeling of displea-sure*" (GM III.17)—that is, in his determination to keep the lid on that "most dangerous of all explosives, *ressentiment*" (GM III.15)—one of the priest's fa-vorite prescriptions is "mechanical activity": "this regimen alleviates an exis-tence of suffering to a not inconsiderable degree. . . . The alleviation consists in this, that the interest of the sufferer is directed entirely away from his suffering—that activity, and nothing but activity, enters consciousness, and there is consequently little room left in it for suffering: for the chamber of human consciousness is *small!*" (GM III.18). Given that mechanical activity need not always be manual activity, Nietzsche's "modest and worthy" schol-ars are model patients: their regimen makes them "happy in their little nooks; and because they are happy there, they sometimes demand rather immod-estly that one ought to be content with things today, generally" (GM III.23). In swallowing the priest's cure whole, then, and in allowing themselves to be anaesthetized by it, these scientists offer no threat to the ascetic ideal at all. Their way of life—their participation in what one might term the industri-alization of knowledge—represents a special determination *not* to challenge that ideal or offer any alternative to it.

1. Actually, as I shall suggest in section 5, the distinction is really between those with a bad form of the *bad* bad conscience and those with a good form of the same. But this becomes baroque . . .

In sharp contrast to this sort of scientist stand "the last idealists left among philosophers and scholars . . . in whom alone the intellectual conscience dwells and is incarnate today" (GM III.24). For these, the pursuit of truth is not an evasive engagement designed to provide refuge from feelings of displeasure, but is rather a sign of the "passion, love, ardor, and *suffering*" which truth itself inspires in them. Nietzsche is more expansive in *The Antichrist*: "At every step one has to wrestle for truth; one has to surrender for it almost everything to which the heart . . . cling[s] otherwise. That requires greatness of soul: the service of truth is the hardest service. What does it mean, after all, to have *integrity* in matters of the spirit? That one is severe against one's heart, . . . that one makes of every Yes and No a matter of conscience" (AC 50). "*Not to question*, not to tremble with the craving and the joy of questioning . . . that is what I feel to be *contemptible*" (GS 2). Nietzsche's own investment in the "intellectual conscience" is considerable,[2] and it is tempting to equate this notion directly with that *good* bad conscience which he seeks, for the most part, to promote. There is certainly real warmth in his description of these truth lovers as "hard, severe, abstinent, heroic spirits who constitute the honor of our age" (GM III.24), and one does half expect to be told that such "last idealists" might, after all, have it in them to offer an alternative to the ascetic ideal. But no. It turns out that science, "where it still inspires passion, . . . is not the opposite of the ascetic ideal but rather *the latest and noblest form of it*" (GM III.23). Why? Because

> That which constrains *these* men, . . . this unconditional will to truth, . . . is the faith in a *metaphysical* value, the absolute value of *truth*, sanctioned and guaranteed by this ideal alone. . . . I cite the fifth book of my *Gay Science* (section 344): "The truthful man, in the audacious and ultimate sense presupposed by the faith in science, *thereby affirms another world* than that of life, nature, and history; and insofar as he affirms this 'other world,' does this not mean that he has to deny its antithesis, this world, *our* world? . . . It is still a *metaphysical faith* that underlies our faith in science." (GM III.24)

Thus the scientist in whom "the intellectual conscience dwells and is incarnate today" is still held captive by the expressly ascetic conviction that the one true value to be found is a transcendental value, an otherworldly value, which is "inestimable and cannot be criticized"; and so it is that a "depreciation of the ascetic ideal unavoidably involves a depreciation of science" (GM III.25). God and heaven may be absent from the scientist's scheme of things, but he is still animated by the desire to leave the real, immanent world behind him, to count life as merely "a bridge to that other mode of existence"

---

2. I defer detailed discussion of the intellectual conscience until section 5.

in which "'nature,' 'world,' the whole sphere of becoming and transitoriness" is denied (GM III.11). The scientist's form of the ascetic ideal is said to be the "noblest" because he manages, at least, to do without God; but his "unconditional honest atheism . . . is therefore *not* the antithesis of that ideal, as it appears to be; it is rather only one of the latest phases of its evolution, one of its terminal forms and inner consequences—it is the awe-inspiring *catastrophe* of two thousand years of training in truthfulness that finally forbids itself *the lie involved in belief in God*" (GM III.27).

Thus the scientist's faith in truth—a faith that undermines Christianity—represents not so much a "remnant" of the ascetic ideal as its "kernel." And it may be expected to forbid itself more: "All great things bring about their own destruction through an act of self-overcoming. . . . In this way Christianity *as a dogma* was destroyed by its own morality; in the same way Christianity *as morality* must now perish, too: we stand on the threshold of *this* event. After Christian truthfulness has drawn one inference after another, it must end by drawing its *most striking inference*, its inference *against* itself; this will happen, however, when it poses the question '*what is the meaning of all will to truth?*'" (GM III.27). The ascetic ideal will self-destruct, Nietzsche seems to suggest, when this question is confronted, when the last of asceticism's own "inner consequences" is turned back against it. "The will to truth requires a critique," he says. Indeed, and as he puts it in one of his stranger formulations, "the value of truth must for once be experimentally *called into question*" (GM III.24).

So what we seem to have is this. The best scientists and scholars—those in whom the intellectual conscience is alive and well—are unconditionally committed to the truth. Unconditional commitment to the truth, however, turns out to be the kernel of the ascetic ideal, because such commitment constitutes faith in a metaphysical value. Faith in truth undermines faith in other metaphysical values, such as God, by showing them to be contingent, false, or unintelligible. But faith in truth will remain the "strictest, most spiritual formulation" (GM III.27) of the ascetic ideal until it turns its own spotlight back on itself. Only then will the ascetic ideal end "in its own destruction through an act of self-overcoming."

II

It is far from clear that Nietzsche really commands the terminology, or is bothered enough about terminology, to express the thoughts that his discussion of the scientist gestures toward. Certainly the outline I've just given flirts with incomprehensibility; and this, given Nietzsche's lack of concern with consistency at what one might charitably call the surface level of argument, is hardly surprising. But the thought that there is something intriguing going on in this discussion—something to which Nietzsche himself must have attached considerable importance, given that the whole *Genealogy* seems to lead up to it—should not, I think, be given up except as a last resort.

So perhaps we should look first at the next worst resort. On the strength of passages such as those cited, it might be tempting to conclude (as people often have) that Nietzsche is simply an out-and-out relativist of the standard, self-refuting kind. His position certainly appears to contain the usual confusions. On the one hand, he denies that truth is "inestimable and cannot be criticized." He denies, that is, the absolute authority of truth: he seems to think that the belief that some things are just true and others are just false is a superstition that ought to be given up. Yet each of his claims and denials about truth appears to be offered as (just) true. Thus Nietzsche apparently finds himself in the position of saying that the only unquestionable truth is that there are no unquestionable truths—a position which has precisely nothing to recommend it. Nor is the situation evidently improved when we learn that the scientist's commitment to the supreme value of truth marks him out both as the "honor of our age" and as the latest and most spiritual enemy of life and "the whole sphere of becoming and transitoriness." How can he be marked out as both? Or, to put the question another way, given that Nietzsche himself appears and reports himself to be a man of "intellectual conscience"—profoundly committed to "the service of truth"—how can he even hope to do harm to the ascetic ideal if, as he says, such devotion is really no more than an expression of the ascetic ideal in its purest form, "with all external additions abolished" (GM III.27)? Does he believe in the intellectual conscience or not? Does he or doesn't he think that a commitment to truth is always an expression of the ascetic ideal? Can he even begin to address these questions, given his seeming espousal of the daftest kind of relativism?

Perhaps the least contentious starting point is to observe that—whether or not he ought, in the light of his other views, to believe it—Nietzsche clearly does believe that some things are true and some are false. At the very beginning of the *Genealogy* he speaks of "plain, harsh, ugly, repellent, unchristian, immoral truth" and assures us that "such truths do exist" (GM I.1); at the end he describes belief in God as founded on a "*lie*" (GM III.27); and in between we learn that "'the doer' is merely a fiction added to the deed" (GM I.13), that we are "obliged for truth's sake" to reject the claim that the origin of "justice is to be sought in the sphere of the reactive feelings" (GM II.11), that a certain "fact once came insidiously into the mind of Spinoza" (GM II.15), that the priest's insistence that one is to blame for one's own suffering is "brazen and false enough" (GM III.15), and so on. There is no indication anywhere that Nietzsche did not take most of what he said to be true, nor that he doubted that his own genealogy of morals was truer than any genealogy produced by the "English psychologists" (GM I.1). In short, Nietzsche helps himself to the notions of truth and falsity, fact and fiction, as if they were altogether *un*problematic. Moreover, his own proclaimed method for arriving at truths is thoroughly scholarly, scientific: one should turn to "what is documented, what can actually be confirmed and has actually existed, in short the entire long hieroglyphic record, so hard to decipher, of the moral past of mankind!" (GM P7).

The question whether Nietzsche was especially wedded to this method in practice is less significant in the present context than the fact that he seriously suggests it *as* a method. And the impression of sober empirical-mindedness is heightened when he remarks, in *Twilight of the Idols*, "what magnificent instruments of observation we possess in our senses! . . . Today we possess science precisely to the extent that we have decided to *accept* the testimony of the senses—to the extent to which we sharpen them further, arm them, and have learned to think them through. The rest is miscarriage and not-yet-science" (TI, Reason 3). Again, the attitude expressed is hard-nosed, realist—certainly not the kind of thing one would expect to hear from someone who has decided to call the value of truth into question. Indeed, not the sort of thing one would expect to hear from someone who had any doubts at all about the propriety of truth, or about the distinction between true and false, between fact and fiction. So what on earth does Nietzsche mean when he suddenly insists that "the will to truth" has become "a *problem*" (GM III.27), that there is somehow something *wrong* with having faith in truth?

The reason he gives for saying this is, as we have seen, that faith in truth "is the faith in a *metaphysical* value, the absolute value of *truth*"—a faith which entails a denial of "this world, *our* world" (GM III.24). So faith in truth—the thought that truth is "inestimable and cannot be criticized" (GM III.25)—is an expression of the ascetic ideal. But it isn't yet clear why one should believe this. Surely one could have faith in truth without "thereby" affirming "*another world* than that of life, nature, and history" (GM III.24). Couldn't one, for instance, simply hold that true beliefs are what one should aim at having? Wouldn't that count as faith in truth? I think that Nietzsche would have to concede that it did—certainly if he wants to hold on to his own "repellent, unchristian, immoral" truths as true.

Yet this would be to miss the thrust of his point. We should ask instead what Nietzsche thinks faith in truth and faith in God have in common, given that he apparently regards both as expressions of the ascetic ideal. Faith in God is the means whereby "the man of bad conscience . . . ejects from himself all his denial of himself, of his nature, naturalness, and actuality, in the form of an affirmation, as something existent, corporeal, real, as God, as the holiness of God, as God the Judge. . . . [In it] resides . . . the *will* of man . . . to cut off once and for all his own exit from this labyrinth of 'fixed ideas'; his *will* to erect an ideal—that of 'holy God'—and in the face of it to feel the palpable certainty of his own absolute unworthiness" (GM II.22). If one substitutes "truth" for "God" in this passage, one begins to get a sense of the kind of faith in truth that Nietzsche is bothered about. God serves to justify existence for those who find their lives impossible to affirm; and the priest, in encouraging entry into this particular "labyrinth of 'fixed ideas,'" aims to "become master . . . over life itself, over its most profound, powerful, and basic conditions" (GM III.11). Thus the solution being offered to the man of bad conscience consists in the giving of a *total* and *final* explanation of existence which is couched in terms of an "ideal" defined precisely so as to rob "this world, *our* world" of its value. Having accepted this solution, the believer acquires an otherworldly warrant for the slave morality to which *ressentiment* has, in any case, already driven him. Thus faith in God provides (at least) five things: a *complete* explanation of the essential character of existence; an *ultimate* ("fixed") explanation of the character of existence; a metaphysical court ("God the Judge") before which existence is to be held accountable; a devaluation of everything that makes existence distinctive ("nature, naturalness"); and a transcendental ground for detesting everything noble. The first, second, and fifth of these involve truth claims that lend authority to the slavish values enunciated in the final three. One might therefore conclude that these claims, in their pretensions to completeness, finality, and transcendence, exhibit just the qualities that drive Nietzsche to describe faith in truth as the "kernel" of the ascetic ideal. It is not, in other words, the fact that these claims are offered as *true* that arouses Nietzsche's ire; rather, the irritation lies in the *character* of truth (complete, final, transcendent) that they are presented as having.

This point is important for a number of reasons. For one thing, it serves to limit the scope of Nietzsche's attack on faith in truth: only faith in truth as complete, final, and transcendent can properly be seen as an expression of the ascetic ideal. Second, provided that Nietzsche's own truths are not presented by him as having this character, there is no longer any necessary conflict between his willingness to make truth claims and his insistence that the value of truth must be called into question. So the specter of relativism and confusion recedes. But also, we are now in a position to appreciate better why Nietzsche's discussion of truth is pursued through a discussion of *science* specifically. In a well-known passage, he laments the stubbornness of those who, having "got rid of the Christian God," now "cling all the more firmly to Christian morality": "Christianity is a system, a consistently thought out and *complete* view of things. If one breaks out of it a fundamental idea, the belief in God, one thereby breaks the whole thing to pieces. . . . Christian morality is a command: its origin is transcendental; it is beyond all criticism, all right to criticize; it possesses truth only if God is truth" (TI, Expeditions 5). But people refuse to recognize this, and the morality of *ressentiment* persists despite the removal of its underpinnings. Which is bad enough, no doubt. But the thought that the morality of *ressentiment* might somehow— however spuriously—acquire a *new* set of underpinnings is, for Nietzsche, quite unendurable. And it is precisely from science, or rather from a certain attitude toward science, that he sees this threat arising. He remarks of an English genealogist (i.e., of someone who, in Nietzsche's view, gives "passive, automatic, reflexive, molecular" [GM I.1] explanations of prevailing, that is Christian, values) that "he had read Darwin—so that in his hypotheses . . . the Darwinian beast and the ultramodern unassuming moral milksop . . . politely link hands" (GM P.7). Motivated by "petty subterranean hostility" and "a secret, malicious, vulgar, perhaps self-deceiving instinct for belittling man" (GM I.1), the English genealogist uses science to justify an interpretation of human existence that is, if not Christian, at least still fully characteristic of *ressentiment*—man as automaton. "The democratic idiosyncrasy," which is prepared to be "reconciled even to the absolute fortuitousness, even the mechanistic senselessness of all events . . . has permeated the realm of the spirit . . . to such a degree that today it has forced its way . . . into the strictest, apparently most objective sciences . . . —to the detriment of life, as goes without saying, since it has robbed it of a fundamental concept, that of *activity* . . . [replacing it with] a mere reactivity" (GM II.12).

What is the attitude toward science that underwrites this particular devaluation of life? The answer, presumably, is: faith in science as a "system," as "a consistently thought out and *complete* view of things"—in science as total and final explanation. Part of Nietzsche's problem with science, then, is that unconditional faith in *it* threatens to take over and do the job that unconditional faith in God has done hitherto—the job of providing life-denying valuations with a grounding that is "beyond all criticism, all right to criticize."

Nietzsche, no doubt, was thinking principally of those social Darwinists who were his contemporaries, and perhaps also of a certain kind of Marx-inspired historical materialist. But one has only to look around today at the cultural dominance of various forms of scientism to appreciate the point: people think that *the* truth is what science reveals, and that the answers to our most pressing questions are always to be sought from experts who are versed in it, from scientific witnesses. Thus we allow our sufferings to be given sense by explanation in terms of "the mechanical senselessness of

all events" and our misfortunes to be "blamed" on our genes, our upbring-
ing, or our social and economic circumstances. Nietzsche's fears were well
founded.[3] And this, surely, is the point of his claim that "there is no such
thing as science 'without any presuppositions'"; for "a philosophy, a 'faith,'
must always be there first of all, so that science can acquire from it a direction, a meaning . . . a *right* to exist" (GM III.24). If we simply assume that
science is somehow its own justification, we buy in—more or less inertly—
to the ideal it already serves, to faith in a transcendental value.[4] Which is
why, as David Owen puts it, faith in "the 'inestimable' value of truth is the
central feature of the ascetic ideal . . . because it involves the metaphysical
presupposition of the value of truth"[5]—in this case, of the value of scientific
truth. And Owen's quote from Max Weber goes to the heart: science "presupposes that what is produced by scientific work should be *important* in the
sense of 'being worth knowing.' And it is obvious that all our problems lie
here, for this presupposition cannot be proved by scientific means."[6] Thus,
so long as one believes that science necessarily enjoys a unique authority, an
altogether uncriticizable monopoly on truth, one is committed to faith in a
"*metaphysical* value, the absolute value of *truth*"—metaphysical, because science is accorded its status a priori; absolute, because nothing whatever is permitted to vitiate it. And this, according to Nietzsche, is asceticism—the
"kernel" of asceticism.

III

I have spoken so far as if the connection between completeness, finality, *and*
transcendence with respect to truth were obvious. Certainly Nietzsche regards them as an indivisible package. But it will be helpful to investigate his
reasons in more detail. His position, as I shall try to show in this section, is
broadly this: to say that there is or could be a complete and final explanation
of things is to say that that explanation is or would be true quite *regardless* of
our own relation to it. Which is to say that its status as truth could not *possibly* be impugned by us, or by any other being whose interests we would
recognize as cognitive. Thus truth as complete and final is, quite literally,
"inestimable"—that is, in principle not estimable by any knower—and

3. Even if his own physiological and dietary speculations might look a bit dodgy on the same
grounds.
4. And this inert scientism, indeed "our whole attitude toward nature, the way we violate her
with the aid of machines and the heedless inventiveness of our technicians and engineers, is *hubris*"
(GM III.9).
5. David Owen, *Nietzsche, Politics and Modernity* (London: Sage, 1995), p. 95.
6. Max Weber, "Science as a Vocation," in P. Lassman and I. Velody, eds., *Max Weber's "Science
as a Vocation"* (London: Unwin Hyman, 1989), p. 18.

therefore *cannot* be of "this world, *our* world." So to have faith in ultimate explanation is always to have a metaphysical faith: it is always to posit a truth that is true-in-itself of a world that is as it is in-itself, quite irrespective of any of the ways that that world might have of appearing to its (apparent) "inhabitants." And—as we will see—it is Nietzsche's contention that this picture is not merely undesirable (because ascetic) but unintelligible.

It must come as a surprise to those who think of Nietzsche as an irrationalist to find that one of the things he holds against the ascetic ideal, apart from its "hatred of the human, and even more of the animal, and more still of the material," is its "horror . . . of reason itself" (GM III.28). He links these rejections together:

> To renounce belief in one's ego, to deny one's own "reality"—what a triumph! not merely over the senses, over appearance, but a much higher kind of triumph, a violation and cruelty against *reason*—a voluptuous pleasure that reaches its height when the ascetic self-contempt and self-mockery of reason declares: "*there* is a realm of truth and being, but reason is *excluded* from it!" . . . . [Thus] the Kantian concept of the "intelligible character of things" . . . signifies . . . that things are so constituted that the intellect comprehends just enough of them to know that for the intellect they are—*utterly incomprehensible*. (GM III.12)

Nietzsche is railing, then, against precisely the kind of otherworldly "realm of truth" that is posited by metaphysical faith in the "*value* of truth"; and he connects this with "cruelty against *reason*." Why? The answer consists of two intimately related claims.[7] The first, which is presupposed but not directly argued for in the *Genealogy*,[8] is that it is irrational to believe in a "realm of truth and being" *as distinct from* a realm of appearance. The second is that it is irrational to think of truth as independent of any possible knower.

The first claim consists in a rejection of "the typical prejudgment and prejudice which give away the metaphysicians of all ages": that "the things of the highest value must have another, *peculiar* origin—they cannot be derived from this transitory, seductive, deceptive, paltry world, from this turmoil of delusion and lust. Rather from the lap of Being, the intransitory, the hidden god, the 'thing-in-itself'—there must be their basis, and nowhere

7. For what follows I am much indebted to Maudemarie Clark's *Nietzsche on Truth and Philosophy* (Cambridge: Cambridge University Press, 1990). I have also benefited from Brian Leiter's essay "Perspectivism in Nietzsche's *Genealogy of Morals*," in Richard Schacht, ed., *Nietzsche, Genealogy, Morality: Essays on Nietzsche's* On the Genealogy of Morals (Berkeley: University of California Press, 1994), pp. 334–57.

8. Although one might regard the discussion of the origin of the "subject" in GM I.13 as part of an indirect argument for Nietzsche's claim.

else" (BGE 2). This "prejudice" stands or falls with the intelligibility of distinguishing a real world of "things-in-themselves" from the illusory world of "mere" appearance that we actually inhabit. But what, Nietzsche asks, is conceivably to be understood by "appearance" here? "Certainly not the opposite of some essence: what could I say about any essence except to name the attributes of its appearance! Certainly not a mask that one could place on an unknown X or remove from it!" (GS 54).

The very idea of a "thing-in-itself"—of an essence, an "unknown X"—to which appearances somehow accrue is "a *contradictio in adjecto*" (BGE 16), since the removal from a thing of all of its possible appearances would simply constitute the abolition of the thing itself. As Maudemarie Clark puts it, "we can have no conception" of something stripped of all its adjectives (its appearances) "because to conceive of something is to conceive of it as satisfying some description or other."[9] Thus the hard appearance/reality distinction upon which the metaphysicians' prejudice rests evaporates once it is recognized that one side of the divide—the "reality" side—is occupied by nothing at all. Nietzsche draws the moral in the section of *Twilight* called "How the 'Real World' At Last Became a Myth": "We have abolished the real world: what world is left? the apparent world perhaps? . . . But no! *with the real world we have also abolished the apparent world!*" Because the very notion of "appearance" gains its sense through contrast with "the real," neither side of the distinction survives the collapse of the other, and we are left, not with the "real" world of the metaphysicians, but with the real, ordinary world that is "this world, *our* world." To posit, to have faith in, a "realm of truth" in opposition to this world is therefore, on Nietzsche's view, irrational.

The second claim can be construed as a response to a possible objection to the first. As Clark admits, someone might concede that if a thing's essence is bound up with its appearances, we cannot grasp a thing's essence independently of them; but "this seems compatible with understanding its essence as independent of its possible appearances to human beings, thus insisting on the possibility of a metaphysical world."[10] The trouble with this suggestion, however, is that it would establish the possibility of a metaphysical world only if the phrase "independent of its possible appearances to human beings" is construed in a very particular way. Suppose that our own best theory of a thing's essence were false. By this we might mean that some other being with superior cognitive abilities could produce a better theory. What would *make* it a better theory? Or, to put the question another way, what would make it intelligible for us to concede that there might (in principle) *be* this better theory? It is not, surely, necessary that we should be able to ar-

9. Clark, *Nietzsche on Truth and Philosophy*, pp. 46–47.
10. Ibid., p. 100.

rive at this theory ourselves; for there is no obvious reason, other than arrogance, to hold that the truth about things must be made answerable to our own, perhaps very limited, cognitive abilities. But surely it *is* necessary that we should be able to recognize the superiority of this theory if, by magic, we were granted the cognitive abilities required to arrive at it. Otherwise there would be no sense to *our* imagining (here and now) that such a theory might indeed *be* better. Thus, the operative sense of "better" must be the same sense as that in which we already say that some of our own theories are better than others—that is, that some of them give us more of what we want from a theory than others do. To imagine, then, that a being with superior cognitive abilities might be able to produce a better theory than our own best theory is to imagine it producing a theory which better satisfied our own standards of rational acceptability—our own "cognitive interests" in such properties as "simplicity, comprehensiveness," explanatory power, and so on.[11] So, while it is intelligible to imagine that a theory better than our own best theory might be true independent of our own cognitive *abilities*, it is not intelligible to imagine its being true independent of our own cognitive *interests*. Which means that there is nothing in this thought experiment that establishes the possibility of a metaphysical world. For in order to establish that, we would have to be shown not merely that (1) the "real" truth might be independent of all "possible appearances to human beings," in the sense that the "real" truth might elude our cognitive abilities, but also (2) that the "real" truth might be independent of all "possible appearances to human beings," in the more dramatic sense that the "real" truth might be orthogonal to the cognitive interests of any being that we could conceive of as making truth claims. The first of these two requirements, as we have seen, is perfectly intelligible—but it allows only for the possibility of a theory that accounts more satisfactorily for more of a thing's appearances than our own best theory does, and so includes no reference to a "realm of truth" distinct from a realm of appearance—while the second, which would establish the possibility of a "realm of truth" in which truths were true of things-in-themselves, independently of any conceivable knower, is, as we have seen, unintelligible. The very notion of truth is dependent upon the notion of cognitive interests; and there can be no cognitive interests without knowers who have them.

Nietzsche's way of making this point is to insist on the impossibility of a view from nowhere, of a view from no particular point of view:

> Henceforth, my dear philosophers, let us be on guard against the dangerous old conceptual fiction that posited a "pure, will-less, painless, timeless knowing subject"; let us guard against the snares of such contradictory concepts as

11. Ibid., p. 48.

"pure reason," "absolute spirituality," "knowledge in itself": these always demand that we should think of an eye that is completely unthinkable, an eye
turned in no particular direction, in which the active and interpreting forces,
through which alone seeing becomes seeing *something*, are supposed to be lacking; these always demand of the eye an absurdity and a nonsense. (GM III.12)

In other words, beware of the thought that there is some determinate way
that things-in-themselves *are*, independently of the ways in which they appear. Beware of the thought that there might be a stand-point from which
"knowledge in itself"—that is, knowledge divorced from our cognitive interests, from our temporality, from our will—might be had. Beware of demanding absurdities, of banishing reason in the name of "pure reason."

If Clark's interpretation is plausible, as I believe it is, then in his later works
Nietzsche discovers grounds to reject any view which is committed to a metaphysical conception of truth—that is, to any conception of truth as true of
things-in-themselves and true independently of our own best standards of
rational acceptability. Which is to say that Nietzsche rejects metaphysical realism; and in doing so, if he and Clark are right, he justifies his claim that
the ascetic ideal, in its hatred of "this world, *our* world," also exhibits a hatred of reason.

Some will doubtless feel that, following Clark, I have made rather a lot of
what are, after all, only some scattered remarks, most of them more assertive
than demonstrative. But the present reading is consistent with what Nietzsche does say, makes sense of why he says it, and serves to explain how his
discussion of truth fits in with his diagnosis of faith in science as implicitly
ascetic. It also, of course, makes clear precisely why Nietzsche equates faith
in complete and final explanation with faith in transcendental explanation.
If there were an ultimate truth about things, then it would—as I said at the
beginning of this section—be "inestimable" and beyond criticism; which is
to say that its truth would be independent of our best standards of rational
acceptability; which is to say that it would be true independently of any
knower; which is to say that it would be true of things as they are in themselves, that is, metaphysically true. And so it is that—because Nietzsche has
grounds to reject as unintelligible the notion of the thing-in-itself and the
notion of interest- or knower-independent knowledge—he also, and by the
same token, has reason to reject the possibility of complete, final, and "inestimable" truth.

IV

In the second section I noted the temptation to conclude that Nietzsche
must be mired in the confusions of relativism. The position on that is now

as follows: Nietzsche does indeed, as I suggested, appear to regard his own claims as true; and he does indeed reject faith in truth—but only faith in truth *as metaphysically conceived*. So there isn't as yet any warrant for thinking him confused. Nor will any warrant for such a thought arise so long as we can establish what his own conception of truth is, and can establish that, in the absence of the metaphysical conception, his own one doesn't collapse into relativism anyway (i.e., that it doesn't render his own truth claims—for instance about the unintelligibility of metaphysical realism—redundant or self-refuting).

Plainly Nietzsche's conception must construe truth as estimable and subject to criticism, as dependent on possible knowers and as dependent on our cognitive interests. What he actually says about it is this: "precisely because we seek knowledge" we should not be discouraged by the sorts of tricks that the ascetic ideal plays on us. Rather, "to see differently in this way for once . . . is no small discipline and preparation of the intellect for its future 'objectivity'—the latter understood not as 'contemplation without interest' (which is a nonsensical absurdity), but as the ability *to control* one's Pro and Con and to dispose of them, so that one knows how to employ a *variety* of perspectives and affective interpretations in the service of knowledge" (GM III.12). Thus, in becoming practiced in and alert to the kinds of interpretation that have been given of knowledge, we become attuned to the partiality of every interpretation and alive to the fact that all such partiality is the product of "contemplation" *with* "interest"—of the deployment of "[some]one's Pro and Con." And this leads Nietzsche to his main statement of the doctrine known as "perspectivism": "There is *only* a perspective seeing, *only* a perspective 'knowing'; and the *more* affects we allow to speak about one thing, the *more* eyes, different eyes, we can use to observe one thing, the more complete will our 'concept' of this thing, our 'objectivity,' be. But to eliminate the will altogether, to suspend each and every affect, supposing we were capable of this—what would that mean but to *castrate* the intellect?" (GM III.12).

To some extent, of course, this passage does no more than restate in positive terms Nietzsche's rejection (as "unthinkable") of "an eye turned in no particular direction, in which the active and interpreting forces . . . are supposed to be lacking." In fact, according to Clark, that is effectively all that the passage does: "perspectivism is designed to free us from the snares of the idea that knowledge could obtain . . . 'pure truth'—that knowledge is of things-in-themselves." [12] But such a limit can be placed on Nietzsche's doctrine only at the price of ignoring or discounting half of what he says. For

12. Ibid., p. 133.

while it is true that his claim that there is "*only* a perspective seeing" serves to discount the notion of "pure truth," nothing in this includes the thought, on which Nietzsche is equally insistent, that we should learn "how to employ a *variety* of perspectives" or that "the *more* eyes, different eyes, we can use to observe one thing" the better. In other words, Nietzsche seems to claim *both* that there is no such thing as perspectiveless knowing *and* that we should adopt as many perspectives as possible.

Clark recognizes Nietzsche's insistence on the desirability of multiple perspectives but regards this as an unwitting hangover from an earlier phase of his thought. She is drawn to this conclusion, it seems, by taking Bernd Magnus's word for it that Nietzsche is really recommending a form of omni-perspectivism — a sort of view from everywhere that would somehow transcend the limits of perspectivism and reinstate the possibility of "pure truth": "a God's-eye-view, a view from no point whatsoever save from all the possible perspectives seen simultaneously."[13] If this were right, then Clark's diagnosis of Nietzsche's position as a confused remnant of his various pre-*Genealogy* thoughts about truth would be abundantly justified: Nietzsche has no business whatever to be claiming that there "really" is a way that things are in themselves, or that there is a final, "inestimable," omni-perspectival truth of the matter.[14]

But it seems to me that Magnus's reading of the passage in question is something of a red herring. Nowhere does Nietzsche suggest that one should somehow strive to *amalgamate* as many perspectives as possible or that one should try to adopt as many at once as one can. Indeed, what he says cuts in quite the opposite direction. The "future 'objectivity'" of the intellect depends on "the ability *to control* one's Pro and Con and to dispose of them" — that is, on the ability to explore "a *variety* of perspectives" by adopting, by trying out, by suspending, by abandoning, a variety of different and perhaps incompatible interests.[15] There is no perspective whatever from which *every* "active and interpreting" force, "through which alone seeing becomes seeing *something*," is absent; there is no knowledge "without interest." But the attempt to amalgamate all possible perspectives, or to adopt as many as possible simultaneously, would be intelligible only on the assumption that every perspective can somehow be taken by itself, in isolation from the in-

13. Bernd Magnus, "The Deification of the Commonplace: *Twilight of the Idols*," in Robert Solomon and Kathleen Higgins, eds., *Reading Nietzsche* (Oxford: Oxford University Press, 1988), p. 153.

14. For Clark's discussion of this point, see *Nietzsche on Truth and Philosophy*, pp. 144–50.

15. That this is what he means emerges more clearly from Carol Diethe's translation: we should "be able to *engage* and *disengage*" our "'pros' and 'cons'" (my emphasis). *On the Genealogy of Morality* (Cambridge: Cambridge University Press, 1994).

terest which prompts it. Omni-perspectivism, that is, makes sense only if the *variety* of interests which various perspectives serve can somehow be suppressed. And this is precisely what Nietzsche says cannot be done: "to eliminate the will altogether, to suspend each and every affect, supposing we were capable of this—what would this mean but to *castrate* the intellect?" Omni-perspectivism, then, is a recipe not so much for "the service of knowledge" as for the abolition of it.

But if Nietzsche is not advocating omni-perspectivism, what is the point of his claim that "the *more* eyes, different eyes, we can use to observe one thing, the more complete will our 'concept' of this thing, our 'objectivity,' be"? One answer to this question lies in the scare-quotes around the word "concept," which are there, I suggest, because of Nietzsche's view that "all concepts in which an entire process is semiotically concentrated elude definition; only that which has no history is definable." The example he gives is "punishment":

> the concept "punishment" possesses in fact not *one* meaning but a whole synthesis of "meanings": the previous history of punishment in general, the history of its employment for the most various purposes, finally crystallizes into a kind of unity that is hard to disentangle . . . and, as must be emphasized especially, totally *indefinable*. . . . At an earlier stage . . . this synthesis of meanings can still be disentangled . . . ; one can still perceive how in each individual case the elements of this synthesis undergo a shift in value and rearrange themselves accordingly, so that now this, now that element comes to the fore and dominates at the expense of the others. (GM II.13)

—and he concludes the section with a long (but, he suggests, incomplete) list of the diverse purposes to which punishment has been put. His discussion of punishment illustrates what he calls "a major point of historical method": one must recognize that "the cause of the origin of a thing and its eventual utility, its actual employment and place in a system of purposes, lie worlds apart. . . . The 'evolution' of a thing, a custom, an organ is thus by no means its *progressus* towards a goal . . . —but a succession of more or less profound, more or less mutually independent processes of subduing. . . . The form is fluid, but the 'meaning' is even more so" (GM II.12).

Thus, in his tracing of the "fluid" history of the meaning of punishment, Nietzsche arms himself against the temptation to assume that the concept has a single fixed definition, or that there is some unique purpose which various forms of punishment have served more or less well. He arms himself, in other words, against the essentialist temptation to think that there is *a* "concept" of punishment. Hence the scare-quotes around the word. But of course the "concept" can still be investigated. And in his own investigation of it, Nietzsche adopts the only approach consistent with his "major point of historical method": he explores the various "system[s] of purposes" within which the word punishment has been given meaning; he reconstructs the various interests it has been made to serve; he employs "a *variety* of perspectives and affective interpretations in the service of knowledge." One point of the claim that "the *more* eyes, different eyes, we can use to observe one thing, the more complete will our 'concept' of this thing . . . be" is thus the very opposite of what Magnus suggests. Far from being a curious attempt to smuggle a quasi-essentialist "realm of truth" back in through the side door, it is actually a consequence of Nietzsche's determination to reject essentialism altogether. (Indeed, and as one might expect, the insistence on variety expresses precisely the "ephectic bent" that Nietzsche claims is characteristic of the true philosopher: see Chapter 3.)

One might describe the foregoing as a diachronic multi-perspectivism—one which traces shifting perspectives over time. But Nietzsche is clearly committed to a synchronic version too, according to which one tries out different perspectives in order to discover which best satisfies one's interests—to discover what, from the point of view of a particular "system of purposes," is worth knowing. The "objectivity" of the intellect for which one thus prepares oneself, then, is objective in its recognition of the impossibility of interest-free truth claims, and hence in its recognition that one had better experiment with one's truth claims in the light of whatever interests apply in a given case (for instance, is a *scientific* answer what I really want when I ask: Was Nietzsche mad?).

So perspectivism does serve, as Clark says, to free us of the "idea that knowledge could obtain . . . 'pure truth,'" but it also alerts us to the necessity of "variety" in our interpretations. Moreover, in his emphasis on the role of purpose, will, affect, or interest, together with temporality and history, Nietzsche underlines just how rooted in "this world, *our* world" the activity of knowing is. As David Owen puts it, for Nietzsche "consciousness is neither disembedded nor disembodied; knowing, like seeing, is an activity which attends the embedded and embodied character of human subjectivity. Consequently . . . our cognitive constitution is not separable from our affective constitution, our cognitive interests are not independent of our affective interests. . . . [P]erspectivism . . . emphasizes the contextual character of our knowledge." [16] It is this emphasis that allows Nietzsche to construe truth and knowledge as necessarily estimable, as necessarily open to criticism, for if knowing is always rooted in interests, is always part of a "system of purposes," no knowledge will satisfy every interest, nor will every "sys-

16. Owen, *Nietzsche, Politics and Modernity*, p. 33.

tem of purposes" have a place for every item of knowledge. Nietzsche makes the point rather strikingly when he says that "physics, too, is only an interpretation and exegesis of the world (to suit us, if I may say so!) and *not* a world-explanation"—that is, not a complete and final account of the world (BGE 14). Physics expresses and answers to certain of our interests; but other systems of purposes are possible, and in these the findings of physics may have no place at all. (No one was ever worse at chess for the want of a bit of physics.) Truth—and physics, for Nietzsche, is certainly a source of truth—is never "inestimable."

But doesn't this mean that Nietzsche is committed to relativism after all? Doesn't it mean, for example, that physics is only true if you think that it is—that it's all a matter of opinion? And, if so, wouldn't that mean that perspectivism itself is just a matter of opinion?

I'll take the last question first. It certainly looks tempting to say that perspectivism is self-refuting. It appears, after all, to announce that every knowledge claim is perspectival except the claim that every knowledge claim is perspectival. Indeed, it *does* say that. But this only looks problematic if one forgets what sort of thing perspectivism is supposed to exclude. "The crux of the matter," as Maudemarie Clark puts it, "is that perspectivism excludes only something contradictory" [17]—that is, it excludes only the unintelligible notions of the thing-in-itself and the view from nowhere. Thus, in insisting that all knowledge is perspectival, perspectivism doesn't set up some *new* paradigm of knowledge only to find that it falls within its own scope; rather, it identifies conditions *already* implicit in the idea of knowledge, and without which the idea of knowledge would be (would always have been) contradictory and senseless. So perspectivism represents an *analytic* of knowledge rather than a redefinition of it, and is a matter of opinion only if you think that acceptance of the principle of noncontradiction is a matter of opinion—which, since acceptance of that principle is itself a condition of the possibility of thought, might prove rather an unrewarding line to run. So perspectivism does not refute itself: knowledge is always knowledge from a point of view, and points of view are always embedded and embodied in interests and systems of purposes.

But what about the suggestion that the very embeddedness of knowledge, the contingency of it, makes for an "anything goes" conception of truth—for the view that every *particular* truth is just a matter of opinion? This suggestion misses the point too, however, and for much the same reasons that the previous one did. Both trade on the suspicion that perspectivism somehow takes away from us something that we had enjoyed in our conception

17. Clark, *Nietzsche on Truth and Philosophy*, p. 134.

of knowledge before. And so it does: if we were wedded to the existence of a perspective-free "realm of truth," it robs us of confusion and inconsistency. But it doesn't take away anything that we could intelligibly *want* to retain. Consider the sort of worry that a person who wouldn't like to see the floodgates opened might have. "If it's all about point of view," such a person might say, "then what's to stop someone claiming that witchcraft is just as good (true) as modern medical science, or that astrology is just as good (true) as physics? People *do*, after all, hold such views." The proper response to this is to ask the objector how he himself would respond. Presumably he would answer that modern medical science and physics enjoy massive advantages in explanatory power, predictive power, comprehensiveness, and so on over their alleged competitors, and so that it would be simply *irrational* to regard the respective halves of each pair as, cognitively, on a par. And the perspectivist would agree. For to respond thus is to do no more than to acknowledge the role of our cognitive interests in the production of truth. We justify our acceptance of one account over another by pointing to its superior capacity to satisfy the standards of rational acceptability immanent to the "system of purposes" within which it has its place. Astrology, if offered as a rival to physics, simply doesn't measure up to the standards of acceptability immanent within the "system of purposes" to which physics answers— it either satisfies none of the same interests or satisfies some of them, only less well. In this sense, perspectivism proposes nothing that should be found obnoxious by those of us who find anything-goes relativism obnoxious— because perspectivism deprives us of *nothing* that we could cogently want. Clark puts it neatly when she says that just as "creative power is not limited by the inability to make a square triangle," so "cognitive power is not limited by the inability to have nonperspectival knowledge." [18]

Perspectivism leaves everything as it was. Within a given "system of purposes" the truth is whatever (currently) best satisfies the standards of rational acceptability immanent to that system. Between perspectives there may be no rivalry at all (as, for instance, there is no rivalry between the truths of physics and the truths of chess); there may be rivalry which is resolvable by resort to a more general perspective that embraces both of the original ones (as, for instance, the rivalry between Newtonian mechanics and special relativity is resolved under the perspective of general relativity); and there may be rivalry which is simply, or is as far as we can see, irresolvable (as, for instance, the rivalry between a perspective from which noble values seem attractive and one from which they do not appears irresolvable). If this is a plausible way of presenting Nietzsche's own conception of knowledge

18. Ibid.

and truth—that is, as a version of what Hilary Putnam calls "internal realism"[19]—then there is no warrant at all for concluding that Nietzsche is either confused or mired in relativism. He thinks that some things are true while others are false—for example, his own genealogy versus those of his English predecessors. And he believes that nothing whatever is true in the sense presupposed by "faith in truth"—that is, he holds that the very idea of a complete, final, inestimable, transcendent truth, perspectivelessly true of things as they are in themselves, is self-contradictory.

V

We are now in a position to return to a matter touched on earlier—the "intellectual conscience." That Nietzsche regards himself as the possessor of such a conscience seems beyond question: his description of the "greatness of soul" required for "the service of truth"—"the hardest service"—and his demand that one should make a matter of conscience "of every Yes and No" (AC 50) does not sound like someone describing somebody else, certainly not like Nietzsche describing somebody else. And we now know under what conception of truth he serves. But what, then, are we to make of his claim that the scientist who has "faith in truth" is one of those "in whom alone the intellectual conscience dwells and is incarnate today" (GM III.24)? For one would have thought that, even if he has forbidden himself "*the lie involved in belief in God*" (GM III.27), this scientist certainly hasn't forbidden himself the lie involved in faith in truth (as final, inestimable, and so forth). In this much, surely, he hasn't done enough trembling with "the joy of questioning" (GS 2).

The obvious answer, I suppose, is that intellectual conscience is a matter of degree. The scientist is prepared to be "severe" against his own "heart" (AC 50) in the ruthless application of the standards of acceptability immanent to the practice he engages in; but he is not quite ruthless enough to recognize that that practice is itself an interest-dependent "system of purposes" (rather than, for example, something transcendentally self-justifying). So he has a reasonably well, but not quite a fully, developed intellectual conscience. This seems like the right sort of thing to say. But perhaps things are more complicated, too: for in GM III.27 Nietzsche quotes approvingly his own derivation of the intellectual conscience from "Christian morality itself, the concept of truthfulness taken more and more strictly, the confessional subtlety of the Christian conscience translated and sublimated into the sci-

19. See, for instance, Hilary Putnam, "A Defense of Internal Realism," in Putnam, *Realism with a Human Face*, ed. James Conant (Cambridge: Harvard University Press, 1990), pp. 30–42.

entific conscience, into intellectual cleanliness at any price" (GS 357). This serves partly to reaffirm what we have already seen, that Christianity plays a central role in its own downfall: it destroys itself "through an act of self-overcoming" when "Christian truthfulness" draws "one inference after another"—against "Christianity *as a dogma*" and against "Christianity *as morality*." But it serves also to situate the very idea of the intellectual conscience firmly within the conspectus of Christianity; and this makes one wonder whether, once the last and "*most striking inference*" has been drawn, the inference drawn by "Christian truthfulness . . . *against* itself," the intellectual conscience hasn't thereby been inferred against as well (GM III.27). If it has been, then Nietzsche's attribution of such a conscience to the scientist who has "faith in truth" is entirely unproblematic: the scientist hasn't drawn the final inference yet. But what in that case *does* start to look odd is Nietzsche's attribution of an intellectual conscience to himself: for here, in the *Genealogy*, the crucial inference is not just drawn but trumpeted.

We seem, then, to have two ways of understanding the intellectual conscience. One, which is wedded to truthfulness (of some sort), forbids itself lies of every kind, including the lie involved in "faith in truth." This seems to be the sense in which Nietzsche might accord an intellectual conscience to himself but ought not to accord one to the scientist. The other, wedded to a specifically "Christian" version of truthfulness, strives for "intellectual cleanliness at any price" but still *within* the ambit of the penultimate inference. This type of intellectual conscience would appear to be the scientist's, but not Nietzsche's. So what is the difference between Nietzsche's truthfulness and "Christian" truthfulness?

Nietzsche appears to relate truthfulness (of every kind) to "the confessional subtlety of the Christian conscience"; and this gives us something to go on. Some amateurish theology (though not more amateurish than Nietzsche's own) would suggest that part of what is involved in the confessional is the making of a clean breast of things. To some extent this is doubtless supposed to remove a burden from the one who confesses; to some extent, too, it must be meant to reinforce the power of the confessor (the priest). But both of these ends are secured in the context of the assumption that God knows everything anyway, already. He sees to the heart of things and nothing is hidden. Thus, one strives to tell the *whole* story so far as one can, in an effort to make one's own account match God's (there would be no point in trying to hide anything, after all). The assumption, then, is that there *is* some ultimate truth about oneself, a truth finally graspable only from a God's-eye-view, and that one must try, with whatever "subtlety" one has, to approximate it. One must tell it as it "really" is. So construed, "the confessional subtlety of the Christian conscience" presupposes precisely the metaphysical realism that Nietzsche associates with "faith in truth." This makes perfectly good sense of the truthfulness involved in the intellectual conscience of the scientist: "faith in truth" is precisely what distinguishes him. And since "faith in truth" is ascetic, the scientist's intellectual conscience turns out to be a form of the *bad* bad conscience (perhaps, since he is the "honor of our age," a good form of the *bad* bad conscience?—which would make the "worthy laborer's" conscience a bad form of this same conscience?). But what does any of this tell us about Nietzsche's own, apparently non-Christian, truthfulness?

Back to the confessional. Central to the attempt to keep nothing hidden—to bare one's soul, to tell it as it "really" is—must be a profound willingness to distrust oneself: indeed this is one of the positive things that Nietzsche credits to the priest's influence. The priest exploits feelings of *ressentiment* in order to foster "self-discipline, self-surveillance, and self-overcoming" (GM III.16). Self-surveillance: what makes me construe my thoughts, my actions, *that* way? Am I trying to fool myself? Do I have some *reason* for giving prominence to this rather than that? How sure am I of my own motivations? Would I know if I was deceiving myself? Can I be trusted? Given the assumption that one is, in a sense, trying to tell God nothing that he doesn't already know, this kind of scrutiny of one's own perspectives on oneself must be essential. One asks: which *interests* do these perspectives of mine serve? And the minute one frames the question that way, one recognizes that one has arrived in Nietzsche-territory. Divorce Christian self-surveillance from the metaphysically realist "system of purposes" embodied by the confessional and one has Nietzsche's own, non-Christian, version of truthfulness: it consists in trembling with "the joy of questioning" one's own motivations for holding the views one does; it consists in what he calls "integrity" (AC 50)—a quality exhibited in one's willingness to adopt "a *variety* of perspectives" on oneself "in the service of knowledge." Nietzsche's version differs from the Christian version, then, in a single crucial respect: it is not predicated on the assumption that there is a "realm of truth" within which God's view of the matter holds unquestionable sway ("really" and "finally"). There is no self-in-itself of which knowledge might be sought (or confessed). But that still leaves the important task in place. It still leaves one to assess and to question, self-critically, one's motivations for thinking what one does think; it still leaves one to be "severe against one's own heart" and to make "of every Yes and No a matter of conscience." (One can see this as Nietzsche's adopting or advocating the kind of "ephectic" self-relation discussed in Chapter 3, a self-relation predicated on an ascetic *procedure* but not on the ascetic *ideal*. Or, to put it another way, one can see the intellectual conscience as the philosophical conscience freed from the dominion of priestly morality.)

The *Genealogy* bears ample witness to Nietzsche's fascination with one's attitude toward one's own perspectives on oneself—perhaps especially when the question of lying is raised. In the previous chapter I reported Nietzsche's claim that in art "the *lie* is sanctified and the *will to deception* has a good conscience" (GM III.25). What does this mean? The "lie," evidently enough, is that the world is as beautiful as it is represented as being; and the lie is told in "good conscience" when the artist "arrives at the ultimate pinnacle of his greatness" and "comes to see himself and his art *beneath* him—when he knows how to *laugh* at himself" (GM III.3). Thus the artist's good conscience consists in his achieving a perspective on himself from which he can acknowledge, cheerfully, that his own beautifications are also deceptions. He is *truthful* with himself. In sharp opposition stands the "moralistic mendaciousness" of the modern soul: "good people"

> do not tell lies—that is true; but that is *not* to their credit! A real lie, a genuine, resolute, "honest" lie (on whose value one should consult Plato) would be something far too severe and potent for them: it would demand of them what one *may* not demand of them, that they should open their eyes to themselves, that they should know how to distinguish "true" and "false" in themselves. All they are capable of is a *dishonest* lie; whoever today counts himself a "good man" is utterly incapable of confronting any matter except with *dishonest mendaciousness* . . . : who among them could endure a single *truth* "about man"? (GM III.19)

Nietzsche rather spoils the effect of this passage by going on to condemn the tendency of nineteenth-century biographers to suppress the more private or shameful aspects of their subjects' lives. Nowadays, having had a surfeit of the opposite tendency in the meantime, it is hard to concur. But Nietzsche's point survives the datedness of his example. The "good man"—that is, the man who subscribes to slave morality—either cannot or will not recognize that his valuations are rooted in *ressentiment*, that his "goodness" is an expression of vengefulness against "a hostile external world" (GM I.10). He is either unable or unwilling to be straight with himself about the interests underpinning his judgments—he refuses to open his eyes to himself. And this, for Nietzsche, is what his dishonesty consists in. That Nietzsche is less concerned here with the lie (i.e., the lie that everything of value is ultimately otherworldly) than with the attitude with which the lie is told is clear from his rather admiring reference to "genuine, resolute, 'honest'" lies—that is, to lies told by those who *can* "distinguish 'true' and 'false' in themselves." The invocation of Plato's authority is significant too. His own noble lie is of course the *locus classicus* of unflinching mendacity; but it is also his chief point of kinship with the artist. For in his own truthful untruthfulness, the great artist is "fundamentally opposed" to the ascetic (i.e., the Platonic) ideal—a point "instinctively sensed by Plato, the greatest enemy of art Europe has yet produced" (GM III.25). Honest liars, it seems, can recognize one another. But the crucial point is that Nietzsche is resting his criticism of a certain form of lying—the lying that "good people" do—on a conception of truthfulness which, although traceable to the "confessional subtlety of the Christian conscience," is not itself a symptom of that conscience. Rather, the readiness or the capacity to open one's eyes to oneself is presented, not as a prerequisite for baring one's soul to God, but as a sign of one's "ability *to control* one's Pro and Con," to be ruthless with oneself in one's estimation of one's own purposes and interests.

If this is right, then the version of the intellectual conscience which Nietzsche attributes to himself (and ought not to attribute to the scientist) is one founded on a commitment to truthful "self-surveillance"—to a ceaseless vigilance over and questioning of one's own motives, including one's own motives for being tempted to believe "that truth is *divine*" (GM III.24). It is a *good* bad conscience. The scientist's intellectual conscience, on the other hand, while it is also founded on a commitment to self-surveillance, is so because he fears that an insufficient amount of it might debar him from that "realm of truth" in which he still has unconditional faith. Thus the scientist's conscience, unlike Nietzsche's, is rooted in, and draws its legitimation from, a transcendental "system of purposes."

I say "Nietzsche's" conscience—with warrant, I think, from the passages of the *Genealogy* cited and also from the *Antichrist*. But another passage from the *Genealogy*, parts of which I have already discussed in a slightly different context, may seem to pull in a different direction. Nietzsche begins the whole book by announcing that, far from being masters of self-surveillance,

> We are unknown to ourselves, we men of knowledge—and with good reason. We have never sought ourselves—how could it happen that we should ever *find* ourselves? . . . Present experience has, I am afraid, always found us "absent-minded": we cannot give our hearts to it—not even our ears! Rather, as one divinely preoccupied and immersed in himself into whose ear the bell has just boomed . . . we sometimes rub our ears *afterward* and ask, utterly surprised and disconcerted, "what really was that which we have just experienced?" and moreover: "who *are* we really?" . . . So we are necessarily strangers to ourselves, we do not comprehend ourselves, we *have* to misunderstand ourselves, for us the law "Each is furthest from himself" applies to all eternity—we are not "men of knowledge" with respect to ourselves. (GM P1)

There are three ways one might construe this passage. The first is to take it perfectly literally, as a mysterious disavowal of the possibility of Nietzsche's ever placing himself under surveillance. If this is right, then either I am wrong about Nietzsche's own version of truthfulness or else the beginning and the end of the *Genealogy* contradict each other. The second way is to take the passage as a kind of chiding banter addressed to the best of his contemporaries — those "hard, severe, abstinent, heroic spirits" who still have faith in truth. This seems plausible: there is more than an echo here of the quote from *The Gay Science* given in GM III.24: "we men of knowledge of today, we godless men and anti-metaphysicians, we still derive *our* flame from the fire ignited by a faith millennia old . . . that truth is *divine*" (GS 344). Given that he then goes on in GM III.24 expressly to call "the *value* of truth into question," it seems safe to say that the "we" invoked there is not really intended to include Nietzsche himself. And the impression is confirmed three sections later when he touches again on "our problem, my *unknown* friends (for as yet I *know* of no friend): what meaning would *our* whole being possess if it were not this, that in us the will to truth becomes conscious of itself as a *problem*?" (GM III.27). On this construction, the passage from the preface actually prefigures rather than contradicts the final sections of the *Genealogy*. Nietzsche is taking his "heroic spirits" to task for not being quite heroic (truthful) enough: they are "preoccupied" with themselves in the wrong way ("divinely"): they assume that there is something final to be known about themselves that lies in a "realm of truth" *behind* experience. But that is a metaphysician's folly; and for as long as "we" cling to it "we are necessarily strangers to ourselves . . . , we *have* to misunderstand ourselves," we are *doomed* to overlook in ourselves that "faith in truth" which, Nietzsche assures us, is the "kernel" of the ascetic ideal. The third way of taking the passage is consistent with the second but has a slightly different emphasis. On this reading, Nietzsche is chiding himself for the same offenses, or for being subject to the temptation to commit them. He acknowledges the need for his version of truthfulness but cannot be quite sure that he won't slip back into being "divinely preoccupied." His self-surveillance may falter: he may not be quite "ephectic" enough.

For what it's worth, the second reading seems most plausible to me (perhaps seasoned with a dash of the third). Nietzsche is setting out to needle his imagined readers with the suggestion that they are "unknown" to themselves; and he is wooing them at the same time by including himself among their number.

VI

What we have so far, then, is a reasonably detailed account of Nietzsche's diagnosis of "faith in truth" as intrinsically ascetic; an exegesis of (or at least a series of suggestions about) the anti-metaphysical conception of truth that Nietzsche defends instead; and a way of understanding the notion of truthfulness as it enters into Nietzsche's own version of the "intellectual conscience." What we haven't yet looked into, however, is the full significance of Nietzsche's claim that the "*value* of truth," and of the will to truth, must be called into question (and "experimentally" called into question, at that). Nor have we investigated the relation between the calling into question of the value of truth and the advent (or the threat) of nihilism.

In one sense, of course, Nietzsche's critique of metaphysical realism just *is* a critique of the will to truth; and in this much we have already seen what questioning the value of truth consists in. If truth, as presupposed by the scientist's "faith in truth," is "inestimable" and otherworldly, then the "will" to it is the will to transcend "this world, *our* world" in favor of another world. The will to truth is thus an expression of the ascetic ideal, and the truth so willed has whatever value that ideal itself has. Furthermore, if, as Nietzsche claims, the truth of the metaphysical realist is predicated on the unintelligible notions of the thing-in-itself and the view from nowhere, then the ascetic will to truth has whatever value attaches to the pursuit of unintelligible ends. Thus—one might suggest—Nietzsche's critique of "faith in truth" as "divine" is already an investigation into the value of truth as traditionally conceived; and his conclusion—that "faith in truth" is faith in a self-contradictory lie—strongly indicates a negative valuation. Moreover, because "faith in truth" is an expression of the ascetic ideal, that negative valuation is predicated not only on the falsity or incoherence of truth so conceived, but also on the general undesirability of attitudes rooted in *ressentiment*. And this, one might think, is all that needs to be said.

But one would be wrong. For one thing, the foregoing makes neither reference to, nor evident sense of, Nietzsche's odd-looking claim that "the value of truth must for once be experimentally *called into question*" (GM III.24)—where the emphasis should be on "experimentally." For it would seem pretty pointless, on the face of it, to conduct an empirical enquiry into the value of something that has already been shown to be inconceivable. No one, presumably, would think it worthwhile to call the value of, for example, square triangles experimentally into question. Nor is the *scope* of the foregoing self-evidently appropriate. To be sure, Nietzsche does subject the truth of the metaphysicians to a withering critique. But he still has his own conception of truth; and nothing that he says suggests that that conception should somehow be immune to the trials of questioning. Indeed, he suggests the opposite: "From the moment faith in the God of the ascetic ideal is denied, a *new problem arises*: that of the *value* of truth" (GM III.24)—which is to place the origin of the problem at precisely the point where the destructive work against metaphysical truth is complete. It seems, then, that the conception of truth which needs to be called experimentally into question must be Nietzsche's own and not the scientist's at all. But what does this mean?

I have argued that for Nietzsche the truth is whatever best satisfies our cognitive interests—or, to put it more fully, the truth is whatever best satisfies the standards of rational acceptability immanent to a particular "system of purposes." This allows one to imagine calling truth experimentally into question in (at least) two different ways. The first pertains to individual truths. One might ask of some particular knowledge claim whether it really is true, whether it really does best satisfy our cognitive interests—and put it to the test. This way of calling truth experimentally into question is essentially a matter of being honest and open minded in the face whatever sort of evidence is relevant to the practice one is engaged in. As such, it is given exemplary expression by the empirical methods characteristic of natural science, and also by the synchronic version of multi-perspectivism mentioned earlier. But to call for this kind of experimental questioning would hardly be very radical, and it is impossible to believe that Nietzsche would make such a fuss about it if this were all that he meant.

The second kind of experimental questioning is more interesting. The focus here is not on particular (putative) truths but on the framework within which such truths are sought. The object of experimental questioning becomes the "system of purposes" whose standards of acceptability are being applied in particular cases. Hilary Putnam gives an example that illustrates the point:

> Suppose a rumor reaches me that my colleague, Professor X, has engaged in sexual misconduct with his students (perhaps the rumor was started by enemies of Professor X). . . . Suppose out of sheer curiosity I investigate the rumor, find the evidence very insubstantial, and publish a "carefully stated finding" that . . . "there is not enough systematic evidence to evaluate . . . [the rumor] carefully." . . . The point, quite simply, is that if you investigate slanderous charges, then merely concluding that "there is not enough systematic evidence to evaluate the claims carefully" does not let you off the moral hook. By giving the charges respectful attention, you take on a responsibility.[20]

—and Putnam concludes that Professor X could probably sue him for libel, and win. What this illustration shows, narrowly, is that the pursuit of truth within a framework of interests that might be appropriate for, say, investigating the claim that a certain kind of manual labor produces repetitive strain injury, may be wholly inappropriate when engaged in under other cir-

20. Putnam, "Scientific Liberty and Scientific License," in *Realism with a Human Face*, p. 206.

cumstances. More generally, it shows that one must assess not merely the status of particular claims relative to the standards of acceptability immanent to a given "system of purposes" but also the relevance of those standards to the kind of case that is being addressed. Otherwise one will find oneself giving priority to a particular perspective—to a particular set of interests— as if it were not a *perspective* at all but instead some kind of unconditional and "inestimable" view from nowhere. In this much, then, the experimental questioning of the value of truth consists, first, in remembering that truth is dependent upon interests and, second, in assessing which *set* of interests should be given (conditional) priority in particular cases. One must have the ability, in other words, "*to control* one's Pro and Con."

This, as I say, is more interesting; it reflects Nietzsche's claim that "there is no such thing as science 'without any presuppositions,'" and also Max Weber's remark that the importance of scientific findings "cannot be proved by scientific means." But, even so, we haven't really done much more here than to reiterate the doctrine of perspectivism and then to emphasize the role that Nietzsche's version of truthfulness must play in it. Nothing yet shows quite why Nietzsche should have insisted so hard that it is the "*value* of truth" that must be called into question.

We do get an indication, though, if we glance back at Putnam's example. There, the truth claims of science are shown to be entered inappropriately in the case of Professor X; and the standard by which they are held to be inappropriate is an explicitly *moral* standard. The interests embodied by this application of scientific method, in other words, are (quite properly) held accountable to standards of acceptability immanent to another "system of purposes" altogether. What this shows is not only that scientific truth is not true of things as they are in themselves (i.e., not only does science lack *otherworldly* authority) but also that science, because scientific truth needn't take precedence over our other interests, has no inalienable authority of a *this*-worldly kind either. It can *gain* authority only when co-opted by a "system of purposes" that is itself of the appropriate sort. Science is not "self-reliant," as Nietzsche puts it, because "it first requires in every respect an ideal of value, a value-creating power, in the *service* of which it could *believe* in itself—it never creates values" (GM III.25). Thus the value of science is always parasitic upon the values of the ideal which it serves. And this of course means that, since science is functioning for Nietzsche as an exemplar of the pursuit of truth in general, the value of truth is parasitic in the same way. Truth doesn't create values, it serves them. Which is why the "*value* of truth" becomes a problem just as soon as "faith in the God of the ascetic ideal is denied": truth had value—indeed had transcendental value—in the service of *that* ideal. But once "Christian truthfulness" has drawn "its *most striking inference*, its inference *against* itself," the ascetic ideal no longer has the clout to underwrite the value of anything. "Science" (truth) "henceforth *requires* justification" (GM III.24). It is this that prompts Nietzsche to ask, in *Beyond Good and Evil*, "Suppose we want truth: *why not rather* untruth?" (BGE 1) and why not "recognize untruth as a condition of life"? (BGE 4). That is, why not experiment with ideals that radically downgrade our *cognitive* interests (in favor of other interests) and that, therefore, reverse the values that the ascetic ideal has always accorded to truth and falsity? Would this not be precisely the way in which "the value of truth" might "for once be experimentally *called into question*"?

This brings us to the heart of Nietzsche's critique. We can now see the rather dramatic sense in which the value of the "will to truth" becomes problematic once Christian truthfulness draws its final inference against itself. But more than that: we can also see what sort of void the ascetic ideal must leave behind once its terminal "act of self-overcoming" is complete. The ascetic ideal has owed its hegemony so far to the fact that it is a "closed system of will, goal, and interpretation": its

> goal is so universal that all the other interests of human existence seem, when compared with it, petty and narrow; it interprets epochs, nations, and men inexorably with a view to this one goal; it permits no other interpretation, no other goal; . . . it rejects, denies, affirms, and sanctions solely from the point of view of *its* interpretation . . . ; it submits to no other power . . . —it believes that no power exists on earth that does not first have to receive a meaning, a right to exist, a value, as a tool of the ascetic ideal, as a way and means to *its* goal, to *one* goal (GM III.23).

Its success, in other words, has been attributable to its totalitarian nature, to its capacity to (pretend to) offer a complete, final and—therefore—transcendentally self-justifying account of existence. "Why has it not found its match?" Nietzsche asks (GM III.23). The answer, historically, is that its status as a (mere) interpretation has been occluded precisely by the fact that the ideal was completely "victorious" (GM I.7). But now?—now that the "inner consequences" of the ascetic ideal are playing themselves out, and its very "kernel" is busy drawing inferences against itself? Mightn't it (or we) at last find its match? The answer is a resounding *no*. For only *another* "closed system of will, goal, and interpretation" could possibly take its place; and it is precisely in the realization that *any* transcendentally self-justifying account of existence must be unintelligible that the last inference of asceticism consists. Thus, when it overcomes itself, the ascetic ideal doesn't merely vacate the playing field, it abolishes it as well. In the form of its own self-destruction it precludes, once and for all, the possibility of anything ever taking its place.

It is this fact that leads Nietzsche to describe the gradual self-overcoming of the ascetic ideal as an "awe-inspiring *catastrophe*" (GM III.27). For in its interpretation of "this world, *our* world" as "a wrong road," as a "bridge to that other mode of existence" (GM III.11)—to that transcendental "realm of truth" which is the "real" home of all value—the ascetic ideal had at least "*offered man meaning!* . . . the only meaning offered so far"; and "any meaning is better than none at all" (GM III.28). Asceticism had, in effect, given the will of man something to will, by directing it, under the auspices of a "monstrous . . . mode of valuation" (GM III.11), to a self-contradictory goal. "But all this notwithstanding—man was *saved* thereby, he possessed a meaning, he was henceforth no longer like a leaf in the wind, a plaything of nonsense—the 'sense-less'—he could now will something; no matter at first to what end, why, with what he willed: *the will itself was saved*" (GM III.28). Yet the respite is temporary. For with its demise (when "the will to truth becomes conscious of itself as a *problem*")—and its preemptive strike against any possible successor—the ascetic ideal *unlocks* the will from its "closed system" and effectively unleashes it: "this is the great spectacle in a hundred acts reserved for the next two centuries in Europe" (GM III.27). And the spectacle may be grim: for deprived of a goal, the will will continue willing, indeed "would rather will *nothingness* than *not* will" (GM III.28). Which is why the truthful self-critique of truth threatens to eventuate, not in relativism (which one might live with), but in nihilism.

That's where the *Genealogy* ends—on the threshold of a spectacle that Nietzsche describes as "most terrible" and "questionable." But he also suggests that it might be "most hopeful" (GM III.27). Why? Well, for one thing—if he's right (and there's no sign that he is yet)—the morality of *ressentiment* ought to wither away, or ought at any rate to become more contestable now that its transcendental underpinnings are gone. Or, to put the matter more hesitantly still, a space has at least been opened up for ideals that do not "advocate the 'beyond,'" that do not slander life (GM III.25). But of course no such counter-ideal can hope to do quite the job that the ascetic ideal did. No counter-ideal can ever pretend to offer itself as a "closed system of will, goal, and interpretation." Nor can any putative counter-ideal restore to the pursuit of truth its previous, uncriticizable status. Rather, because of the recognition upon which perspectivism is founded—that truth is necessarily bound up with our interests—prospective counter-ideals must content themselves with proposing (nontranscendentally grounded) *hierarchies* of interest. David Owen puts it like this:

our cognitive constitution is not separable from our affective constitution . . . .
[I]nsofar as different perspectives are rooted in different affects and since the

different affective interests of perspectives may clash . . . , the ranking of perspectives is a function of the ranking of affects and our "best" standards of rationality are the product of this ranking of our affective interests. . . . Thus, for Nietzsche's perspectivism, the question of how we rank our affective interests becomes [the] central question for reflection about rationality and truth.[21]

Or—to put the point more generally—if in the absence of the ascetic ideal we are to avoid the collapse into nihilism, we must provide the will with a goal; and, given that transcendental goals are no longer possible, that goal must be an immanent one, grounded in our ambitions for ourselves as denizens of "this world, *our* world"; which means that we must decide what *sort* of creature we want to be (i.e., we must decide how we should rank our interests). That we are free to do this, now that God is dead, is the great promise: man's "future digs like a spur into the flesh of every present" (GM III.13), so that "he gives rise to an interest, a tension, a hope, almost a certainty, as if with him something were announcing and preparing itself" (GM II.16). That we may not be *able* to do it is the great peril: we will never be able to lock the will again into a "closed system," but if we cannot create *some* sort of this-worldly meaning for ourselves then "nothingness" beckons.[22] Nietzsche pins his hopes on the "man of the future, who will redeem us not only from the hitherto reigning ideal but also from that which was bound to grow out of it, the great nausea, the will to nothingness, nihilism; this bell-stroke of noon and of the great decision that liberates the will again and restores its goal to earth and his hope to man; this Antichrist and antinihilist; this victor over God and over nothingness—*he must come one day*—" (GM II.24).

That Nietzsche yearns for a counter-ideal is beyond doubt: he calls for one repeatedly. But it is much less clear that he actually has one in mind. His diagnosis of the present is compelling: he is brilliant on the *whats* and *whences*. But has he anything to say about the *whither*? That is the question for the next chapter.

21. Owen, *Nietzsche, Politics and Modernity*, p. 38.
22. Or so Nietzsche claims. See Chapter 6, section 5, for discussion.

CHAPTER SIX

THE NOBLE

In a lizard a lost finger is replaced again; not so in man.

—*Beyond Good and Evil*, sec. 276

At the end of the second essay of the *Genealogy*, Nietzsche imagines himself being asked: "What are you really doing, erecting an ideal or knocking one down?" (GM II.24)—and we have certainly seen him doing a lot of knocking down. The question is a crucial one for Nietzsche, and his uncertainty in the face of it is amply signaled by the fact that he raises it *in medias res* before relaxing, as it were with a sigh, back into further acts of demolition. The fact that these further demolitions culminate in a diagnosis—that the ascetic ideal, the only remotely successful ideal so far, is now engaged in the final scenes of its own self-destruction—makes the question more pressing still. One somehow feels entitled to expect that Nietzsche, having exposed the impending nihilism of the modern condition, ought also to be prepared to remedy it, or should at least have some idea of what a remedy might look like. To be told by one's oncologist precisely how one's cancer is going to kill one, and by what mechanism, is all very well: but one would like to know how to cure it too. One might forgive the oncologist: if his best effort falls short of a cure that's not his fault. But Nietzsche can't use that defense (nor in fact, if Nietzsche is right, can the oncologist). It is part of his account of truth—about impending nihilism, terminal cancer, whatever—that truth serves interests. And so, having offered it as a truth that nihilism threatens, he is faced immediately with the question: Why, if true, is that worth knowing? What does that knowledge give us?—to which there would appear to be three sorts of possible answer. The first is that recognizing the depth of our predicament ought to make us want to listen to the following solution to it . . . The second is that the recognition of the depth of our predicament ought to spur us *all* on to find a solution, and finding a solution matters because . . . The third is that the prophecy of nihilism is liable to prove self-fulfilling, and nihilism is better than what we currently have because. . . . Only the most charitable would read Nietzsche as offering an answer of the first sort. An answer of the second sort does seem vaguely to be on offer. But it is hard to avoid the suspicion that Nietzsche's answer is really of the third sort, and that he is half in love with nihilism because he senses that only the experience of *that*—preferably rather dreadful and colorful—will persuade people that our current predicament actually is one, or is deep. But before saddling him with that view, we should see whether the *Genealogy* has anything less apocalyptic to offer instead.

I

I said a moment ago that only a very charitable reader would emerge from the *Genealogy* feeling that some sort of replacement for the ascetic ideal had been proposed in it. But that isn't quite right. For very *un*charitable (or careless) readers have often felt that way too. The view dies hard that what Nietzsche really wanted was a new barbarism, a return to the nobles of the first essay and that "disgusting procession of murder, arson, rape, and torture" at which the "splendid *blond beast*" excels (GM I.11).[1] Why do people think so?

The answer, I suspect, lies in a vague hotchpotch of reasons: Nietzsche is much nicer about the nobles in the first essay than he is about the slaves; Nietzsche regards the triumph of the slave over the noble as a disaster; Nietzsche is nasty about the virtues of slave morality (things like pity); Nietzsche would prefer a morality of self-affirmation to one of *ressentiment*, that is, he would prefer a noble morality. The only noble morality we are clearly told about in the *Genealogy* revolves around "murder, arson, rape, and torture"; hence Nietzsche is in favor of murder, arson, rape, and torture. I don't think that leaves out much. Certainly Nietzsche nowhere goes so far as to make the announcement "I want a new barbarism." But the evidence that he did want that is supposed to be strong enough without it. That evidence is, however, extremely weak. Nietzsche's glamorization of the original nobles, particularly in turning them into artists or beasts of prey, can't be denied. He plainly finds them fascinating and alluring (perhaps too fascinating and alluring). But we should at least consider why.

The *Genealogy* ends in crisis, in a crisis of value, which I will try to state

1. It would be tiresome to list all the people who have thought so. One will do: Bertrand Russell, the doyen of careless and uncharitable Nietzsche readers, makes most other misreaders look half-hearted—see his *History of Western Philosophy* (London: George Allen and Unwin, 1979), pp. 728–39.

as I think Nietzsche understood it. (I ask whether he understood it correctly in section 5 below.) With the death of God—with the impossibility of believing any longer in an otherworldly metaphysical realm—the foundations of Western morality are kicked away. The metaphysical realm was invented in the first place, according to Nietzsche, as a means of justifying valuations which implicitly or explicitly said no to "a hostile external world" (GM I.10). That is, the morality of *ressentiment* first posited another world in order to take maximum revenge against "this world, *our* world," and then granted itself a transcendental foundation in the very world it had invented in order to justify its increasingly subtle devaluations of the real world. Take away the transcendental world, however—which is just what happens when "Christian truthfulness" draws "its *most striking inference*, its inference *against* itself" (GM III.27)—and all you have left is a morality that says no to this world without affirming anything else instead (however imaginary). What you have, in other words, is the breeding ground of nihilism. Therefore, if you are to avoid nihilism, you need a style of valuation that affirms what's left after the abolition of the metaphysical world—you need a style of valuation that affirms "this world, *our* world" and the lives we lead immanently in it. In light of this, then, it is perhaps not surprising that Nietzsche should have felt rather excited when he thought that in the pre-Socratic Greeks he had discovered a mode of valuation, a "noble" morality, that seemed in some important respects to fit the bill. Nor is it surprising that he should have thought that there might be lessons to be learned from it; nor is it strange that he should have viewed its demise at the hands of a world-denying morality with dismay. In short, Nietzsche's attachment to the original nobles is not merely an intelligible but a mandatory response to the crisis he believes himself to have diagnosed: the nobles' morality, as he describes it, is a life-affirming one, and a life-affirming morality is precisely what is needed now that God is dead.

Whether life affirmers are bound also to be murdering, rapacious, pyromaniacal torturers, however, is an entirely separate question (i.e., not one settled either way by the observation that Nietzsche prefers the original nobles, unattractive habits notwithstanding, to the slaves whom they oppress). The question is, in fact, an empirical one: for there is no conceptual connection between the adoption of a style of valuation which affirms life for what it is, including the suffering in it, and the desire to *increase* the amount of suffering that the world contains (and hence that needs affirming). You could say yes to life, that is, without being then obliged by any logical consideration to go out and burn something down. That Nietzsche's original nobles felt so impelled is, I suggest, more an interesting fact about them than about the necessary appurtenances of *ressentiment*-free living. The "*blond beast*" has no monopoly on nobility. And Nietzsche would agree; indeed he quite obviously *does* agree. He has a lot to say, for instance, about the extreme *stupid-ity* of his original nobles: they do not "honor cleverness," for among them cleverness "is far less essential than the perfect functioning of the regulating *unconscious* instincts" (GM I.10). This relative mindlessness sits rather easily with the recreational pursuits that Nietzsche envisages the nobles engaging in; and Nietzsche is not a celebrator of mindlessness. Indeed he emphasizes that it was precisely not in the nobles' way of doing things but in the slaves' that "man first became an *interesting animal*" (GM I.6)—that is, an animal "*pregnant with a future* . . . as if man were not a goal but only a way, an episode, a bridge, a great promise" (GM II.16). Bestial mayhem, then, is not the way forward; and if Nietzsche is promoting a resurgence of noble moral-ity, it isn't the morality of the original nobles that he's after.

This point is borne out further when one considers Nietzsche's alleged contempt for the nicer sounding virtues of slave morality. It is easy to read him as a straight opponent of all of them. But read a little harder, and it be-comes clear that it is the *attitude* behind them that he deplores, not (always) the virtues themselves. In *Daybreak* he puts it like this: "It goes without say-ing that I do not deny—unless I am a fool—that many actions called im-moral ought to be avoided and resisted, or that many called moral ought to be done and encouraged—but I think the one should be encouraged and the other avoided *for other reasons than hitherto*. We have to *learn to think differently*—in order, at last, perhaps very late on, to attain even more: *to feel differently*" (D 103). Thus, in the *Genealogy*, he waxes lyrical about justice, for instance: "it ends, as does every good thing on earth, by *overcoming itself*. This self-overcoming of justice: one knows the beautiful name it has given itself—*mercy*" (GM II.10). He is also keen on loving one's enemies (GM I.10) and on respect and gratitude (GM I.11). But one of the most striking in-stances comes in *Zarathustra*, where gentleness is commended—gentleness with "claws" (Z, Of the Sublime Men). *With* claws, because gentleness is valu-able only when shown by a person who has the wherewithal to act otherwise.

Similarly with mercy: Nietzsche celebrates mercifulness when it is exhib-ited by those who have claws enough to contemplate alternatives: "As the power and self-confidence of a community increase, the penal law always be-comes more moderate. . . . The 'creditor' always becomes more humane to the extent that he has grown richer. . . . It is not unthinkable that a society might attain such a *consciousness of power* that it could allow itself the noblest luxury possible to it—letting those who harm it go *unpunished*. 'What are my parasites to me?' it might say. 'May they live and prosper: I am strong enough for that!'" (GM II.10).

Mercy is a virtue, then, when it is an expression of self-affirmation, of strength rather than weakness. Pity too, against which Nietzsche inveighs rather reliably, may have its noble incarnations. The kind he doesn't like is pity as one-upmanship, where one portrays the sufferer as a victim (as someone *even* weaker than oneself) in order to gain a vicarious sense of superiority over him, and hence, in a roundabout way, to affirm oneself. But nothing in this precludes either compassion for the suffering of others or the desire to alleviate it. And so with most of the other "traditional"—that is, Christian—virtues.[2] The noble versions of these virtues differ from the slavish versions, not in the sorts of behavior they promote—that is, not in the sense that noble gentleness, unlike slavish gentleness, might somehow be compatible with rape or arson—but in the attitudes toward oneself and toward the world upon which they are founded. Thus the slavish versions have their origin in the impossibility of affirming either self or life except indirectly through the denigration of something else. These virtues arise when "Weakness is . . . lied into something *meritorious*" (GM I.14), when weakness has, "thanks to the counterfeit and self-deception of impotence, clad itself in the ostentatious garb of the virtue of quiet, calm resignation, just as if the weakness of the weak—that is to say, their *essence*, their effects, their sole ineluctable, irremovable reality—were a voluntary achievement, willed, chosen . . . the sublime self-deception that interprets weakness as freedom, and their being thus-and-thus as a *merit*" (GM I.13).

The virtues of the slave are the inventions of *ressentiment* turned creative; and they are sustained, Nietzsche suggests, only at the cost of truthfulness—a virtue which, as we saw in the previous chapter, is both the mainstay of the Christian conscience and also, finally, its poison chalice. Nothing in Nietzsche's attitude toward the virtues per se, then, suggests that he is opposed to them (and hence that he favors murdering people). He is opposed only to those *expressions* of virtue that are founded on an inability or a refusal to say yes to "this world, *our* world." So, again, there are no grounds to believe that Nietzsche is urging a return to the original nobles (with all that being like them would entail).

Nor, of course, *could* he urge that. The considerations I've offered so far are persuasive, perhaps. But the real clincher is to be found at another level—when we ask, What makes the original noble possible? The answer, baldly, is: his relatively low degree of internalization. The nobles, as I said a moment ago, are stupid: the will to power, in them, is not yet mediated very much through consciousness, through meaning—and they strive to maintain themselves in this condition by going "outside" and compensating "themselves in the wilderness for the tension engendered by protracted confinement and enclosure within the peace of society" (GM I.11). Their pro-

2. I have a feeling that humility might be unrescuable. Reverence is fine, though.

cessions of "murder, arson, rape, and torture" function precisely so as to keep "the entire inner world, originally as thin as if it were stretched between two membranes," from expanding and extending itself, from acquiring "depth, breadth, and height" (GM II.16). Their stupidity, in other words, prompts them to indulge in torture; but their torturings also keep them stupid. The significance of this, in the context of the story that Nietzsche tells in the *Genealogy*, is that the nobles were always, in the long run, onto a loser. They were always going to be defeated in the end by the much less stupid (much more "interesting") people whom their oppressive behavior had produced. Actually, "defeated" isn't quite right here: "co-opted" would be better. Increasing civilization civilizes.

One might summarize the process in question under the title "How the Original Noble At Last Became An Impossibility":

1. He begins by oppressing people and imposing customs on them. For this he needs the capacity to make and keep promises, which presupposes that he, too, has been to some degree internalized. He works off his frustrations, his non-creative *ressentiment*, by going outside.

2. He organizes the law as a system of equivalences for injuries so that *ressentiment* is given both a target and a limit: this reinforces the doer/deed distinction integral to slave morality. The people he oppresses become cleverer, subtler, more resentful, and even, in the end, creative. They resort to a war of words (of meanings). This requires the noble himself to become subtler, cleverer, and more articulate if he is to remain on top. (Less time now for extracurricular activities.)

3. He's getting quite clever now. But since cleverness is a product of internalization and repression, this involves an increase in his suffering (inward suffering). Thus his success in keeping his subjects under control eventually brings his own predicament—and indeed his own conceptual resources for dealing with it—much more into line with theirs.

4. As the institution of law becomes stronger, his own freedom of action is increasingly curtailed: "the law-giver himself eventually receives the call": submit to the law you yourself proposed (GM III.27). There is no longer much outside for him to go and discharge his energies into. More internalization; more *ressentiment*; more cleverness; more reason to wonder whether the slaves' solution to suffering mightn't be the right one (it seems to work for them, after all).

5. Becomes Pope. Convergence with public attitudes continues.

6. Becomes democratic politician. Convergence complete. The original noble has overcome himself.

This progression, I suggest, represents rather accurately the trajectory described in the *Genealogy*. The original noble isn't personally eliminated by slave morality: rather, the inherent instability of his relation to the slaves, coupled with his desire to remain in charge of them, ensures that his title to original nobility (a title founded on minimal internalization) must eventually lapse. He is *sure* to become cleverer; his will to power is *sure* to become more and more mediated through consciousness; he is *sure* to become less and less like a "beast of prey"; and so he is *sure* to become more and more like those he formerly preyed upon. The original noble was doomed from the moment he oppressed his first slave.

If this is Nietzsche's version of power corrupting, and absolute power corrupting absolutely, then his version shares with the better known one the property of irreversibility. From the standpoint adopted at the end of the *Genealogy*—a perspective from which the ascetic ideal is busy destroying itself—the conditions required to produce a *return* to the original noble are simply not present. The whole culture, after two thousand years of training in cleverness, is saturated with consciousness and meaning to such an extent that any reversion to the unfathomably shallow stupidity of the original noble is out of the question. Man cannot be magically disinternalized. Given which, there would be no point at all in hoping that the place vacated by the self-overcoming of the ascetic ideal might be occupied instead by the ideal of original barbarism. It is for this reason that Nietzsche describes Napoleon as "the most isolated and late-born man there has ever been, and in him the problem of the *noble ideal as such* made flesh—one might well ponder *what* kind of problem it is: Napoleon, this synthesis of the *inhuman* and *superhuman*" (GM I.17). Napoleon is *late*-born, note: an anachronism, a throwback to antiquity. And the problem he poses, in David Owen's formulation, is that "the good conscience and noble morality (the overhuman) are maintained in antiquity only because the noble has the opportunity to express his instinctive drives (the inhuman) outside of society. . . . [A]t this juncture it appears that the overhuman is non-contingently tied to the inhuman. Thus Nietzsche's characterization of this synthesis [represented by Napoleon] as a *problem* reveals . . . the central ethical concern of his genealogical reflection: *how is it possible to have the overhuman without the inhuman?*" [3] Or, to put it another way, the problem is that the noble ideal (the superhuman) has always been predicated upon an uninternalized stupidity (the inhuman), which is no longer—except in rule-provingly exceptional cases—to be had. The problem, then, is how to predicate nobility on what we *do* have, on the all-too-clever, all-too-human condition that a couple of millennia of internalization has left us in.

Nietzsche wants man to become noble again, to be sure. But he recognizes that it is only as an "interesting animal" that man can now be considered

3. David Owen, *Nietzsche, Politics and Modernity* (London: Sage, 1995), p. 74.

"*pregnant with a future.*" And such a pregnancy is not about to be brought to term by having a few more rapists around.

II

Nietzsche, then, is not advocating a return to the original nobles. What he wants is some sort of new nobility—one built out of the human materials we actually have to hand. And he wants it because the self-overcoming of the ascetic ideal leaves us both without a goal and without the capacity ever again to avail ourselves of transcendental interpretations. Hence the only solution (the only way of avoiding nihilism) is to come up with an ideal that is immanent through and through—with a noble ideal, in other words. So what sort of ideal is Nietzsche recommending? What sort of vision of human life does he want to promote? I devote this and the next two sections to the somewhat shadowy suggestions (or perhaps the wish list) that Nietzsche seems to offer.

By far the nearest thing in the *Genealogy* to a series of *measures* that one might take in order to improve oneself along Nietzschean lines is this: "Man has all too long had an 'evil eye' for his natural inclinations, so that they have finally become inseparable from his 'bad conscience.' An attempt at the reverse would *in itself* be possible—but who is strong enough for it?—that is, to wed the bad conscience to all the *unnatural* inclinations, all those aspirations to the beyond, to that which runs counter to sense, instinct, nature, animal, in short all ideals hitherto, which are one and all hostile to life and ideals that slander the world" (GM II.24). On the face of it this looks straightforward: one should learn to feel bad about oneself for one's transgressions against immanence. But stop to think what this might involve, and matters at once become thornier. It is, I take it, evident that the "bad conscience" concerned here is not the *bad* bad conscience of slave morality (see Chapter 1). There would be no point in trying to wed one's unnatural inclinations to that, since it is thoroughly implicated in them already. Indeed, the *bad* bad conscience of slave morality is precisely the *source* of those judgments against natural inclination that Nietzsche wants to see rescinded. So the "bad conscience" in question must, instead, be bad conscience in its "raw state."

But how easy is it to make sense of someone's wedding their unnatural inclinations to the bad conscience in its "raw state"? The idea is presumably meant to be this: one turns back one's unnatural inclinations into one's "raw" bad conscience, thereby generating a *good* bad conscience about one's natural inclinations and a moralized (bad) form of good bad conscience about the rest; and success in this would render one immune to the charms of slave morality, the ascetic ideal, etc. But the idea is incoherent. The first problem with it is that one wouldn't *have* any unnatural inclinations on Nietzsche's view unless one already had a *bad* bad conscience—a state of affairs that supersedes one's initial possession of the bad conscience in its raw state, and so which cannot somehow be discharged back into it. But even if we supposed, for the sake of argument, that one could in fact have both unnatural inclinations and a (still) "raw" bad conscience at the same time, it wouldn't do any good. Bad conscience in its raw state, remember, is caused by the "instinct for freedom" being "pushed back and repressed, incarcerated within," so that it is "finally able to discharge and vent itself only on itself" (GM II.17). Bad conscience in its raw state, in other words, just *is* the internal space produced by the repression of instinct. Therefore, if one wanted to push one's unnatural inclinations back into it one would already have to have repressed one's natural ones first; and this, apart from leaving one in a somewhat paradoxical state, would also leave one in the position of having no outwardly directed inclinations of any sort. Indeed the *only* way that Nietzsche's model of conscience could be squared with having one's natural inclinations entirely out from under the "evil eye" would be to have no conscience at all (hence, as we saw in Chapter 1, Nietzsche's rather confused affection for beasts of prey).[4]

Nietzsche is certainly right to think that his new nobility, whatever it comes to, requires "ideals that slander the world" to be somehow ousted. But he is quite wrong to think that it "would *in itself* be possible" to oust them by tinkering about with the mechanisms of bad conscience. Better, then, to avert one's eyes from this particular suggestion. Much more promising would be a line of attack that sought either to neutralize "unnatural inclinations" by *deploying* the resources of bad conscience that we actually do have, or to show how the very conditions of bad conscience might eventually be superseded. Nietzsche gestures in both of these directions; and the following two sections will be given over to an assessment of what those gestures come to.

III

In Chapter 5 I discussed Nietzsche's attribution of the origins of intellectual conscience (good and bad) to the "self-surveillance" promoted by "the confessional subtlety of the Christian conscience" (GM III.27). The passage I want to come back to is this:

> You will guess what, according to my idea, the curative instinct of life has at least *attempted* through the ascetic priest, and why it required for a time the

4. Were it not for the fact that Nietzsche's use of the terminology of bad conscience is always so muddled and inconsistent, one might construe GM II.24 as the closest he comes to advocating a return to the original noble.

tyranny of such paradoxical and paralogical concepts as "guilt," "sin," "sin-fulness," "depravity," "damnation": . . . to direct the *ressentiment* of the less severely afflicted firmly back on themselves ("one thing is needful")—and in this way to *exploit* the bad instincts of all sufferers for the purpose of self-discipline, self-surveillance, and self-overcoming (GM III.16)

The attempt to exploit "the bad instincts of all sufferers" in order to effect the improvement of the "less severely afflicted" clearly meets with Nietz-sche's approval. And his reference—"one thing is needful"—to the task out-lined in *The Gay Science*, the task of giving style to one's character, suggests that he envisages the possibility of an analogous attempt in the service of nobility—an attempt that would repudiate such concepts as "guilt," "sin," and the rest, but which would still attempt to turn certain of our "bad in-stincts" to good account. When one notes, moreover, that the "bad instincts" in question are those of the internalized bad conscience (among the possi-bilities of which are "this secret self-ravishment, this artists' cruelty, this de-light in imposing a form upon oneself" [GM II.18]), it becomes clear that Nietzsche is toying with precisely the first of the two options mentioned at the end of the previous section: he is wondering whether one mightn't de-ploy the resources of the bad conscience *against* the "unnatural inclinations."

What we are dealing with here, of course, is the soul-artistry discussed in Chapter 4—Nietzsche's recipe for outdoing the priest on his own territory. "*One thing is needful*," he says—"that a human being should *attain* satis-faction with himself": "To 'give style' to one's character—a great and rare art! It is practiced by those who survey all the strengths and weaknesses of their nature and then fit them into an artistic plan until every one of them appears as art and reason and even weaknesses delight the eye" (GS 290). The idea, clearly enough, is that we should somehow reinterpret ourselves (landscape ourselves, in effect) so that concepts like "guilt" and "sin" can gain no purchase—so that the *bad* bad conscience remains an unrealized possi-bility. But what, actually, are we to make of this? Why might anyone think it a good thing? Suppose I perform a series of vile and spiteful acts and then lie to you about what I've done. Suppose, too, that "through long practice and daily work at it" (GS 290) I succeed in reinterpreting the former as a sublime expression of my own rich and overfull nature and the latter as a magnanimous attempt to spare your sensibilities. Doubtless I might manage by these means to avoid feeling sinful or guilty: I might attain "satisfaction" with myself. But at what cost? Does my self-exculpatory self-aestheticization somehow make me more noble? Is my soul *really* more beautiful now for the work that I've done on it? Indeed what—apart from providing me with an arena for narcissism—might my stylish new character be *for*?

Part of what Nietzsche is getting at here, no doubt, is the futility of excessive self-recrimination—and also the undesirability of it: if one hates oneself too much one will swiftly find oneself hating the world, and that way asceticism lies. But disapproving of excessive self-recrimination is one thing; deciding to abolish self-recrimination altogether is another. And Nietzsche's sole motivation for apparently wanting to pursue the latter course lies in a (seeming) commitment to the value of aesthetic self-satisfaction at any price. But if that price includes wholesale self-deception, it is far from clear that we, or Nietzsche, should be ready to pay it. It is a mark, he says, of "the man of *ressentiment*" that he is "neither upright nor naive nor honest and straightforward with himself" (GM I.10). The man of *ressentiment* is a great self-deceiver; but so too, it would seem, is the man of stylish character. How, then, do they differ from one another?

We can sharpen this point if we recall that Nietzsche refers to the one "needful" thing in the context of self-surveillance. This suggests that giving style to one's character is somehow related to Nietzsche's own nonpriestly versions of "self-discipline, self-surveillance, and self-overcoming"—that is, to his own (good, post-Christian, postscientific) intellectual conscience, to his own form of truthfulness. But as we saw in Chapter 5, that form of truthfulness is very demanding: "one has to surrender for it almost everything to which the heart" clings; for only if "one is severe against one's heart" can one aspire to "*integrity* in matters of the spirit" (AC 50). Which sounds most unlike the self-beautification of a moment ago: those maneuvers, after all, seemed designed precisely so as to gratify the heart, precisely so as *not* to surrender anything to which the heart might cling. So is it a case of style *or* integrity, beauty *or* truthfulness? And—if it is—why does Nietzsche apparently run them all together in GM III.16?

The answer, I think, lies in the role that Nietzsche's version of truthfulness is supposed to play. I argued in the previous chapter that truthfulness was a precondition of being able "*to control* one's Pro and Con" (GM III.12), of having the "ephectic" ability to avoid deceiving oneself about one's own motivations—even if one does deceive other people. I also suggested that the true artist (the soul-artist) is one who is able to deceive with a good conscience precisely insofar as he is *not* himself taken in by his own beautifying lies (i.e., insofar as he refuses to seal them with the move to judgment). Considered together, these points serve both to complicate the sense of the "one thing is needful" passage, and also to strip it of some of its horticultural complacency. For if the one "needful" thing is to give style to one's character *truthfully*, the specter of self-serving self-*deception* recedes. One might regard the stylish results of one's art with satisfaction, no doubt; but, if one has been truthful, one will not be misled by those results into thinking that one "really" is as one portrays oneself to oneself as being. But in that case, what is the point of trying to give style to one's character at all? If I reinterpret myself as thus-and-thus while remaining fully aware of my own self-evading motives for doing so, how, in the event, have I solved (or evaded) anything? What "need" has my newly stylish character even remotely met? Nietzsche's answer can be glimpsed in the following: "it might be a basic characteristic of existence that those who would know it completely would perish, in which case the strength of a spirit should be measured according to how much of the 'truth' one could still barely endure—or to put it more clearly, to what degree one would *require* it to be thinned down, shrouded, sweetened, blunted, falsified" (BGE 39). This appears to gesture toward a rather less comfortable motive for self-beautification than the mere attainment of "satisfaction." The emphasis is now on self-preservation: if one does not at *some* point thin down and falsify one's image of oneself, one will perish.

But the passage may be problematic. On the face of it, it might look as if Nietzsche is appealing to some sort of in-itselfness of things—to a terrifying reality lying behind the everyday world of appearances. And if so his appeal is atavistic: by this time he should have purged himself of that "real" world which only a metaphysician would see lurking beneath the "apparent" one. But if the passage looks like a throwback from one angle, it doesn't look like that from every angle. Specifically, it doesn't look like that if one situates it, not in the context of *Birth of Tragedy*-like glimpses of the Dionysian, but in the context of remarks like the following: "*Fundamental insight.* —There is no pre-established harmony between the furtherance of truth and the well-being of mankind" (HH 517). This "insight" is Nietzsche's crispest expression of the "tragic" view of existence—the view that there is or may be an ineliminable mismatch between what we would like to be the case and what in fact is the case. Such a view entails no inappropriate metaphysical commitments (e.g., to a realm of "truth" in itself). Rather, it entails only what Nietzsche's perspectivism insists upon: that it is not our interests that determine truth or falsity but our best standards of rational acceptability. And these standards may yield truths we don't like—even truths we can't live with.

For Nietzsche himself, the clearest example of such a truth (and something to which he was acutely, even abnormally, sensitive) is the reality of the suffering of others. In *The Birth of Tragedy* he puts it like this: suppose someone "put his ear, as it were, to the heart chamber of the world will and felt the roaring desire for existence pouring from there into all the veins of the world . . . —how could he fail to break suddenly? How could he endure to perceive the echo of innumerable shouts of pleasure and woe . . . ?" (BT 21). In *Human, All Too Human* he says it again: "whoever would be truly able to participate" in the "vicissitudes and suffering" of others "would have to despair about the value of life; if he were to grasp and feel mankind's overall consciousness in himself, he would collapse with a curse against existence" (HH 33). And his confession in *The Gay Science*—"I only need to expose myself to the sight of some genuine distress and I am lost" (GS 338)—is generalized in the *Genealogy*, so that the suffering of others poses a threat to everyone who is "happy, well-constituted, powerful in soul and body": "it is disgraceful to be fortunate," they are tempted to say: *"there is too much misery!"* (GM III.14)—misery made unbearable by its meaninglessness. In *The Birth of Tragedy* Nietzsche evades, shrouds, and falsifies the object of his horror with his metaphysics: he deceives himself into believing that transcendental consolation is to be had through art. But by the time of *Human, All Too Human*, and certainly by the time of the *Genealogy*, no such sweetener is available to him, and other measures begin to take its place. We find Nietzsche frantically warding off "collapse" and its attendant "curse on existence" by appeal to the alleged pleasures of cruelty and to the redemption of suffering through "spectacle." We read increasingly strident celebrations of the sort of person who might actually be able to deal with suffering on these terms. As Henry Staten puts it, "Without the cruel hero, Nietzsche would have to shut himself off entirely from the perception of a universe of suffering that he would not be able to bear. He needs the cruel hero precisely so that he can receive back into himself, *absorb* and *endure* the greatest quantity of sympathetic perception of suffering, and in fact experience it as the ultimate pleasure, the 'feeling above all feelings.'"[5] And in this fantasy, the fantasy of the "cruel hero," Nietzsche's requirement that the truth of the suffering of others be "thinned down, shrouded, sweetened, blunted, falsified" continues to be met, despite his surrender of metaphysical consolation. But the sado-masochistic consolation he settles for instead (*that* feature of his late "style") is none the less founded on self-deception for that.[6]

But we needn't suffer from Nietzsche's own particular (and admirable) sensitivities in order to require the shrouding of unacceptable truths. To take only the most obvious example: from the vantage point of any recognizably human perspective it is a truth that I must one day die. If I am honest, moreover, I will deny myself the more seductive (religious/transcendental) compensations for this realization. But can I—really—look it squarely in the eye, without the *least* softening of *any* of its implications? The end of *me*—

5. Henry Staten, "Masochism and Aestheticism in Nietzsche's View of History" (unpublished manuscript).
6. The kind of self-deception involved here may be similar to the failures of acknowledgment that Stanley Cavell discusses in *Disowning Knowledge* (Cambridge: Cambridge University Press, 1987): it's not that one doesn't know what the truth is, it's that one fails to acknowledge the truth as true.

my memories, my thoughts, my hopes, my longings, my attachments—all gone; and gone for—what? To think this thought "completely" would surely destroy me: I evade it, shroud it, sweeten it, blunten it, falsify it. And, in falsifying it, it is an ordinary, this-worldly truth that I "*require*" to be "thinned down"—not the "real" truth of some redundant metaphysics. When Nietzsche says that "life is no argument. The conditions of life might include error" (GS 121), included in the "error" are the evasive measures one is bound to take in the face of suffering and of one's own mortality.[7] And there may be other errors too.[8]

If what I have said is right, *every* character needs sooner or later to deceive itself, and Nietzschean truthfulness can only ever be taken so far, no matter how much strength of spirit one has. And if this is right, the last role of truthfulness is truthfully to surrender to the necessity of deceiving oneself, having stood firm against one's heart's desire to capitulate sooner. Style, on this reading, is not so much a matter of opportunistic self-exculpation as the (honest) last resort of a soul that can face no more. ("As an aesthetic phenomenon existence is still *bearable* for us" [GS 107] .)

But—and I think what I've said is right as far as it goes—how does all this relate to the question of nobility? I suggest the following. Put aside for a moment the possibility of actually *perishing* of truthfulness. Think instead of the point raised earlier, that an *excess* of self-recrimination is apt to sour people against themselves and against the world. According to Nietzsche, "the degree to which life has been spoiled for them might be inferred from the degree to which they wish to see its image falsified, thinned down, transcendentalized, deified" (BGE 59). Existence "transcendentalized" and "deified": this is the end point of the priestly version of self-surveillance. If one is not to succumb to it, one must plainly prevent one's life from being "spoiled"—that is, one must prevent one's life from becoming unaffirmable. Indeed, insofar as one's truthfulness is of the Nietzschean kind—the kind that forbids itself not merely "the *lie involved in belief in God*" (GM III.27) but also the lie involved in any transcendentalizing move whatever—one is *impelled* to prevent one's life from being "spoiled." There comes a point, in other words, at which one is truthfully driven to say, "Enough!—any more (Nietzschean) truthfulness and I must either perish or abandon truthfulness: die, or mendaciously begin to slander 'this world, *our* world' in favor of an-

7. For a supremely sensitive exploration of the extent to which it is possible, without otherworldly compensations, to face up to the fact of death, see Henry Staten, *Eros in Mourning* (Baltimore: Johns Hopkins University Press, 1995).

8. Suppose, for instance, that Richard Dawkins's "selfish gene" hypothesis were true. Could one honestly face it, and face it squarely, as true of oneself? (What self?) Surely an "error" of some kind would be needed here.

other." And the measure of one's "strength of spirit," of one's nobility, will be how much severity against one's own heart one can put up with first: the more that that turns out to be, the more of existence and the world one will have been able to affirm.[9]

Style, on this reading, is the one "needful" thing if the last limit of affirmation is not also to prove the first step into vengefulness. Nietzsche calls the honest pressing of this limit the "discipline of suffering": a "tension of the soul in unhappiness which cultivates its strength, its shudders face to face with great ruin, its inventiveness and courage in enduring, persevering, interpreting, and exploiting suffering, and whatever has been granted to it of profundity, secret, mask, spirit, cunning, greatness" (BGE 225). And this, I think, gives the sense of Nietzsche's efforts to imagine how the resources of the internalized bad conscience might be exploited to noble ends. The bad conscience in its "raw state" is an inward arena carved out by the repression of instinct, rich with the potential for suffering and *ressentiment*, but also with the potential for that "*active* 'bad conscience'" exhibited in the "joyous labor of a soul voluntarily at odds with itself that makes itself suffer out of joy in making suffer" (GM II.18). This latter potential—what I have called the *good* bad conscience—is realized and maintained only against the odds and with much hardship. It is achieved when Nietzsche's version of truthful self-surveillance is continually (that is, ephectically) taken to its very limit. One interprets and reinterprets oneself at the furthest edge of one's capacity for affirmation, constantly striving to render more and more of existence affirmable, one's latest interpretation and "style" always the only and most fragile bulwark against collapse into *ressentiment*, *bad* bad conscience, and asceticism. Or to put it another way: if one is not to "perish," one is *impelled* to occupy the wafer-thin space between self-exculpating self-deception on the one hand (forbidden by truthfulness) and transcendental solutions on the other (also forbidden by truthfulness); and this slender region—the limit of one's character, the limit of one's ephectic capabilities—is constituted by whatever lies about oneself one cannot, right now, live without ("untruth as a condition of life" [BGE 4]). Style, thus, is a kind of continually evolving last-ditch fiction and self-deception which one cannot help but interpose between oneself and those more dangerous fictions and deceptions that spoil the world. The "No" and the "critique" that one burns into oneself (GM II.18) are the marks of that integrity which obliges one to be "severe against one's heart"; and the "discipline of suffering" that one thereby under-

9. The space across which this Nietzschean self-surveillance takes place is the "*pathos of distance*" internalized—"the craving for an ever new widening of distances within the soul itself, the development of ever higher, rarer, more remote, further-stretching, more comprehensive states" (BGE 257).

goes constitutes both the practice of truthfulness and its (life-affirming) reward. On this reading, truthfulness, self-surveillance, nobility, the *good* bad conscience, and the one "needful" thing come fruitfully into confluence with one another, as Nietzsche surely intended that they should. On this reading, too, the differences between the man of stylish character and the self-deceiving self-exculpator, on the one hand, and the man of *ressentiment*, on the other, are explicit. The man of character differs from the first in his ruthlessness with himself: self-deception is his last resort and barrier, not his ticket to an easier life. And he differs from the second in his determination not to have existence and the world "spoiled": the man of *ressentiment* has let those things be spoiled already.

In my view, the sketch of a new "interesting" nobility that Nietzsche gives here (or my reconstruction of it) is his most successful attempt to imagine what a truly immanent ideal of living might be like. It also, unlike the positions canvassed in the previous two sections, exploits conditions that we do, as a matter of fact, have to hand. The reading that yields it, I have to admit, sits rather uneasily with the tone (undynamic, country parkish) of the passage in *The Gay Science* from which it largely derives, here treated more as a hint or a seed of an idea than as an actual expression of one. But I think I have warrant for that: nowhere in the *Genealogy* is Nietzsche reluctant to refer us directly to *The Gay Science* when it suits his purposes; but in this case he merely makes an allusion in passing—"one thing is needful"; and I'm content to regard that as a license to interpret broadly, as I have done. I suspect that Nietzsche thought better of *how* he said what he said in *The Gay Science* while remaining attached to something in the idea itself. And, if what I have argued here is plausible, he was right in both cases.

IV

I turn now to the other of the stratagems mentioned earlier: the attempt to imagine how the very conditions of bad conscience might eventually be superseded. It will helpful first, however, to make a distinction. The phrase "self-overcoming," apparently univocal in translation, is in fact used to convey two quite separate ideas.[10] There is self-overcoming in the sense that is achieved by severity against one's heart: one overcomes one's own inclinations, one's own laziness, etc. And there is self-overcoming in the sense exhibited by the transformation of justice into mercy (GM II.10) or by the destruction of the ascetic ideal in accordance with its own "inner consequences" (GM III.27): here the logic immanent to a concept or an institu-

---

10. And is used, moreover, to translate distinct German words. Kaufmann translates both *Selbstaufhebung* and *Selbstuberwinding* as "self-overcoming," and both *aufzuheben* and *aufgehoben* as "overcome." See his footnotes to GM II.10 and GM III.27.

tion finally brings about its transformation (or destruction). In the first sense of self-overcoming, the self is as it were divided against itself and goes to work on itself on that premise. In the second sense, the self is overcome in virtue of structural features intrinsic to its very constitution.[11] The nobility of style discussed in the previous section is Nietzsche's attempt to make something of out the first sort of self-overcoming (the man of "raw" bad conscience overcomes his tendency to become a man of *bad* bad conscience). But I think that Nietzsche hoped that, like "every good thing on earth" (GM II.10), the whole apparatus of the "raw" bad conscience might one day overcome itself in the second sense. That is the subject of the present section.

I was properly intolerant in Chapter 1 of Nietzsche's ambition to accord "innocent" consciences to beasts of prey (GM I.11). But the same strictures need not, I think, apply to his description of the "*sovereign individual*" who stands at the end of the "tremendous process" of internalization:

> the man who has his own independent, protracted will and the *power to make promises*—and in him a proud consciousness, quivering in every muscle, of *what* has at length been achieved and become flesh in him, a consciousness of his own power and freedom, a sensation of mankind come to completion. . . . The proud awareness of the extraordinary privilege of *responsibility*, the consciousness of this rare freedom, the power over oneself and over fate, has in his case penetrated to the profoundest depths and become instinct, the dominating instinct . . . : this sovereign man calls it his *conscience* (GM II.2, translation adjusted).

On the face of it, certainly, one might be inclined to raise an eyebrow at this: the conscience, good or bad, is precisely what *supplants* instinct on Nietzsche's view. And the "quivering" of consciousness "in every muscle" has a physicalism about it which both cuts against Nietzsche's account of what the internalized space of consciousness *is* and conjures up unwelcome specters of "blond beasts," "unconscious" artistry, and the like. But perhaps one should take more seriously Nietzsche's claim that the sovereign individual occupies a place at the *end* of "this tremendous process"—that is, perhaps one should construe the sovereign individual as a prediction or a wish or a hope about that future with which man is said to be pregnant. The attractions of such a move, I think, become most apparent if we place ourselves for a moment at the *beginning* of the process of internalization:

> The situation that faced sea animals when they were compelled to become land animals or perish was the same as faced these semi-animals . . . : suddenly

11. The old Marxist view that capitalism would collapse because of its own inherent contradictions is an example of (faith in) the second kind of self-overcoming.

all their instincts were disvalued and "suspended." From now on they had to walk on their feet and "bear themselves" whereas hitherto they had been borne by the water: a dreadful heaviness lay upon them. They felt unable to cope with the simplest undertakings; . . . they were reduced to their "consciousness," their weakest and most fallible organ! I believe there has never been such feeling of misery on earth! (GM II.16).

This rather wonderful description captures something essential to the acquisition of "raw" bad conscience as Nietzsche figures it—the fact that man suddenly feels *at odds* with himself, at sixes and sevens with his own endowments and capacities. And it is from this mismatch with himself, from man's failure, as it were, to fit his own skin that his sufferings—and his *ressentiment*, his doer/deed distinctions, his yearnings for the beyond, his idealism, his *asceticism*—all derive. That the very fact of being conscious (i.e., internalized) *ensures* that our experience will be problematic for us is something that Nietzsche insists upon. In *The Gay Science* he puts it like this: "consciousness does not really belong to man's individual existence but rather to his social or herd nature. . . . Consequently, given the best will in the world to understand ourselves as individually as possible . . . each of us will always succeed in becoming conscious only of what is not individual but 'average' . . . . Fundamentally, all our actions are altogether incomparably personal, unique, and infinitely individual; there is no doubt of that. But as soon as we translate them into consciousness *they no longer seem to be*" (GS 354). Again we have a picture of consciousness as something that alienates us from ourselves, as something that forces us to think of ourselves as distinct from what we do, so that there is a mismatch between what we are and what we can conceive of ourselves as being. But, just as sea animals eventually become adapted to their lives as land animals, and feel at home with themselves on land, why shouldn't man at last come to feel at home with himself as a conscious, "interesting" animal, at ease with his capacities and once more "borne" up by them? Why should he not, somewhere on the *other* side of consciousness, become "conscious" of himself and of his actions as "incomparably personal, unique, and infinitely individual." Is this what the "sovereign individual" has achieved?

I suspect that that is how Nietzsche means him to be understood. If one lays aside the beastly connotations of the relevant passage, it is quite easy to read it as an attempt to imagine what fitting one's own skin might be like. One's "consciousness" quivers "in every muscle": that is, one's consciousness no longer figures in one's experience as a *separate* inner arena, a space within which one seems a "doer" to oneself, forever dislocated from one's deeds. Instead, the inner and the outer are somehow intersuffused, so that the thought of consciousness "quivering," the thought of consciousness *in* one's muscles, is neither figurative nor oxymoronic. In this condition, consciousness is not the theater of pain that the newly internalized experience: it is the medium that bears one up, the medium through which one experiences one's actions as unique, as incontestably one's own (the dancer *is* the dance). Thus, what I described earlier as "physicalism" might much more appropriately be described as the spiritualization of the body. And this new consciousness, in which the sovereign individual is maximally at home, has "penetrated to the profoundest depths and become instinct." *Become* instinct, note: the instincts *we* know about are there to begin with, are not the products of development; but in the sovereign individual "instinct" is a result, an achievement made "flesh in him": the *meaning* of "instinct" is different now. So nothing in this involves a return to the pre-internalized condition of the beast of prey. What it does involve is a journey through to the other side of internalization, where one arrives—not at a "synthesis of the *inhuman* and *superhuman*" (GM I.16)—but at the superhuman itself.

Nietzsche did, I think, have some such transformation of consciousness in mind—a transformation best described as the self-overcoming of the bad conscience. But where does imagining this transformation get us? Have we the least idea what it would be like to be the sovereign individual—to match up with ourselves, to be at home with ourselves as he is? David Owen (in a slightly different context) suggests an example: "Playing tennis," he says, there are moments at which "I am caught in a sense of complete certainty that I can do no wrong"; I "play without the need for conscious reflection on what I'm doing"; I enjoy "mastery of the activity" in which I am engaged until "something does go wrong" and "the mood is broken." [12] One has an immediate sense of what this experience is like (even if only for two or three shots). And one can get the same sort of thing at the piano—just the odd bar here and there when the piano seems almost to be playing itself, a couple of phrases during which one gains an intimation of what pianistic mastery might actually be like. [13] At such moments there really is no gap between who one is and what one is doing, no reflective distance between thought and action. One might, without undue pretension, describe one's consciousness as "quivering" in the muscles of one's fingers and arms, and one's (brief, fragile) mastery as "instinct." For these moments, at least, there is no "dreadful heaviness," no mismatch between means and ends; one feels utterly at home—perhaps like a sea animal who has learned to live on the land.

There is, I am sure, an inkling in these experiences of what it would be

12. Owen, *Nietzsche, Politics and Modernity*, pp. 107–8.
13. See D 537 for Nietzsche on this sense of mastery.

like to relate differently to one's own consciousness. But so what? How do such inklings relate to the search for a new nobility? The answer, I suspect, is that they hardly do at all. For one thing, these experiences—although real enough—do appear typically to be encountered in activities that are *not* part of the mainstream of one's life, indeed in activities that are often a kind of *alternative* to the mainstream of one's life. Moreover, such experiences cannot be *willed*: you can't sit down at the piano and decide to have a few bars of mastery. If those bars come at all, they come of their own accord. Nor do such experiences survive scrutiny: if one catches oneself having one, that is usually the end of it; indeed one often doesn't realize one is having the experience until it's over. These considerations certainly limit the significance of whatever inklings we have. Indeed, I think we must admit that we have absolutely no idea what it might be like to lead life as a whole in that way. Mastery of the piano, of tennis—yes, perhaps. But mastery of existence *in toto*, of existence as an "interesting animal" . . . ? If Nietzsche does have something of this sort in mind (and I think his description of the sovereign individual points in that direction), then neither he nor we should place too much weight on it. There is no guarantee whatever that consciousness, bad conscience in its "raw state," will eventually be transformed in its own self-overcoming. (It is striking that the internal logic that leads to the self-overcoming of justice and the ascetic ideal becomes apparent only at a very late stage, or afterward.) Nor, if consciousness were so transformed, have we the resources—now—to imagine what on earth that might be like. At best, then, I think that the thought of the "sovereign individual" should be taken as a rather misty, if beautiful, kind of hope for man's future, as a wish, the vaguest prophecy. As such, it might predispose us in favor of mastery; it might also prompt us to cherish certain experiences more, as intimations of something. But what it seems not to be able to do is to suggest by itself any course of action that we could take now in order to bring its realization closer. Nietzsche might, I suppose, see mastery of life as the inevitable outcome of sufficient ruthlessness in self-surveillance: perhaps with enough "discipline of suffering" we might become such virtuosic stylists of character that living on the furthest edge of the affirmable becomes second nature to us, "instinct." But if so, the sovereign individual really functions here only as a carrot, as a sort of enticing appendage to the far more grueling regime laid out earlier in section 3. The mere possibility—the wish—that consciousness might eventually overcome itself *cannot*, alone, provide a goal for the human will. The interpretation it offers is much too thin—there is nothing sufficiently substantial in *these* inklings to qualify as an ideal. However inspiring Nietzsche's vision may be, then, it simply isn't the sort of thing to be counterposed by itself to nihilism: it's a fancy, a morale booster, not a solution.

V

That completes my survey of what seem to be the most positive suggestions in the *Genealogy*, Nietzsche's best shots at a solution to the problem he claims to have diagnosed (none of which bears the least resemblance to a return to the original nobles). But so far I have refrained from investigating the diagnosis itself—a task which can be postponed no longer.

Nietzsche requires a new sort of nobility because, according to him, the self-overcoming of the ascetic ideal leaves us entirely bereft of a goal; and without a goal we will be catapulted into nihilism. Thus the search for a new kind of nobility is rendered essential by the threat of nihilism. But this way of putting the matter elides an important issue—an issue, moreover, which Nietzsche shows himself only too happy to slide past. He assures us that "man would rather will *nothingness* than *not* will" (GM III.28)—and it all sounds horribly plausible. But it is plausible only if a suppressed premise is also plausible. Expanded, his claim should read: man would rather will nothingness than not will *in accordance with an ideal*. The suppressed premise is that *some ideal or other* is always essential. If it were not, there would be no reason to regard the fact and the manner of the collapse of the *ascetic* ideal as such a (potential) catastrophe. Nietzsche's suppression of this premise reveals or underlines a number of things. The first is the depth of his own commitment to idealism (one *must* have an ideal). The second is his commitment to a model of "the ideal" drawn from asceticism. The authority of the ascetic ideal is complete, final, and transcendent until it overcomes itself, at which point its claim to authority—its status as an ideal—is entirely lost. Therefore, Nietzsche seems covertly to conclude, any subsequent ideal can function as one only if it too lays claim to complete, final, and transcendent authority. But that of course is just what the ascetic ideal's last inference against itself declares to be impossible. Which leaves Nietzsche with a choice. He can insist on the truth of his suppressed premise together with the conception of an "ideal" that it seems to presuppose—in which case nihilism really will be the only option left once the ascetic ideal has self-destructed. But this has the paradoxical consequence that it turns nihilism itself into a complete, final, and transcendent ideal: if man necessarily needs such an ideal to will in accordance with, and if such ideals appear now to be ruled out of court, it becomes an uncriticizable truth not only that man will "will *nothingness*" rather "than *not* will"—but also that he will will it as an inestimable ideal, as a "closed system of will, goal [nothingness], and interpretation [existence is no longer sustainable]" (GM III.23).

Nietzsche was unquestionably drawn to this position—and drawn to it by the very idealism that he seeks at a larger level to overcome: it is, for in-

stance, hard not to notice that his default response to the dilemma he has diagnosed is usually to want everything and everybody destroyed (of which
more in a moment). But he does have another choice. He can admit what he
really has to admit if he is to continue to see man as an "interesting animal,"
as an animal "pregnant with a future." He can admit, that is, that man is perfectly capable of willing in accordance with less-than-transcendent ideals (a
less-than-transcendent ideal is, after all, the most positive thing that Nietzsche or anyone else, according to him, can offer). But if less-than-transcendent ideals are enough, this raises the possibility that man (some men, most
men) might not care all that much about ideals of *any* kind (i.e., that they
may be content with *much* less than transcendent ideals, or even with no
ideals at all). Or, to put the matter another way, Nietzsche must face the possibility that people won't value value enough to be driven to nihilism (to *that*
value) if all other values fail. And Nietzsche knows that this possibility is almost certainly, in almost all cases, realized: "We can see nothing today that
wants to grow greater, we suspect that things will continue to go down, down,
to become thinner, more good-natured, more prudent, more comfortable,
more mediocre, more indifferent, more Chinese, more Christian—there is
no doubt that man is getting 'better' all the time" (GM I.12). It is against the
background of this that the following is to be read:

> What is to be feared, what has a more calamitous effect than any other
> calamity, is that man should inspire not profound fear but profound *nausea*;
> also not great fear but great *pity*. Suppose these two were one day to unite,
> they would inevitably beget one of the uncanniest monsters: the "last will" of
> man, his will to nothingness, nihilism. . . . And therefore let us have fresh
> air! . . . So that we may, at least for a while yet, guard ourselves, my friends,
> against the two worst contagions that may be reserved just for us—against the
> *great nausea at man!* against *great pity for man!* (GM III.14)

Notice that nausea and nihilism here are "reserved just for us"—for Nietzsche and his "friends"; and remember, too, that "as yet" he knows of no
friends (GM III.27). The implication is inescapable: one needs a very special
quality in order to be filled with "nausea at man," to be driven to nihilism;
and the only quality that fits the bill is that of valuing value enough to prefer nihilism to (the sight of) life without ideals. The *object* of one's nausea
wouldn't much mind, of course; but then that, to Nietzsche and his "friends,"
is just what makes the nauseating nauseating.

Nietzsche's deepest fear is not nihilism. A general outbreak of nihilism
would actually be rather encouraging for him: it would suggest that most
people were, after all, idealists. No, what seizes him with horror is the thought
that the ascetic ideal might overcome itself and precisely nothing happen as

a result—that the inhabitants of contemporary culture might prove so un-interested in the question of value that they regard the demise of asceticism with indifference. This is partly what motivates Nietzsche's attack on those who, having "got rid of the Christian God, . . . cling all the more firmly to Christian morality": such people do not take the question of value seriously enough to recognize that morality has become a *problem* (TI, Expeditions 5). Indeed, for them it hasn't become a problem. This specter—the specter of mass indifference to the question of value—haunts Nietzsche's whole proj-ect and represents the deepest difficulty for him. He is resigned to the fact that he won't be preaching to the converted; but he does at least need to be preaching to the convertible; and those who don't much value value are not that—Nietzsche's concerns are irrelevant to them.

This leaves him, it would seem, with just two options. He can try to awaken a sense of the value of value by showing what it looks like to take the issue passionately and seriously. This, together with the pretense that we are all idealists really ("man would rather will *nothingness* that *not* will"), seems to be his strategy in the *Genealogy*: he attempts to excite and flatter us (his readers) into recognizing that there's a very important problem here, and that we too ought to get worked up about it. The other strategy is to try to shock and disgust us out of our indifference by showing us a portrait of our-selves. The best example of this strategy is to be found in *Zarathustra*. I quote the whole passage:

Behold! I shall show you the *Last Man*.

"What is love? What is creation? What is longing? What is a star?" thus asks the Last Man and blinks.

The earth has become small, and upon it hops the Last Man, who makes everything small. His race is as inexterminable as the flea; the Last Man lives longest.

"We have discovered happiness," say the Last Men and blink.

They have left the places where living was hard: for one needs warmth. One still loves one's neighbour and rubs against him for one needs warmth.

Sickness and mistrust count as sins with them: one should go about warily. He is a fool who stumbles over stones or over men!

A little poison now and then: that produces pleasant dreams. And a lot of poison at last, for a pleasant death.

They still work, for work is entertainment. But they take care the enter-tainment does not exhaust them.

Nobody grows rich or poor any more: both are too much of a burden. Who still wants to rule? Who obey? Both are too much of a burden.

No herdsman and one herd. Everyone wants the same thing, everyone is the same: whoever thinks otherwise goes voluntarily into the madhouse.

"Formerly all the world was mad," say the most acute of them and blink.

They are clever and know everything that has ever happened: so there is no end to their mockery. They still quarrel, but soon they make up—otherwise indigestion would result.

They have their little pleasure for the day and their little pleasure for the night: but they respect health.

"We have discovered happiness," say the Last Men and blink (Z, Zarathustra's Prologue 5).

If this passage doesn't provoke a thrilling horror of self-recognition one should go back and read it again. Indeed it is one of those (many) Nietzschean moments that seem to become more and more acute, and ever closer to the bone, with each rereading—superbly calculated, one would have thought, to fill one with self-revulsion (I *am* the Last Man).[14]

But suppose it doesn't. Suppose one were to read it, recognize oneself . . . and blink. What might Nietzsche possibly say next? This, it seems: "You want, if possible—and there is no more insane 'if possible'—to *abolish suffering*. And we? It really seems that *we* would rather have it higher and worse than ever. Well-being as you understand it—that is no goal, it seems to us an *end*, a state that soon makes man ridiculous and contemptible—that makes his destruction *desirable*. The discipline of suffering, of *great* suffering—do you not know that only *this* discipline has created all enhancements of man so far?" (BGE 225). Which isn't, it will be granted, very likely to move things along. But it does illustrate the problem: faced with the Last Man (someone not much interested in human enhancement), all that Nietzsche can find it in himself to do is rather strenuously to announce that—as far as he himself is concerned—nihilism would be preferable. But this is just to revert to the first, paradoxical option outlined at the beginning of the present section— to nihilism as a transcendent ideal. And why should the Last Man care anyway? Given that we pretty well all *are* Last Men, why should we heed the ravings of some bizarre malcontent who seems to think it better that the human race should die out altogether than that we should attempt to live as contentedly, as healthily and as long as we can—something, moreover, that we're getting better at doing? Surely the Last Man should just make sure that the gun control laws are tight enough.

Perhaps. Indeed, no doubt. But this still doesn't show exactly how pivotal a place the Last Man occupies in Nietzsche's thought. It is not just that the Last Man is unreachable and unspeakable. His significance goes deeper; and to see how, we need to return to *Zarathustra*. If Nietzsche confronts the Last

14. For a brilliant attempt to shame a subset of contemporary Last Men into self-recognition, see chapter 4 of Michael Tanner's *Wagner* (London: HarperCollins, 1996).

Man most directly in that book, he also—and by no coincidence—comes closest there to confronting the peculiar conflict that the Last Man foments in him. Zarathustra, recovering after his experiment with the thought of eternal recurrence,[15] finds one thing uniquely difficult to bear:

> "'Alas, man recurs eternally! The little man recurs eternally!' . . .
> "The greatest all too small!—that was my disgust at man! And eternal recurrence even for the smallest! that was my disgust at all existence!
> "Ah, disgust! Disgust! Disgust!" Thus spoke Zarathustra and sighed and shuddered; for he remembered his sickness (Z, The Convalescent 2).

What we see here is Zarathustra being *tempted* to nihilism—tempted to say that the little man, the Last Man, makes the "destruction [of mankind] *desirable*." But he resists. And it is in his capacity to affirm even the endless repetition of the Last Man that his nobility, finally, resides.

Thus the Last Man acts on Zarathustra in two ways. First, he nauseates him, tempts him to nihilism. But second, he is the catalyst of that *overcoming* of nausea which constitutes Zarathustra's greatest moment. And the Last Man is capable of performing these functions precisely because his existence proves that transcendental ideals are not merely impossible (the final inference of asceticism) but unnecessary as well (life, in the Last Man, goes on). Thus the Last man is, for Zarathustra, both the strongest argument *against* affirming life and the final demonstration that life *can* be affirmed without a transcendental ideal—without a "closed system of will, goal, and interpretation." As Zarathustra's animals put it to him: "how should this great destiny not also be your greatest danger and sickness!" (Z, The Convalescent 2). Nietzsche, however, crucifies himself on the combination: he finds it infinitely easier to think of the Last Man as making nihilism an all-but-irresistible ideal for an idealist like him than he does to recognize or remember that the existence of the Last Man also shows nihilism (or any other transcendental ideal) to be something one can live without. And yet it is precisely in this second role that the Last Man *ought* to be significant for him—for it is only if nihilism, and transcendental ideals generally, are unnecessary that he can hope to discover the noble, immanent ideal that would, from his point of view, make life worth living. Indeed, it seems as if the thought of the Last Man—the "little man"—marks the point at which Nietzsche himself says "Enough!" and finds his character forced and squeezed into apoca-

---

15. The odd doctrine of eternal recurrence may well have a bearing on Nietzsche's project to instigate a new nobility. Nowhere, however, is that doctrine referred to or even alluded to in the *Genealogy*—so (with some relief) I won't discuss it here. For such thoughts as I do have on the matter, see Ridley, "Nietzsche's Greatest Weight," *Journal of Nietzsche Studies* 14 (1997), 19–25.

lyptic shapes: nihilism is *his* last-ditch fiction, the self-deception he cannot live without.

When he thunders, then, against the Last Man—as something that "makes man ridiculous and contemptible—that makes his destruction *desirable*"—he falls short of the nobility of Zarathustra and threatens to undermine his own positive ambitions as well. And it is surely worth noticing that the relative absence of such (overt) thundering in the *Genealogy* is accompanied by a comparable absence of (direct) references in it to the Last Man; for it really does seem that while Nietzsche was *just* able to imagine someone else rising above the thought of lives lived without ideals, he was himself more or less incapable of doing so. "Whatever is profound loves masks," he says in *Beyond Good and Evil* (BGE 40): and his own self-seduction to nihilism, together with his capacity to deal with it, are both far more profound—or at any rate more fecund—when well disguised.

VI

We saw in the previous chapter that Nietzsche cannot provide a principled method for ranking competing claims to represent our most basic interests. And the impasse in communication outlined just now is the result of precisely that. The Last Man's version of our most basic interests—of the court of appeal before which it is to be decided whether certain things are worth knowing—simply excludes Nietzsche's version, and his truths along with it. Nietzsche's version is expressed as follows: "But grant me from time to time—if there are divine goddesses in the realm beyond good and evil— grant me the sight, but *one* glance of something perfect, wholly achieved, happy, mighty, triumphant, something still capable of arousing fear! Of a man who justifies *man*, of a complementary and redeeming lucky hit on the part of man for the sake of which one may still *believe in man!*" (GM I.12). And this, while it rules out comfort and longevity as ends in themselves, will scarcely appeal to anyone who regards human life as perfectly worthwhile (i.e., as sufficiently worth believing in) even in the absence of human excellence. Which is why Nietzsche must deploy and depend upon rhetorical strategies—either the incitement and flattery of the *Genealogy* or the hideously acute portraiture of *Zarathustra*—to get us to take him (value, excellence) seriously. He can't *demonstrate* to the Last Man that the Last Man's way sells us short; he can only attempt a seduction.

Nietzsche states the position very clearly in *Daybreak*: "Only if mankind possessed a universally recognized *goal* would it be possible to propose 'thus and thus is the *right* course of action': for the present there exists no such goal. It is thus irrational and trivial to impose the demands of morality upon mankind. —To *recommend* a goal to mankind is something quite different: the goal is then thought of as something which *lies in our own discretion*" (D 108). A universally recognized goal is, of course, exactly what the impossibility of transcendental ideals rules out; and the lack of such a goal renders the attempt to *impose* on people an account of our basic interests futile. Thus one can appeal only to people's "discretion": one can attempt only to "recommend" an ideal, to incite people to take it seriously, to seduce them into adopting it. And the *Genealogy*, one must suppose, is Nietzsche's effort to do just that.

Yet recommendings and seducings are tricky. Anyone can recommend anything, of course. But in order to recommend something successfully one needs authority—precisely the commodity that the absence of a universally recognized goal, the absence of any transcendental imperative, renders problematic. Therefore Nietzsche needs actually to perform a double seduction: not merely does he need to seduce us to his own account of our most basic interests, he needs first of all to seduce us to *him*. We need to be brought to think of him as someone whose views are peculiarly worth listening to, are peculiarly worth knowing about. And this, I think, he can do only by impressing us with the power of his account of how we have come to be what we are—with the acuity of his insight into *us*. Just as people will listen more eagerly to a fortune teller who appears to understand them or know something about them, so Nietzsche's authority is predicated on whatever sense he can produce in us that his grasp on what we are about is better than our own. He coaxes us into recognizing the hostility behind our altruism, the fear behind our love; he persuades us that our gentleness is vanity; he shows us to ourselves in a light that is at once shocking and at the same time (oddly) glamorous. And when he foretells catastrophic events, he offers to demonstrate how these await just such creatures as those we now recognize ourselves to be (while not of course forgetting to assure us that we, too, are idealists at heart—which is important, because if he can persuade us to take, say, Christian truthfulness seriously, then he can hope that "the will to truth" will eventually become "conscious of itself as a *problem*" in us [GM III.27], and hence that we will be prepared for a *new* idealism). In short—and if it works—his authority is built on that most peculiar form of flattery, the kind that makes welcome even the most unpleasant revelations about ourselves provided that it also makes us feel more interesting (to us and to him). And at all of this, I think, Nietzsche is a master.

It is, in fact, a measure of his success that one can come away from the *Genealogy* disappointed at just how few recommendations it appears to contain: one is seduced enough by him to want to listen. What we eventually hear, I've suggested—the second stage of seduction—is the proposal that one should live a life of truthful self-surveillance and self-overcoming, that one should practice that noble "discipline of suffering" which permits one to say yes to as much of existence and the world as one can bear. And in this way, one is cajoled into feeling, it might *just* be possible to attain to that ideal and enviable condition enjoyed by the "sovereign individual." The fact that one knows next to nothing of what that condition might consist in, or even— really—how a sufficiently stylish bad conscience could either be achieved or be expected to lead to its own self-overcoming, signals the point at which Nietzsche's imagination reaches its limit. It also, therefore, marks the point beyond which we should refuse to be seduced (and should start thinking for ourselves).

But Nietzsche's seductive powers have proved a good deal more far-reaching. Indeed, in many contemporary readers those powers have induced a style of interpretation which, as Peter Berkowitz remarks, "confuses Nietzsche's intention to overcome morality with its actual overcoming, mistakes the desire to discover or invent new modes of thought for their discovery or invention, and mixes up the ambition to found new forms of life with their successful establishment. Propelled by a combination of credulity and enthusiasm, the new orthodoxy equates Nietzsche's wishes and promises with their fulfillment." [16] I will single out here just one example of this impulse at work—perhaps its most attractive expression in the present context. This is the view that Nietzsche should be read not only as recommending an ideal (such as nobility) but also as *realizing* it in recommending it. One can see why it would be nice to think this: if the *Genealogy* really were an example of what it seeks to promote, one could assume not only that the relevant ideal was available but also that the really hard work toward it had already (somehow) been done. This view is discernibly operative in the interpretations of a number of writers. But only David Owen, so far as I am aware, has actually troubled to produce an argument in support of it. It goes like this: someone who recommends an ideal but does not "exhibit commitment" to it is "engaged in a performative contradiction which utterly undermines . . . the process of recommendation"; from which it follows that "if Nietzsche's argument is to legitimate its right to recommend an ideal . . . it must exhibit in the performance of its argument the ideal which it seeks to recommend." And since, in Owen's view, Nietzsche does succeed in recommending an ideal, he concludes that the argument must itself be exemplary *of* that ideal (a contention he then attempts to illustrate).[17] But there is a confusion here.

16. Peter Berkowitz, *Nietzsche: The Ethics of an Immoralist* (Cambridge: Harvard University Press, 1995), p. 5.
17. Owen, *Nietzsche, Politics and Modernity*, p. 127.

Owen appears to equate the exhibiting of commitment to an ideal with the exhibiting of the ideal itself. But the first can easily happen without the second: for instance, I can exhibit the depth of my commitment to the ideal of chastity by castrating myself for my failure to exhibit chastity—a measure which would, if anything would, lend authority (sincerity) to my recommendation of that ideal. Similarly, Nietzsche can succeed in recommending his ideal in the *Genealogy* without actually enacting it in the book: indeed I have tried in this section to suggest what his (nonexemplary) authority for doing so consists in.

From Nietzsche's point of view, it seems to me, the fact that he doesn't have to go for exemplarity is just as well. Much of the pressure and urgency of his recommendation appears clearly to spring from "disgust," from "nausea" at man. If the thought of the "little man" were not so vile to him, his *need* to inspire a new nobility would be that much less. And one doesn't, really, have to be all that uncharitable to conclude that "nausea" is merely the misleading label he gives to his own brand of *ressentiment*—the brand that culminates in the self-deceptions of transcendental nihilism.[18] Nietzsche is far too caught up in the condition he is busy exposing and denouncing to make the break. But if the *Genealogy* does succeed in recommending nobility, and if it doesn't do so by showing us what fully achieved nobility might look like, it does nonetheless show us something very important. It exemplifies not the ideal itself but commitment to that ideal—it shows us what idealism, in Nietzsche's sense, comes to. And by this, supposing ourselves to be seducible at all, we might well allow ourselves to be (i.e., try to be) seduced. For in Nietzsche's extraordinary wrestlings with his own allegiances and aversions, in his fraught attempts to negotiate between good and bad forms of bad conscience, he makes almost everybody else seem complacent, boring, and morally unserious—as well he knows. Nor is he inclined to be pointlessly modest about the fact: "today," he says, "there is perhaps no more decisive mark of a '*higher nature*,' a more spiritual nature, than that of being divided in this sense and a genuine battleground of these opposed values" (GM I.16). And it is in showing us what it looks like to be such a battleground that Nietzsche, whose nature on these criteria was about as high and spiritual as anyone could survive having, succeeds most triumphantly. It ought to be impossible to emerge from the *Genealogy* not feeling more divided, less complacent, and—at least in intention—much, much more of an idealist. Which is where, as I suggested a moment ago, the hard work and independent thought need to begin.

18. For a somewhat different route to a similar conclusion see chapter 2 of Henry Staten's *Nietzsche's Voice* (Ithaca: Cornell University Press, 1990).

CONCLUSION

I could imagine a music whose rarest magic would consist in its no longer knowing anything of good and evil . . . —an art that from a great distance would behold, fleeing toward it, the colors of a setting *moral* world that had almost become unintelligible.

—*Beyond Good and Evil*, sec. 255

At the end of the second scene of the second act of the second night of Wagner's *Ring* cycle, Wotan, the chief of the gods, finds himself in an impossibly frustrating position: his misuse of power has produced a situation which, so far as he can see, no one but he can understand or rectify. And yet, he also knows, any attempt on his part to intervene—to legislate a solution—will serve only to make matters worse. So he is left to fret: "How can I create one, / who, not through me, / but on his own / can achieve my will? / Oh godly distress!" And he acknowledges that he cannot: "for I have no power to make him; / my hand can only make slaves!" [1] Nietzsche would have known the feeling. His own "extravagant honesty" (BGE 230) has caused "the will to truth" to become "conscious of itself as a *problem*" in him (GM III.27), so precipitating a crisis in value that hardly anyone else, he suspects, will either notice or, if they do, will have the least idea how to address. Yet part of the price exacted from him by his extravagant honesty is the acknowledgment that the absolutely authoritative legislation of value is no longer possible. Any attempt to pretend otherwise will result only in a deepening of the problem (in self-deceiving nihilism, for instance). So he is stuck. Indeed, like

---

1. Wagner, *Die Walküre*, trans. Andrew Porter, *The Ring of the Nibelung* (London: Faber, 1977), pp. 109–10.

Wotan, he is obliged through impotence simply to crave and hanker after the appearance of a world-redeeming hero who will somehow be noble enough to resolve the crisis *without* legislating anything (GM II.24). And he knows it isn't him (GM II.25).

But if Nietzsche is roughly on a par with Wotan, he is at a grievous disadvantage when it comes to Wotan's creator. Wagner was able to do much more than crave and hanker: the music between Brunhilde and Sieglinde at the end of act 3, scene 1, for instance, bodies forth the very solution that Nietzsche and Wotan can only dream about. Music can do something that mere argument can not. As Michael Tanner puts it, Wagner, that "most intellectual of musical dramatists," insists "that we should respond" to his works "by feeling rather than thinking"—and this just because of "the extraordinarily dense quality of the thinking which is going on in both the words and the actions of his dramas." Tanner quotes from Wagner's *Opera and Drama*: "Nothing should remain for the synthesising intellect to do in the face of a dramatic work of art; everything presented in it must be so conclusive that our feeling about it is brought to rest; for in the bringing to rest of this feeling, after its highest arousal in sympathy with it, lies that very peace which leads us to the instinctive understanding of life. In drama we must become *knowers* through *feeling*."[2]

And, in Wagner's case, it works. So "conclusively" is everything presented that, by an astonishing musical alchemy, conviction is conjured out of viscera. Tanner is surely right to suggest that Nietzsche's brilliant, insight-laden animus against Wagner owes much—very much—to envy.[3] I made a lot in Chapter 6 of Nietzsche's seductive techniques and of his need for them. Yet the alchemy of music is what he really wants (indeed, he wants a Socrates who practices music [BT 14]). No one knows how the alchemy of music works; but *that* it works is beyond question. And it is because of this that the claim I made in the introduction—that Delius's *A Mass of Life* is one of the finest commentaries on *Zarathustra*—wasn't merely frivolous: Delius succeeds in alchemically transmuting that will to will backward, that will to overcome the great "It was" of the past (Z, Of Redemption), which Nietzsche's prophet can only splutter about. Viewed most bleakly, then, Nietzsche is caught between a rancorous envy of those like Kant on the one hand, who are still able to legislate values with unshaken faith in their transcendental authority, and of Wagner on the other, who has no need to legislate but only to *show*—and who intoxicates and converts in the showing. In virtue, respectively, of his honesty and giftlessness Nietzsche is unable to do either.

2. Michael Tanner, *Wagner* (London: HarperCollins, 1996), p. 9.
3. Ibid., p. 209.

Whether he fully acknowledges the fact, however, is less clear. His insistence on the necessity of learning his works "by heart" (Z, Of Reading and Writing) is presumably supposed to encourage a kind of para-cognitive digestion of them, so that they enter the viscera and emerge knowledgelike from the fire of feeling. In this much he may be hoping to achieve what Wagner can achieve. But the hope is doomed. For Nietzsche is a *thinker*; and this means that the longed-for Wagnerian alchemy can, even if possible, go to work only on what has already been discursively imagined and worked out. Thus Nietzsche would need first to form a clear view of what a new nobility might be like; and this—for the best of reasons—he cannot do. (If he could, he wouldn't have needed to invent Zarathustra or write the *Genealogy*.) To evoke, concretely, a more-than-human grandeur in prose requires a perspicacity of purely *conceptual* elaboration that is neither possible nor necessary when the same task is attempted in music. And the aphoristic style, whatever else it is, isn't music (which is not to say that it doesn't need to be lived with, digested—only that those processes won't result in musical effects).[4] So if Nietzsche does hope somehow to appropriate the capacities of music—as they are revealed by Wagner, at least—he is deceiving himself. (This fact, incidentally, should put Michael Allen Gillespie's odd claim that *Twilight of the Idols* is composed in sonata form into some perspective.[5] If that book *is* in sonata form—underdemonstrated, in my view—then it is a sonata form of the most banal, music-primer variety, that is, of the kind that is more or less incapable of alchemizing purely musical material, let alone any other sort. And if such a miscalculation accords well enough with Nietzsche's strictly musical gifts, it accords exceedingly badly with his appreciation and understanding of what music can achieve. So, assuming that Nietzsche intended what Gillespie claims to have discovered—which I doubt—the explanation of it can lie only in an uncharacteristically *un*fruitful variety of the envy that he undoubtedly did feel for musicians more gifted than himself. Which is why Gillespie's "discovery," even if it is one, can tell us nothing of any interest about *Twilight*.)

But Nietzsche does have other resources. However much he clearly wishes that he could do what Wagner does, he too can do things—and things that lie beyond the scope of any opera. The evangelical, conviction-producing effect of Wagner's music (*Tristan* most unignorably) is deep, searingly so. But it is also inchoate. One comes away from those operas thinking about *them*. *What*—exactly—have I been seduced to here? How? Why? One doesn't

4. Nor is it to say that Nietzsche doesn't sometimes achieve something else—poetry. But poetry, like prose, is discursive: one *says*, one *conceives*.

5. Michael Allen Gillespie, "Nietzsche's Musical Politics," in Gillespie and Tracy Strong, eds., *Nietzsche's New Seas* (Chicago: University of Chicago Press, 1988), pp. 117–53.

come away from them with a different conception of what thought can do, or of what thought should from now on *aspire* to do. From the *Genealogy*, on the other hand, it seems to me that if one has read it, worked at it (and then, if needs be, learned it by heart), one does emerge with a different and less inchoate set of intellectual priorities. Nietzsche succeeds, as Wagner could not, in making the problem of value explicit. And if Wagner succeeds in producing full-blown intimations of what the far side of that problem might feel like to be on, it is from Nietzsche that we learn why it is a problem in the first place—and why getting to the far side of it might matter. It is in this that his greatness as a moral philosopher ultimately lies. Almost no one before him, and certainly no one since, has exhibited a remotely comparable *intellectual* commitment to the value of value; nor does anyone else flatter us so much by what, in all moral seriousness, he demands that we prove ourselves capable of. And in these twin traits of his thought Nietzsche reveals himself for what, at bottom, he is: an exhilaratingly earnest, terrifyingly exacting optimist—a true creature, in other words, of that momentous efflorescence of Protestantism usually termed Enlightenment.

INDEX